WORKING FICTIONS

POST-

CONTEMPORARY

INTERVENTIONS

· · · · · · · · · · · · · · · ·

Series Editors:

Stanley Fish and

Fredric Jameson

CAROLYN LESJAK

WORKING FICTIONS

....

A Genealogy

of the Victorian

Novel

DUKE UNIVERSITY PRESS   DURHAM AND LONDON   2006

© 2006 DUKE UNIVERSITY PRESS

All rights reserved

Printed in the United States

of America on acid-free paper ∞

Designed by Amy Ruth Buchanan

Typeset in Adobe Caslon by Tseng

Information Systems, Inc.

Library of Congress Cataloging-in-

Publication Data and republication

acknowledgments appear on the

last printed page of

this book.

For my sister Susan
and my mom Doris

CONTENTS

....

ACKNOWLEDGMENTS

....

I hope that Eric Hoffer is right: that "what counts most is holding on." This book has been with me a long time; its beginning and end marked by two deaths: my sister's and my mother's. Fortunately, its writing has also been a time of much life, the peaks of which have been the birth of my daughter, Sophie, and the arrival, just recently, of Mia from China. That life also includes the constant love and encouragement of my father, V. James Lesjak, and my sister, Catherine Lesjak, for which I am grateful.

I thank most of all my mentors at Duke. I feel lucky to have been a graduate student before the drive to professionalization was in full swing. My advisor Eve Sedgwick defines for me real scholarly love and my other committee members—Fredric Jameson, Toril Moi, Michael Hardt, and Clyde Ryals—have served as models of intellectual integrity and political engagement who are always before me in my own work. Many thanks too to the crew at 819 Clarendon, the Marxist reading group, and the current Summer Institute—these, to me, represent the heart of the collective spirit necessary for sustaining good work. Martin Hipsky is also part of this spirit; his reading of many drafts helped me immensely.

I also feel lucky to have gotten to know Nancy Armstrong and Amanda Anderson early on in my career. They have both been incredibly generous with their time and advice and their support has been incalculable.

This book would also be a far lesser thing but for the tireless help of my colleagues Betsy Bolton and Nora Johnson. Especially down the stretch, their encouragement and criticism (perfectly dosed) has been invaluable. Thanks, too, to Swarthmore College for leave support and to my students for providing a great environment in which to teach and learn. Many thanks as well to my editor, J. Reynolds Smith, and the two anonymous readers at Duke University Press.

Finally, Chris Pavsek has been with me through it all. His presence is everywhere in these pages; he has sustained me and just plain made me happy.

When men question not

the fruits of toil but the toil itself

then philosophy in Marx's sense of

human activity has become actual.

. . . .

C. L. R. JAMES,
State Capitalism and
World Revolution

INTRODUCTION

....

A Genealogy of the

Labor Novel

И

Two questions lie at the heart of this book—why do we unthinkingly take our pleasure separately from our work and what might this have to do with the Victorian novel? While a prodigious body of scholarship has unearthed the numerous roles the Victorian novel has played in the production of our own life world, and, accordingly, firmly established us as the novel's rightful inheritors, there has been less critical analysis devoted to labor and almost none to the relationship between labor and pleasure.[1] This book aims to understand the reasons behind this absence as well as the inseparability of labor and pleasure in the nineteenth-century novel and in our own contemporary situation. Its central argument is that a new genealogy of the Victorian novel can make visible the obscured connections between labor and pleasure. This genealogy not only transforms our understanding of the Victorian novel by placing what I call the problematic of labor at its center but also, more broadly, revives the project of realism by establishing its unique ability to bring this problematic to light.

To be sure, to trace a genealogy of the labor novel is not to make a claim for an originary moment when labor and pleasure come to organize how movements of capital are understood and represented. Instead, following Foucault's notion of genealogical analysis, this analysis historicizes the political uses of labor and pleasure and suggests how they undergo "extraordinary and transforming" changes during the nineteenth century.[2] In so doing, this genealogy also speaks to our contemporary situation: it historicizes what has come to be taken as a given—the divide between labor and pleasure—and offers possible models of a radically "other" social life in which labor and pleasure would be reinvented. The stakes in this history are high: they involve nothing less than the most intimate and most social aspects of our lives—the world of work and our personal pleasures—and how they might be lived otherwise.

The construction of such a genealogy must begin with the difficulties that arise when dealing with labor and literature. The first and most important problem involves the issue of visibility. To put it baldly, one is hard put to find representations of industrial labor in literature. Despite the fact, for instance, that labor and the working class are the industrial novel's explicit objects of inquiry, even a cursory look at its "classics"—Dickens's *Hard Times*, Disraeli's *Sybil*, Gaskell's *Mary Barton*, Brontë's *Shirley*—reveals a marked *absence* of representations of work or workers working. A definite problem in the industrial novel, the situation only gets worse once the industrial novel disappears from the cultural scene. Domestic fiction, the *Bildungsroman*, Victorian aestheticism: traditionally these genres and cultural movements have not been viewed with an eye toward industrial labor; if anything, they have signaled its supersession.

In Catherine Gallagher's influential analysis of the industrial novel in *The Industrial Reformation of English Fiction*, the Victorian novel stops talking about industrial work somewhere around the 1860s when the industrial novel loses its social foundations. As Gallagher argues, the difficult translation between the social and the novelistic that formed the centerpiece of the industrial novel was replaced by "the 1860s discovery of an independent realm of representation."[3] After that, literature, according to Gallagher, moved on to issues less politically contentious than labor and the working class, leaving behind this earlier moment of social criticism and the difficult representational problems it entailed. The novel, in short, became that cultural object with which modern readers are familiar: an autonomous imaginative space free from the struggles of the political fray and thus able to deal in timeless truths rather than time-bound, ideological conflicts.[4] The project of the industrial novel was seen to be at an end.[5]

But what if we do not follow Gallagher's argument, and instead recognize that labor is *always hard to see* in the novel—even in the industrial novel where Gallagher assumes it is really to be found—and that its visibility (or lack thereof) is an integral part of its composition? What if, rather than reproducing the elision of work and workers from the cultural sphere that the novel encourages (and Gallagher's analysis confirms), we were to follow labor in all its inscrutability in order to make visible its continued and often vexed presence, its unwillingness, as it were, to go away? I will argue for a series of perpetual absences of labor in the Victorian novel, in which there are no sudden disappearances, but no moments of clear visibility either. In this light, the industrial novel becomes a place where labor can be "seen" not because it is being directly represented or visibly foregrounded but because the attempt to represent the working class at all necessitates an engagement with labor's overall problematic: how to represent industrial labor and working-class laborers without simultaneously promoting social revolution.

This reconceptualization of the industrial novel and its place within Victorian realism begins to explain why the relationship between labor and pleasure has not received more critical attention. If labor is primarily conceived of in terms of its overt representation in any given novel, then Gallagher's trajectory makes a certain amount of sense. Similarly, if labor is detached from pleasure, the industrial novel appears to be supplanted by various forms of domestic fiction, the social problems it raised replaced by the pleasures of the aesthetic. In her reading of the failure of Elizabeth Gaskell's social criticism in *Mary Barton*, for instance, Gallagher concludes by encouraging us "to remember that [Gaskell's] failure is the foundation of the book's formal significance, for its very generic eclecticism points toward the formal self-consciousness of later British realism."[6] The novel's "formal significance," or the pleasures of the text *as* text, reinforces a lineage for the novel that pits the pleasures of the aesthetic against the labors of the social and, by extension, suggests that "*formal* self-consciousness" (emphasis added) eventually trumps the *content* (the labor and social criticism) of earlier social fiction. In "losing" labor, then, we also lose pleasure as a concept or an experience ineluctably tied to the social; we cede it to the realm of the aesthetic and divorce it from labor, which is positioned as that which the aesthetic overcomes. The conflict between labor and pleasure is seamlessly resolved by placing them in a serial relation to one another: one loss (labor) is more than compensated for by another gain (the aesthetic development of the British novel) down the literary road. This book contends that there was no such trade-off in the nineteenth-century British novel but rather a continuing struggle to come to terms with the relationship between labor and pleasure and the larger social conflicts this relationship embodied.

Importantly, the difficulty with seeing this relationship rests not only with analyses of industrial fiction but also with readings of domestic fiction. In a seminal reading of the domestic novel, Nancy Armstrong's *Desire and Domestic Fiction* (1987) attempts to break down the distinction between political history and the history of sexuality by illustrating the political work gender performs in the Victorian novel. She defines her project as trying "to show how the discourse of sexuality is implicated in shaping the novel, and to show as well how domestic fiction helped to produce a subject who understood herself in the psychological terms that had shaped fiction."[7] The importance of this claim is enormous; it not only repositions domestic fiction as central to the development of the middle-class and bourgeois culture but also politicizes gender by granting to women authors and their female heroines powerful cultural agency.[8] At the same time, Armstrong also warns of the dangers inherent in focusing on sexuality as the foundation of political relationships. Dyadic models of gender, she cautions, have the tendency to subsume all relations of power under the rubric of sexuality. In the wake of Armstrong's and other feminists' work on domestic fiction, this cautionary note has in many ways been borne out in the subsequent detachment of sexuality from other forms of politics. Armstrong presciently describes this political fallout when she notes that "by inscribing social conflict within a domestic configuration . . . one loses sight of all the various and contrary political affiliations for which any given individual provides the site" (24). My dual focus on labor and pleasure is an attempt to build on the strengths of Armstrong's insights regarding the politics of sexuality while simultaneously heeding her concerns about the loss of other "various and contrary political affiliations."[9]

The language of pleasure is part of this work. As Armstrong defines desire in her discussion of the Brontës, desire is precisely what elides political identity: modern desire is synonymous with the formulation of a universal notion of subjectivity. In contrast, my use of pleasure strives to unsettle contemporary invocations of "desire," whether articulated along Foucauldian lines (as in Armstrong's analysis) or Freudian/Lacanian ones, which are premised on the notion of lack or absence. As will become clear in chapters 4 and 5 (on William Morris and Oscar Wilde, respectively), a particular political utility inheres in the notion of pleasure as opposed to desire, both because of pleasure's relationship to an expanded notion of use and its ability to shift the locus of attention away from more individually situated, psychoanalytic approaches to satisfaction and happiness toward a more broadly social project relying on the collectivity for its realization. In the end, such a shift asks us to try to imagine a notion of pleasure which, unlike the Lacanian notion of enjoyment or *jouissance*, is not predicated on loss but rather on a new kind of intimacy with the object-world, an intimacy that escapes the imperialist impulse—the subject's need to devour the object—and instead productively rewrites subject-object relations in revolutionary ways.[10] This also relates to my use of the term "pleasure" as opposed to "happiness" or "leisure" as labor's antithesis. Unlike "happiness," which suggests a certain contentment with one's lot (the sense of being well-adapted to one's environment), or "leisure," which designates the cessation of activities and time specifically free from work, "pleasure" is both about gratification, especially sensual and sexual gratification, *and*, in its utopian permutations, a form of activity, such that it is neither an escape from labor nor a capitulation to the status quo, but always a figure of striving, of something that has to be worked for and is always in the making. By consciously adopting Morris's and Wilde's term, I hope to allow their language to estrange more contemporary readings of desire. My wager is that the nineteenth-century vocabulary of labor and pleasure is enlightening in this regard, not least because it formulates these relationships in ways to which we are now unaccustomed.

The constitutive relation of labor to pleasure has its beginnings in the history of the middle class. As the historian Anna Clark has noted, the middle class was the first to develop a coherent class identity, demarcated at once by the issue of work and the gendering of workers.[11] In the period around the turn of the nineteenth century the separation of masculine work from the feminine home gradually became a defining marker of middle-class status. This concept was then codified in the 1832 Reform Act, which enfranchised middle-class men (as "politically" responsible heads of household) and excluded the working class (exempted by virtue of their work from the benefits of a "family wage" and the domestic arrangements it promoted). As the connection between work and home suggests, the presence of new forms of labor under industrial capitalism was inseparable from the reorganization of social space as a whole. The redefinition of labor not only entailed the gendering of different kinds of social activities and spaces — waged work as opposed to homemaking, the sphere of production versus the domestic sphere — but spoke overall to how social relations were to be envisioned. As I hope to show, pleasure — the possibilities for it, the forces hindering it — served as a potent site for negotiating the new contours of what it meant to be a modern British subject. Pleasure was about new experiential possibilities — sensual, bodily, cognitive, novelistic — as well as a figure for the total constellation of social forces undergoing transformation. It held local meaning as an experience in and of itself while simultaneously functioning as a site for and arbiter of value. As the meaning of labor changed, so too did the meaning of pleasure.

In response, then, to the erasures and divisions that have obscured these connections between labor and pleasure and that continue to structure analyses of industrial and domestic fiction (evident in the very ease with which these two terms are employed), this study argues for a new organization of the history of the Victorian novel. This genealogy extends from the industrial novel and its development in the period from 1832–67 to the late *Bildungsromane* of Charles Dickens and George Eliot in the 1860s–70s to the utopian novels and nonfiction of William Morris and Oscar Wilde in the late 1880s and 1890s. Although these texts might seem to form an odd assemblage, they all actively share in conceptualizing, either implicitly or explicitly, the relationship between labor and pleasure as it evolved over the course of the nineteenth century. The notion of the "labor novel" which forms part of this introduction's title is meant to capture the commonness of purpose or effect drawing these varied texts together, the way in which they share a genealogical relationship to one another. It is also meant to provoke a more general rethinking of generic categories and the ways in which they have operated to suppress or elide the connections between labor and pleasure; the particular texts I examine here exemplify rather than exhaust the new critical possibilities such a rethinking allows.

The degree to which these current categories are entrenched can be measured by the perceived oddness of this grouping of texts, itself symptomatic of divisions currently structuring our conceptions of the Victorian novel: divisions between industrial and domestic fiction, realism and aestheticism, novels and utopian narratives. Unlike the rubric of the "industrial novel," the labor novel is neither confined to one genre nor even a particular form of realism but instead encompasses a range of novels and nonfictional texts that share a preoccupation with what I have been calling the problematic of labor. The treatment of labor as a problematic forgoes any presumption as to what labor should look like and instead repositions it in terms of any number of representational strategies employed in order to represent it. Indeed, within the model I am proposing, the classic social realism of the industrial novel will be seen to have an affinity with the critical realism and "anti-novels" of Morris and Wilde.[12] Yet, while this problematic finds different expression at different historical moments (something that the individual sections of the book trace), it is fundamentally shaped by the underlying concern of the industrial novel: the problem of representing labor without also raising the specter of the economic and social inequalities on which it is based. Whereas the earlier novels perform a variety of exorcisms to keep this threat at bay, those of Morris and Wilde turn the tables by advocating for the social revolution that haunts the industrial novel's and the late *Bil-*

dungsroman's respective depictions of labor. Far from reading the industrial novel as the endpoint of literary concerns with industrial labor, then, this book argues that it is in fact only a beginning.

In the end, the genealogy offered here has three key aims: to revise the commonplace understanding that labor disappears from literary representation once the industrial novel as a genre loses its cultural purchase; to argue that labor cannot be understood apart from the modern pleasures that come to define its antithesis; and to claim, finally, that engaging with these hegemonic and utopian fictions is not only revelatory for our understanding of nineteenth-century British culture but also instructive for moving beyond its established divisions. Together the five chapters that trace this genealogy have as their broadest goal to outline the lineaments of an ongoing response to an increasingly global economy, whose basis lies in particular organizations of labor and pleasure, and their designated spheres, production and consumption. To some readers, the word "genealogy" may evoke a broad survey of Victorian literature, an expectation that this close analysis of six novels cannot hope to meet. I use the term to highlight the "descent" between texts that historically have been treated as disconnected from one another either by generic tradition, subject matter, or political orientation. This genealogy performs important conceptual work in its ability to see the various ideas about labor and pleasure in these texts as "forms of response to a social system as a whole."[13] This conceptual work is not complete until both the constructed opposition between these terms and their interrelations are revealed: a genealogy of the labor novel highlights the centrality of labor and pleasure to Britain's national ideological project in the period from 1848 to 1901 even as it sketches the ideologies by which British culture maintained these central concepts as mutually opposed.

......

How then do we begin to make the presence of labor felt? First, we must recognize that the Victorian novel works to make labor *invisible* by producing aesthetic and domestic pleasures that distract from the issues of labor. The production of these pleasures, in turn, requires the severing of labor and pleasure, which severely limits the kinds of pleasure available and the quality and range of activities associated with labor. In a positive vein, the reciprocal nature of this relationship also implies, however, that revealing the connections between labor and pleasure has the capacity to enhance our understanding and experience of both.

A brief look at one passage in Dickens's *David Copperfield* begins to put flesh on this edifice, providing an exemplary moment of what this process looks like in miniature. Detailing the "golden rules" that pertain directly to David's work as a writer (his learning of shorthand, at this point), Dickens draws our attention not to the work itself but to the manner in which it is approached. As David explains, "My meaning simply is, that whatever I have tried to do in life, I have tried with all my heart to do well; that whatever I have devoted myself to, I have devoted myself to completely; that, in great aims and in small, I have always been thoroughly in earnest."[14] The repetition of "whatever" underscores the lack of specificity attaining to the work; the fact that "it," whatever it is, is being done earnestly and devotedly is of much more importance than the nature of the work actually being done. A final "whatever" makes this abundantly clear: "Never to put one hand to anything, on which I could throw my whole self; and never to affect depreciation of my work, whatever it was; I find, now to have been my golden rules" (560). The vagueness of "whatever" coupled with the elisions it performs—we know, for instance, that David hated his work at Murdstone and Grinby—produces an ethic of abstract labor that is then transferred to realms that are not necessarily realms of labor per se. The real subject here is David's success and its motivation: his "sense of responsibility to Dora and [his] aunts" (559). We are meant to read this novel as a story about the development of David's identity—a process of self-discovery or subject formation in which courtship, coming of age, and matters of the heart carry the day. The refrain of the novel, which captures David's dawning recognition of his incompatibility with Dora—"The first mistaken impulse of an undisciplined heart" (610, 642)—schools us in the pleasures of the right match and the disciplined heart.

There is a story about labor embedded in the novel—and not just the labor of authorship—but that story has been eclipsed in the amorphousness of "whatever." Now the point here is not to develop that story—another version of it will come in a fuller analysis of Dickens's *Great Expectations* in chapter 3—so much as to gesture toward the possibilities that are occluded when we only read along the grain of these texts. For "whatever" leaves so much unexplained, so much open to speculation, when in fact what one does, the kind of work one is involved in, the life one leads as a result of one's work, has a brute specificity to it and, moreover, a real interest for us, at least as important as who and how and to what end we court, one would think. That specificity is all but vaporized in Dickens's formulation; but, significantly, its trace is still there in the repetitions of the passage, in the impulse of a different kind of undisciplined heart, a different kind of pleasure. While it may not be readily apparent, then, labor is nonetheless a structuring presence, a "vanishing mediator" of sorts that facilitates David's development into a properly bourgeois subject and then disappears in the final product.[15] This book intends to make readers attentive to these mediatory processes with respect to work.

Once we accept the mediated nature of labor, and include pleasure in its formulation, even analyses that argue for labor's presence in the later literature of the nineteenth century (long after Gallagher's 1860s), require new scrutiny. In particular, this new skepticism as to the whereabouts of labor and pleasure significantly revises Raymond Willliams's earlier attempts to reestablish the importance of labor within British literature and culture. As readers may recall, in *The English Novel: From Dickens to Lawrence* and *The Country and the City*, as well as elsewhere, Williams makes the case for the centrality of Thomas Hardy and D. H. Lawrence to the English tradition. Arguing against the development of the English novel as a progression from George Eliot to Henry James—which carries with it a belittling attitude toward Hardy as simply a regional or country writer—Williams insists that Hardy's novels "belong very much in a continuing world. He writes more consistently and more deeply than any of our novelists about something that is still very close to us wherever we may be living: something that can be put, in abstraction, as the problem of the relation between customary and educated life; between customary and educated feeling and thought."[16] Crucial to this "border country" between customary and educated life and the mobility it brings are the everyday realities of work and the "harshness of economic processes, in inheritance, capital, rent and trade, within the continuity of the natural processes and persistently cutting across them."[17] These depictions become, for Williams, essential to Hardy's legacy: "But the most significant thing about Hardy . . . is that more than any other major novelist since this difficult mobility began he succeeded, against every pressure, in centring his major novels in the ordinary processes of life and work."[18] Williams's emphasis on "life and work" has been enormously important, in large part because he made visible the (agricultural) laborers who people English fiction and, moreover, made them central to the processes of modernization and historical change.

At the same time, however, his analysis leads to two problems. The first involves the overvaluation of what Williams refers to, time and time again, as "real lived experience" at the expense of a more complicated model of labor, and along with it, of ideology. Labor, and a connection to the land, specifically, come to define authentic experience. As a result, notions of immediacy and authentic "feeling" determine what gets seen by Williams.[19] At its most troubling, Williams's attachment to authenticity risks falling prey to a reductive equation between representation and the real, in which labor is part of the picture only when it is directly represented. Not insignificantly, it also constrains the applicability of his analysis to more contemporary articulations of work, given the increasingly opaque nature of labor within late capitalism. Coupled with this overvaluation of lived experience is a devaluation of domestic life as somehow separate from the "life and work" of so-called authentic laborers. Not only does this raise significant issues regarding the status of female laborers but it paradoxically removes domestic life from lived experience. The denigration of domestic matters is made explicit in Williams's reading of the industrial novel, where any move from the sphere of production to that of the home or consumption is treated as nothing less than a political betrayal; it denotes the novel's disengagement from its realist mission and its inability to remain true to a genuine working-class politics (something I develop more fully in part I). Given the linking of pleasure to the domestic sphere, a linkage that Williams reifies when he divides the industrial novel in this way, the banishment of domestic politics from labor politics leaves no space for pleasure as a legitimate political concern or significant axis of life and work, and no possibility for a dynamic relationship between the two.

Missing in both Gallagher's and Williams's accounts is labor's less visible presence in Victorian novels and nonfiction: its imprint in unexpected places and in a set of problems that extend across the nineteenth century to such unlikely bedfellows as Elizabeth Gaskell and Oscar Wilde. As a result, labor either disappears after 1860 or only appears in the form of male (often agricultural) laborers. So while Hardy's figure of the "reddleman" in *The Return of the Native*—so named because he has so thoroughly absorbed the red dye or reddle that is used to mark sheep that he is literally indistinguishable from his trade—cannot fail to impress us with its dramatization of labor and the way it is physically written on and even in the body, figures like him end up eliding industrial labor and its relations of production. Because they so powerfully captivate us, they fixate our critical gaze on labor's most immediate incarnations. But, as I am contending, industrial labors and modern pleasures find their most telling representation in the interstices of the Victorian novel, nestled, as it were, in the spatial/structural relations formed by the nexus of production and consumption rather than directly represented in or by either sphere alone. The problem thus becomes one of seeing what is structurally present but not readily visible within the strictures of a traditionally realist or "reflective" protocol of reading.

Certainly, the subsumption of labor should come as no surprise. Labor is precisely what needs to be repressed within capitalism—at the same time that it is constitutive of it. But what is surprising is the ease with which critics have read along with these texts, assuming the same absence of work constructed by the novels themselves.[20] In this context, the recognition of a genealogy of the labor novel that extends beyond the industrial novel directly engages the problem of visibility at the heart of capitalism rather than simply reproducing it.

Reading the labor novel against the grain of the industrial novel thus necessarily complicates the story of the realist novel: when labor becomes a problematic rather than an object easily seen, the whole question of authenticity vexing theories of realism and especially earlier studies of labor in the novel can be posed in a more fruitful way. In the past, critics either defended the "reality" of the conditions described or criticized these same conditions for failing to be realistic enough. For leftist critics, in particular, the desire to see industrial labor represented "authentically" (which often meant in politically progressive terms) led in the worst cases to an overly simplistic reading of realism itself: to judge a novel by the veracity of its historical representation (itself obviously a fraught concept) assumed a naive belief in the function of realism as a transparent representation of the social. In contrast, my focus on labor as a problematic makes it equally an aesthetic matter; a question of *how* one represents labor as much as *what* one represents. The introduction of the aesthetic into the discussion of labor produces a more complex version of realism able to walk the "particular tightrope" which defines the uniqueness of the concept of realism identified by Fredric Jameson: its "claim to cognitive as well as aesthetic status."[21] Conversely, the introduction of labor into the aesthetic highlights the work required to produce the aesthetic pleasures of the Victorian novel: the banishing of labor from the scene, and the narrowing of the possible avenues for the expression of pleasure (something I will return to later, in looking at the specific role women are assigned within such an aesthetic order).

This lesson is not, however, merely a negative one, about what is lost in this production. This view of the aesthetic suggests that the knowing and making of the world is one with its pleasures; and that the cognitive and the aesthetic equally enhance rather than detract from one another. In other words, realism and the aesthetic need not be at odds with each other.[22] The broadening of the concept of realism, as in Jameson's use of it, finally admits the utopian into realism, as pleasure and the aesthetic register both what is and what is desired—something, moreover, that does not have to be imported from some theoretical "outside" but instead comes from within the development of the Victorian novel. Once realism is granted its cognitive-aesthetic status, writers as diverse as Morris and Wilde can be seen as crucial participants in realism's project. When their utopianism is no longer assumed to be antithetical to realism, the nature of their aesthetics appears in a wholly different light: as deeply involved in creating new forms and strategies of realism *through* the utopian.

Within the trajectory of the labor novel traced here, pleasure is always inversely related to alienated labor. For this reason, the industrial novel and the late *Bildungsroman* struggle to produce compelling figures of pleasure. In contrast, by re-envisioning labor in an unalienated form, utopian narratives open up new possibilities and sites for pleasure—all the while underscoring, by dint of their utopianism, the present constraints on such pleasures. Pleasure is thus liberated to the extent that its connections to labor are made explicit, thereby reversing the tendencies of the industrial novel, which seeks an escape from labor in pleasure. Likewise, the privatization of pleasure entailed in this "escape" is fundamentally undercut. The more pleasure gets confined to the private recesses of the bedroom (or other sites removed from the realm of production), the more it is rendered ahistorical, thus solidifying the divisions enacted during the nineteenth century. By linking pleasure to labor, the utopian narrative affords the means to rehistoricize, by making public, the practices of pleasure. (Wilde captures the double reversal this entails, the way in which this linkage equally alters both poles of the binary, when a lover says of Dorian Gray, "The curves of your lips rewrite history."[23] Neither lips nor history can be quite the same after this.) No longer an affective "second nature" transcending theorization, this imagining of an intimate relation between labor and pleasure reveals pleasure as a fully material and collective achievement which, in turn, contributes to a retheorization of pleasure itself. From within this dialectic a case is made for the paradoxical seriousness of pleasure—without, hopefully, succumbing to the danger of destroying it in the process, but instead enlarging its scope and potential and heightening its frisson.

As my emphasis on the labor novel rather than the novel of pleasure should suggest, I grant labor in this mutually constitutive relationship a certain Althusserian "determination in the last instance." Or, to put this another way, new conceptualizations of labor generate new theories of pleasure. Whereas commodity production opposes paid labor to pleasure at the same time that it strategically mobilizes pleasure as a site which marks that which is not work, a richer notion of labor—one which breaks down the distinction between paid and unpaid labor, productive and unproductive labor, and necessary and creative activity—works toward the conjoining of labor and pleasure. From this vantage point, Morris's and Wilde's theories of labor come closest to those of more recent critics such as Michael Hardt and Antonio Negri or Oskar Negt and Alexander Kluge. What Hardt and Negri refer to as the "joys of living labor," and Negt and Kluge define as the "liberatory capacities of living labor," involve a notion of labor beyond necessity, expressed not through the abrogation of pleasure but instead fully expressive of it.[24] It is the expansion of labor that brings with it the return of pleasures and enjoyments no longer compromised by the coexistence of gross inequalities and deprivations "elsewhere." Moreover, as Kate Soper argues in her analysis of modernity's "troubled pleasures," "to recognize these 'complications' to modern pleasure is certainly to want to contest much that is currently on offer for consumption (and this includes some indisputably attractive and exciting sources of gratification). It is also to call into question modernity's general definition of pleasure—individualistic, materialistic, nonchalant regarding the future and narcissistic—even while acknowledging its power."[25]

Predictably, restrictions on pleasure come to light in the gender dynamics of these novels. The unredeemed pleasures in all these texts—the impulses of which are often expressed through these novels' heroines—testify both to the oppressive strictures which govern women's lives, specifically, and to a longing, more generally, for social spaces inclusive of larger domains of experience. For these women, who bear the brunt of the violence undergirding current definitions of labor and pleasure, nothing short of terror indicates the cost of these definitions, especially with respect to pleasure. When, in *Daniel Deronda*, Gwendolen feels a "sort of terror" when she comes face to face with Lydia Glasher, "as if some ghastly vision had come to her in a dream and said, 'I am a woman's life,'" her fear speaks for all these heroines.[26]

While the sexual and gendered aspects of this terror are vitally important, the expansion of our notions of labor and pleasure reveals something else as well: that this terror is emblematic of a world in which, as Wilde suggests, having is elevated over being. In this world, objects are viewed simply as things to own and possess, rather than as entities in their own right, which can best be understood when they are allowed to exist in a relationship of alterity to the subjects who would otherwise wish to consume them. This paradoxical intimacy can be felt both in the potential of these novels' heroines—the relation of nonidentity between subject and object, for instance, that permits Esther Lyon to experience herself as a liberating "heap of fragments" until she is forced to submit to Felix Holt's unitary rule—and in its cruel shutting down. The heroines of these novels are left with few options: the industrial novel tellingly confines women to reproducing male labor-power, as both *Mary Barton* and *Felix Holt* end with scenes celebrating their respective heroine's young baby boys; in the late *Bildungsroman* even this option seems unavailable to either Estella or Gwendolen, who are made barren, swallowed up so entirely by their men that they are not even granted a nominal dose of pleasure as wives and mothers. Those who receive that honor—Biddy, Miss Skiffins, Mirah—tend to be submissive from the outset and hence either obsolete or inconsequential to the complications of modern pleasure with which these novels are grappling.

This enlarged framework opens up new critical space, as well, for rethinking the relationship between Marxism and feminism/queer theory, a relationship often marked by the same tensions between labor and pleasure that I am outlining here. If, traditionally, Marxism has concerned itself with issues of work and production, feminist theory and queer theory have had as their domains matters broadly involving pleasure: reproductive and nonreproductive sexualities, sensuality, the construction of gender, and representations of women. As Michael Warner has remarked, in a consideration of the gains of queer theory, "despite powerful work on AIDS and in feminist social theory, the energies of queer studies have come more from rethinking the subjective meaning of sexuality than from rethinking the social."[27] Similarly, Marxist analyses of production and the social, to use Warner's language, have largely precluded discussions of pleasure. Yet, as the example of Gwendolen suggests, by bringing the concerns of pleasure to bear on an analysis of labor and vice versa, the beginnings of a productive rapprochement between the two become possible.

....

The chapters that follow are organized into three parts, each of which examines a different genre and its engagement with the problematic of labor. Together, they outline the stages in the genealogy of the labor novel. The industrial novel, the focus of part I, offers the prototype for the constructed opposition between labor and pleasure. By displacing conflicts in the sphere of production to the sphere of consumption, the industrial novel artificially establishes a divide between production and consumption, and work and pleasure. Labor "disappears" from these novels, much as the laborer John Barton disappears from *Mary Barton* (for the 155 pages chronicling Mary Barton's travails with Jem Wilson), not because it is not there but rather because it has been separated from the domestic concerns which come to occupy the center of these texts—and which can be resolved in a way that the problems of labor cannot. This separation limits the very constitution of labor; it is reduced to something existing outside the social or the larger public sphere, which is defined, in contrast, through workers' pleasures. Production thus becomes nothing other than labor in the narrowest, utilitarian sense—while (cynically) still being characterized as a pursuit that one ought to feel dignified in doing (something that Morris and Wilde harshly criticize).[28] In the more theoretical terms of political economy, labor becomes a commodity, subject to the dictates of capitalist production; like all commodities, it can only realize itself "through the needle's eye of exchange-value."[29] Pleasure, on the other hand, is opposed to abstract labor, while nonetheless tainted by it, for it is available only in commodified or private, sexualized forms. Pleasure thus suffers a similar fate to labor as its social reach or potential expansiveness is equally restricted.

The industrial novel effects this separation by carving out an extra-economic realm independent of production. The shift from production to the pleasures of the home or the pub eclipses the economic inequalities on which the productive sphere is based, transforming them into private, domestic matters rather than collective, political ones. In Gaskell's *Mary Barton* (chapter 1), the use of melodrama and the notion of pleasure it encompasses vitiates the problems her representations of labor and the productive sphere pose for the novel. But, importantly, the novel is only partially successful in its attempts to resolve these problems; their residue, I suggest, delineates a proletarian public sphere in which labor would be organized equitably and collectively and pleasure would be allowed expression in a form other than melodrama, which can only finally imagine pleasure as an antidote to labor, while simultaneously fashioning its working-class subjects as powerless victims. Registering the dramatic alteration in labor politics between 1848 and the Second Reform Bill of 1867, George Eliot's eponymous artisan, Felix Holt (chapter 2), puts forward a complex cultural justification for the exclusion of working men from the franchise. This shift in focus from economic to cultural capital, like the shift toward melodrama in *Mary Barton*, excludes labor from the larger social order or public sphere, using the working class's pleasures rather than their labors as the means by which to determine political legitimacy. In practical terms, the resulting message warns that drunkards do not deserve the franchise. But even when the separation of pleasure from labor is most effectively realized, the work necessary to bring about this separation is fully on display. What we take for granted, in other words, is seen to be actively produced. In the process, the ideologies and aporia required to maintain labor and pleasure as mutually opposed are laid bare. Paradoxically, this is also the promise of the industrial novel: the knowledge that pleasure is deeply entwined in questions of production. So even as the industrial novel engineers the split between them, it nonetheless offers (glimpses of) alternative visions of a public sphere not rent by such divisions.

In the latter part of the nineteenth century, the late *Bildungsroman* reproduces this division, even as it is transformed by the historical specificities of what Eric Hobsbawm calls the age of capital. Part II (chapter 3) locates this new articulation in two *Bildungsromane* written at a time when, as Franco Moretti argues, the primacy of the *Bildungsroman* as a form was nearing its end: Charles Dickens's *Great Expectations* (1861) and George Eliot's *Daniel Deronda* (1876).[30] Whereas the industrial novel putatively represents labor and laborers (even as it renders that labor invisible), the *Bildungsroman* takes up a related but new challenge: how to represent capitalism. In both cases, pleasure figures as a space or site free from the vagaries of production and hence able to escape its conflicts and inequalities. In the industrial novel, the pub or the home serves this function, while in the late *Bildungsroman*, the processes of individual maturation and the development of a properly modern subjectivity subsume labor. The production of the individual, that is to say, takes place outside the sphere of production. Here the work to be effaced is specifically the work of empire, be it the colonial labor of Magwitch in *Great Expectations* or the imperial underpinnings of Zionism in *Daniel Deronda*. In place of labor, the pleasures of consumption and the sphere of circulation—of trade versus labor and of the Jewish Diaspora versus British imperialism—occupy the restorative center of these narratives and, moreover, significantly complicate the problem of seeing (labor) which delimits the industrial novel. Within an increasingly global economy, marked in the late *Bildungsroman* through its figurations of empire, the relations between labor and world market of trade and exchange appear ever more elusive; labor is now transplanted to a geographic "elsewhere" where it is hidden from view and made progressively more abstract.

Yet despite these difficulties, this international traffic nonetheless insinuates itself into the developmental narrative of the *Bildungsroman*. Alongside these novels' more commonly understood biographical, linear narratives, I argue, exist spatial histories: mappings of the geography of work and empire, center and periphery and their interconnectedness. Indeed, the presence of these spatial histories potently reflects the vagaries of "coming of age" in a modern world economy. Only when these two models of history are read in conjunction with one another can the full context and meaning of Pip's and Daniel's development be gleaned. The *Bildungsroman's* figurations of money and empire may appear to take us rather far afield from the framework of labor and pleasure. But it is precisely the insistence on their connection that restores our ability to understand how capitalism produces the incoherences among labor, modes of exchange, and imperialism in the first place and how they are maintained as the structures of global capital become ever more difficult to see the more complicated and far-flung their reach. In short, these *Bildungsromane* offer lessons in "seeing the invisible."

In part III, the utopian fictions of Morris (chapter 4) and Wilde (chapter 5) are shown to directly challenge the distinction between work and pleasure that the industrial novel and the late *Bildungsroman* narrate, and the invisibility of labor that results from this distinction. They thus complete the genealogy of the labor novel by making explicit what has remained largely implicit in the industrial novel and the late *Bildungsroman*: directly identifying labor and pleasure as the framework for modernity, they provide a kind of retrospective Havishamian looking glass to illuminate the ideological contours of the industrial novel and *Bildungsroman* and establish a future project whose completion is yet to come.[31] Their challenge is one of both form and content. The theoretical basis of this challenge leads not only to a new form of realism—critical realism or the utopian novel—but to a reuniting of labor and pleasure, identified in Morris with the notion of pleasurable labor and in Wilde with a nonutilitarian notion of "use" as pleasure. In fact, the uniting of labor and pleasure *requires* a less traditionally realist novelistic form, something that Morris gestures toward when he declares that he will never attempt to write a classically realist novel again (he made one attempt) "unless the world turn topsides under some day."[32]

As the notion of turning the "world topsides under" implies, it is not only English or British culture that forms the object of Morris's critique but rather a *world* economy, which, as Morris sees it, is inseparable from capitalist development and the particular valuations it privileges: mental as opposed to manual labor, exchange-value rather than use-value, utility over and against pleasure or beauty. Just as definitions of labor are incomplete without a consideration of pleasure, then, both of these concepts become activated within an imperial or global context, since it is here that the movements of capital (which locate labor) are to be found. Although I develop an account of these flows of capital and the novelistic structures that manage them most explicitly in part II of the book (in reference to the *Bildungsroman*), they are also present in the industrial novel—and, moreover, come into view precisely when the Victorian novel is viewed in terms of its *organization of labor*. Indeed, the structuring presence of labor goes a long way toward explaining why the empire makes an appearance here at all—whether in *Mary Barton*'s exporting of its titular heroine to Canada at the end, or in *Felix Holt*'s fascination with the Orient. Such references suggest the inextricable connections between so-called local labor politics and (increasingly) global flows of capital.

Perhaps most unexpectedly apparent in Morris's and Wilde's utopias are the extent of the difficulties which surround modern pleasure. Despite their explicit theorizations of and challenges to the present structure of labor and pleasure, they nonetheless have difficulty imagining forms of liberated pleasure for their female characters. Disappointingly, Morris characterizes female pleasure in his utopia as the ability to keep house well and to be appreciated for it; and Sybil Vane is made incapable of sustaining the Wildean pleasures Dorian is granted—even if only for a time. But even as they fail in this regard, they nonetheless locate labor and pleasure at the crux of hierarchies of gender, as when Morris identifies the "family tyranny" which results from private property, and Wilde foresees the disappearance of marriage altogether once private property is abolished and the activity or labor which it has hindered is finally allowed expression. It should be noted that while I maintain a resolute focus on Morris's and Wilde's fiction in these chapters, I also turn my eyes more directly to their essays than I do with earlier authors. I do so because it is in these nonfictional works that their thinking about labor and pleasure is most explicitly articulated. Indeed, I argue that in many ways both Morris and Wilde draw their utopian energies from perceiving and identifying the split between labor and pleasure, a split that had hitherto remained unconscious or repressed. In essence, I am tracing the history of the conditions of possibility for Morris's and Wilde's perception of the split between labor and pleasure as a problem. But, fundamentally, I treat their work—fiction and nonfiction—as a complex of writings deeply related to one another—hence my use of the term labor "novel" to characterize all the texts I am examining in the book. Either directly or indirectly, then, issues of fictional gender, economics, and representation coalesce in the presence of labor and pleasure; in short, the interconnectedness of labor and pleasure is shown to be indispensable both to the life world of the Victorian novel, and by extension, our own, and to any future reconfiguring of that world along terms both more expansive and more intimate.

What I see to be at stake finally in this series of reformulations is the very nature of our relationship to the object world. In order to realize the kinds of changes Morris and Wilde advocate, and the industrial novel and the *Bildungsroman* wish for in their attempts to preserve a realm of pleasure untainted by the conflicts of labor and the sphere of production, nothing less than a thorough reconceptualization of the relationship between labor and pleasure must occur. I envision the genealogy of the labor novel that this book proposes as one experiment in this process of reconceptualization. As I have suggested, a crucial step in such a project is acknowledging the invisibility of labor as central to Britain's social formation in the nineteenth century and to our own, as its legatees. Inconceivable without its counterpart, pleasure, this acknowledgment equally enriches our understanding of the Victorian novel, as it illustrates the limits of an aesthetic hampered by the split between labor and pleasure and, simultaneously, gestures toward a more inclusive notion of pleasure and the possibilities therein.

The nineteenth-century novel "knows" this connection between labor and pleasure in ways that we no longer do, precisely because it was actively negotiated through its texts. In the literature of this period, one can see the ideological work used to contain the power and promise of living labor within the strictures of capitalist valorization; concomitantly, expressions of newfound pleasures also find their way into these texts. That these pleasures may be close to home, that, indeed, they may reside in everyday notions of use and the utopian, is part of the legacy of these novels; but equally they have bequeathed a legacy of divisions, both local and global. Thus the utopian hopes that form this study lie in a kind of global "philosophizing at home," to which, at least for the time being, the categories of labor and pleasure will be central. Utopian in the best sense of the word, these hopes will, of course, have to be continually remade, their realization never-ending.

PART I

Realism Meets the Masses

....

The industrial novel occupies a unique place in the context of debates about realism. As Erich Auerbach suggests, the subject matter of the realist novel —the masses or "the common people"—comes into being as a serious subject for literature as part of realism's inexorable logic:

> But the advance of the realistic mixture of styles which Stendhal and Balzac had brought about could not stop short of the fourth estate; it had to follow the social and political development of the time. Realism had to embrace the whole reality of contemporary civilization, in which to be sure the bourgeoisie played a dominant role, but in which the masses were beginning to press threateningly ahead, as they became ever more conscious of their own function and power. The common people in all its ramifications had to be taken into the subject matter of serious realism.[1]

Within realism's drive to represent the masses lies the search for the ever more novel or strange, the desire for the discovery of new aesthetic material with which to work. Citing the Goncourt brothers as exemplary of this driven fascination with the common people, Auerbach quotes Edmond de Goncourt, who articulates this appeal in terms that strongly echo those of the imperial or colonizing impulse, seeking adventure in foreign places: "the people, the mob, if you will, has for me the attraction of unknown and undiscovered populations, something of the *exoticism* which travelers go to seek" (497).

For my purposes here what is important are the textual and aesthetic determinants of such an attitude. Auerbach argues that the Goncourts' attitude necessarily excludes from representation "everything *functionally essential*, the people's work, its position within modern society, the polical, social, and moral ferments which are alive in it and which point the future" (498, emphasis added). Although Auerbach is not directly addressing the industrial novel, and the distinction is important given the Goncourts' particular fascination with the ugly, the repellent, and the unusual—interests associated specifically with naturalism—nonetheless the problem he identifies in *Germinie Lacerteux* mirrors that posed by the industrial novel: its inability to represent the "functionally essential." Given this, one may ask, what can or does the so-called industrial novel do? If we accept Auerbach's claim that when it comes to the development of realism and its need to incorporate the fourth estate, the "Goncourts were right . . . The development of realistic art has proved it," and, along with this, acknowledge that the impetus motivating realism's representational concerns functionally precludes the representation of its supposed subject matter— "the people's work"—what does the industrial novel in fact represent?

Raymond Williams, in his groundbreaking work *Culture and Society*, reads the industrial novel as a genre defined by its conflicting concerns.[2] These novels, for him, embody a critical response to industrialism, with, in some cases, genuine sympathy for the plight of the working class. A significant aspect of their value resides in their detailed observation and the "intensity of the effort to record, in its own terms, the feel of everyday life in the working-class homes" (99). But in the face of the actual conditions of the working class, they back down from any serious involvement out of fear, opting instead for a backdoor exit involving either the death or the emigration—to a new world, often *the* New World—of their politically engaged and potentially militant protagonists. Williams identifies this ultimate withdrawal, fueled initially out of sympathy, as the determining "structure of feeling" of the industrial novel.

The conflict between sympathy and fear not only determines the internal structure of these novels but constitutes as well their failure realistically to represent the social conditions of their time. The fear of violence, according to Williams, distorts even the best of intentions: Elizabeth Gaskell's *Mary Barton*, which comes closest for Williams to identifying imaginatively with and hence representing the "lived experience" of the working class, is finally unable to sustain its sympathy for that experience once the threat of violence arises and, with it, the potential for that violence to be *organized* through collective solidarity and struggle. This inability is marked in Gaskell's text by the recourse to conventional sentimental fiction, as the novel's center moves from John Barton and his participation in the workers' union to the love trials of Mary Barton and her journey to exonerate her lover, falsely accused of murder. In other cases, such as that of Dickens's *Hard Times*, withdrawal takes the form of confused passivity amid the tangle of complex social forces: Blackpool's "Aw a muddle!" becomes, for Williams, synonymous with Dickens's treatment of the working class in general: a typically adolescent posture in its claim to have "seen through" society while simultaneously rejecting any real engagement in that society, Dickens's work functions more as a symptom than an assessment, realistic or otherwise, of the very confusions of industrial society that it purports to represent (107). Whatever the actual specifics of each individual novel's resolution—be it that of *Alton Locke, North and South,* or *Felix Holt*—the strategy, one of *containment,* remains essentially the same.[3] Moreover, as Williams notes in conclusion, it is a strategy or structure of feeling whose province is by no means limited to the nineteenth century, but whose legacy remains with us today.

While this argument has great explanatory power, most notably in its identification of the structure motivating the oft-noted murky politics of these novels, Williams's own interpretive politics bear further investigation. In the midst of his critique of *Mary Barton*, Williams bemoans what he sees as Gaskell's fall into sentimental fiction: "her [Mary's] indecision between Jem Wilson and 'her gay lover, Harry Carson'; her agony in Wilson's trial; her pursuit and last-minute rescue of the vital witness; the realization of her love for Wilson: all this, the familiar and orthodox plot of the Victorian novel of sentiment, but of little lasting interest."[4] Williams's diagnosis strictly delineates industrial novels as separate from and superior to (if done "authentically") merely sentimental fiction which can be of "little lasting interest." Such a view is problematic for a number of reasons, not the least of which is that Williams's model has served as an exemplar for subsequent interpretations of the industrial novel—although often with the opposite result. While Williams elevates politics above domesticity, within the canon the reverse occurs. In either case, though, politics and the aesthetic development of the novel are seen to take divergent paths. Once categorized as "industrial," a novel is judged on the basis of its political affiliations and its attempt to deal with broad social issues circumscribed in the "public" sphere. Should a novel move from the factory into the home, within a Marxist framework it spells political doom.[5] Conversely, sentimental fiction finds its home in the domestic sphere, with the concomitant valuation that politics, finally, does not make for good novels.

This either/or interpretive model highlights the particular representational quandary of the industrial novel. On the one hand, these novels cannot be "great literature" if and when they stray from their mission of authenticity, which needless to say, they always do. On the other hand, when they enter the realm of properly domestic fiction, they cannot be considered great because sentimental fiction has no real political value. Ultimately, this division implies that domestic fiction deals exclusively with the domestic sphere whereas industrial fiction has as its singular domain the public sphere.[6] It also colludes with broader, dominant views of culture as a realm above the political fray and has served historically to position the industrial novel outside the canon of British literature.

While more recent criticism on the industrial novel has sought to dislodge these cultural assumptions, it seems important to note that this division continues to operate with the ease of second nature. There is a certain unspoken agreement, for instance, that among writers who produced both industrial and domestic fiction—to stick with these categories—the industrial novels represent their worst work. The blurb on the back of the Penguin edition of *Felix Holt* notes that it "is generally regarded as George Eliot's 'political novel.'" Lest this scare readers away, the description goes on to say that the novel is "political in a profounder sense than the immediate one . . . The radicalism [Eliot] portrays is 'an open-ended Radicalism of the emotions.'" The attempt to vitiate the concern a political novel might engender tellingly comes through a claim for a different order of politics altogether that is not part of the public sphere but rather has to do with emotions, and in which a political movement (Radicalism) is transformed into an affective one. Equivocation about the industrial novel may reflect, in part, the current critical bias against didacticism. But I also think it indicates something more fundamental: how intractable the public/private divide remains. In the case of the industrial novel, in particular, this means that no matter the reams of theoretical writing proving the interconnectedness of class and gender politics, they nevertheless continue to be felt as competing and offsetting concerns.

Certainly, further analyses, such as this one, of the coexistence of gender and class narratives in the industrial novel alone will not shake this foundation. My hope is rather that an explicit focus on work will give us new ways of conceiving this impasse and the cultural investments that generate it. Part of this rethinking involves seeing the industrial novel as central, rather than peripheral, to the development of the Victorian novel and to our conceptions, more broadly, of the politics of class and gender.

In addition to the exclusion of the domestic from the public sphere, another exclusion operates with a certain specificity to the industrial novel, given its project, broadly defined, of representing industrialization and its social effects. In response to the demands of the working class for a greater share of social and political power, the ruling class wields the notion of "culture" (here inclusive of more than simply literary culture) as an ideological weapon to exclude the realm of production from the bourgeois public sphere. That is, through the ideology of culture, the ruling class bars the producers of England's wealth from participation and inclusion in the public sphere, deeming them deficient in cultural capital. Culture becomes a litmus test for workers being admitted into the public sphere. Thus the same notion of Arnoldian culture which has worked to situate the industrial novel outside the literary canon also serves to exclude the sphere of production from the public sphere—both in the industrial novel and in Victorian society.[7]

Paradoxically, while Raymond Williams's body of work emphasizes the need to theorize culture as an everyday *process* integral to all social practices, for the most part he leaves out the cultural formation of imperialism and its determining effects on England and English culture.[8] As I will argue, however, the crisis of industrialism, the industrial novel's raison d'être, and its connected attempt to understand the newly emerging experience and processes of modernity cannot be understood outside the context of English nationalism and empire. It is here that the exoticism of the Goncourts is more generally of relevance. In reading the industrial novel as a narrative of "internal" travel, with its respective authors operating as adventure-seeking travelers of sorts, the masses, through metaphoric displacement, are situated much like the exotic, colonial Other, but with the added thrust that their threat to England is if anything greater than that of the colonial, existing as it does within the internal, domestic boundaries of England.[9] Faced with the cultural anxiety wrought by the possibility of *internal* disruption and division, the industrial novel emplots a paradigmatic structure wherein the attempt to represent the fearfully internal Other—the working class—necessitates its eventual absorption into a new community, one whose membership admits an identification beyond that of class interest, in place of class distinctions: the unifying ideology of the national body. The cementing of this national ideology is predicated on the erasure of class and gender inequalities; as Benedict Anderson has formulated it, "regardless of the actual inequality and exploitation that may prevail in the imagined community of 'nation,' the nation is always conceived as a *deep, horizontal comradeship* (emphasis added)."[10]

In chapters 1 and 2, I argue that this process occurs through a series of displacements involving ever-wider spheres: from production to the domestic sphere of consumption, from the domestic sphere to the national sphere, and finally from the national to the imperial sphere, with each move entailing a symbolic resolution of conflict.[11] A central precondition for these symbolic resolutions is the exclusion of work and working-class struggle from representation; an exclusion prompted, on the one hand, by the demands being made by the English working class for political representation and, on the other hand, naturalized almost seamlessly by a politics of culture which shifts the terms of political representation away from the productive sphere altogether. A "crime" committed by an individual member of the working class—be it theft, murder, or some act of violence—functions initially to rob working-class voices of their political legitimacy. But, more significantly, throughout these narratives, the working class is represented in the pub or the home, thereby allowing it to be defined in terms of its pleasures as opposed to its productive activity. Pleasure is thus separated from production; it becomes simply an escape from labor. This realm of pleasure, identified with melodrama in Gaskell's *Mary Barton* and with Esther's romantic education in Eliot's *Felix Holt*, provides the space necessary for the construction of a "moral community"—united under the rubric of "nation"—which symbolically resolves the class divisions inherent in the system of production. In the end the sense of a national community is solidified against what are perceived of as both the external and internal forces threatening its dissolution.

Elizabeth Gaskell's *Mary Barton* only partially performs this suturing of the social. The brief glimpse the novel provides of a proletarian culture whose experiences are not represented in the larger bourgeois public sphere (and indeed are rendered invisible there) blocks its ability, finally, to seamlessly absorb its workers into the national fold. The novel's lack of success in resolving these social tensions puts in high relief the mechanisms necessary to displace issues of production and labor from the public sphere. The loss of pleasure entailed in this displacement testifies both to the vitality of other possible forms of pleasure (identified with the proletarian public sphere) and to their impossibility within the novel's constructed opposition between labor and pleasure. In this way, *Mary Barton* constitutes at once the industrial novel's limits and its promise.

Chapter 2 then turns to a later industrial novel, George Eliot's *Felix Holt* as a site in which to examine the politics of representation surrounding the Second Reform Bill of 1867. Here a similar kind of displacement occurs, but now "culture" itself defines the terms of debate, as the working class is denied admission into the bourgeois public sphere based on its lack of cultural rather than economic capital. The possibility of a proletarian culture at all is rendered moot, silenced by the refusal of any cultural viewpoint to the workers (their pleasures deem them unworthy of such a role) and the removal of production from the public sphere altogether. Employing a paternalistic structure, Eliot positions the workers as not yet ready culturally for inclusion into the public sphere, a point driven home by the extradiegetic "Address to Working Men" appended to the end of *Felix Holt*.

Clearly, these novels participate in the ideological disenfranchisement of the working class. Even as, historically, workers gain representation through the political franchise with the Reform Bill of 1867, the terms of their inclusion have been severely restricted. At the same time, however, these novels position labor at the crux of the battle over workers' representation and dramatize the high stakes involved in silencing the working class. At stake, finally, is not only working-class participation in Victorian Britain's social order but a whole structure of relations regarding work and pleasure that are as applicable to the dominant classes as they are to Gaskell's and Eliot's laborers. While the industrial novel, therefore, may not represent workers working, or even the nature of the work they do, it does something else that, *pace* Auerbach, is far more profound: by addressing the issue of industrial labor at all, it acknowledges, at its best, the constitutive role of labor in modern society, and, at its worst, the need to disavow this insight.

CHAPTER 1

"HOW DEEP MIGHT BE
THE ROMANCE"

....

Representing Work

and the Working Class

in Elizabeth Gaskell's

Mary Barton

There is always a pleasure in unravelling a mystery, in catching at the gossamer clue which will guide to certainty. — Elizabeth Gaskell, *Mary Barton*

Written in 1848, Elizabeth Gaskell's *Mary Barton* was situated at a historical crossroads. In the wake of resurgent Jacobinism in France, Louis Philippe was deposed by the February Revolution, and revolutionary struggles had broken out all across Western Europe, in Italy, the German states, the Habsburg empire, and Switzerland. At stake was the fate of the bourgeois revolutions and the direction they would take: onward to deeper and more democratic revolutionary aims and an alliance with the working class or backward to a retrenchment of bourgeois power and a shoring up of the bourgeoisie's interests with state force. "Eighteen forty-eight failed," Eric Hobsbawm argues, "because it turned out that the decisive confrontation was not that between the old regimes and the united 'forces of progress,' but between 'order' and 'social revolution.'"[1] Or, as Georg Lukács characterizes it, the uprisings and their defeat, especially the June battle of the Paris proletariat, "[produce] a decisive change in the bourgeois camp, accelerating to an extraordinary degree the inner process of differentiation which is to transform revolutionary democracy into compromising liberalism."[2]

Still, at the time of Gaskell's writing, events on the Continent were threatening enough that Britain wished to dampen any incipient feelings of continental camaraderie. Indeed, the possibility of identification with these European movements seemed so real that Gaskell's publishers requested that she write a preface to the completed *Mary Barton* making clear that it was meant in no way to provide grist for revolution. In doing so, Gaskell invoked France as a threat that could obtain in Britain if "merciful deeds" were not speedily deployed to "disabuse the work-people of so miserable a misapprehension" as the thought that the middle classes do not care about their suffering: "At present they seem to me to be left in a state wherein lamentations and tears are thrown aside as useless, but in which the lips are compressed for curses, and the hands clenched and ready to smite."[3]

Against this threat of violence, Gaskell intended *Mary Barton* as a stimulus to the ignorant middle classes, who, the reasoning went, would readily respond with charity and good will if only they knew of the inhumane conditions under which the laboring classes were suffering. The more Gaskell reflected on the "unhappy state of things" between employers and the employed, the "more anxious [she] became to give some utterance to the agony which, from time to time, convulses this dumb people" (3). Her gambit, articulated in the preface, is that "if it be an error that the woes, which come with ever returning tide-like flood to overwhelm the workmen in our manufacturing towns, pass unregarded by all but the sufferers, it is at any rate an error so bitter in its consequences to all parties, that whatever public effort can do in the way of merciful deeds, or helpless love in the way of 'widow's mites' could do, should be done, and that speedily" (3–4). Contrary to her intent, however, she was attacked by many for doing just the opposite: provoking class against class by her detailed descriptions of the working conditions of the Manchester poor. In response, Gaskell defended herself on moral grounds, claiming that "no one can feel more deeply than me how *wicked* it is to do anything to excite class against class."[4] As these potential readings and misreadings make clear, the emergence of the working class as a subject for middle-class literature carried with it unique representational problems. What was the best form for giving expression to the working class without fomenting revolution? Was it possible to depict working-class conditions of life realistically without inspiring class conflict? What was the best way of generating interest in the working class on the part of a middle-class reading public? In short, *Mary Barton* and the industrial novel more generally found itself in something of a Catch-22: if it fulfilled its realist criterion it ran the "wicked" risk of "exciting class against class" and consequently losing its middle-class audience and its moral authority as a cultural force of class conciliation. Faced with this dilemma, *Mary Barton* tries to bridge the gap between realism and morality: suggesting that cross-class solidarity is to be found in another, higher realm of Christian love and "brotherhood," Gaskell hopes, in her "tale of Manchester life," to reconcile "masters and men."

Gaskell's attempts at reconciliation delineate the task critics face: how best to describe and understand the movement within *Mary Barton* between narrative modes or generic conventions. If Raymond Williams sets the stage with his description of the "fall" from realism into sentimentalism or the romance, more recent feminist scholars follow with important reassessments and critiques of that "fall."[5] Nancy Armstrong unearths the politics behind the turn toward the sentimental, arguing for the centrality of female authority in the development of the novel and, in turn, of modern identity itself; Catherine Gallagher counters the neat division of the text into an opposition between realism and sentimentalism, arguing that multiple generic modes operate in the novel and that these modes do not shift progressively (or "fall" from one to the other as Williams would have it) but rather are more loosely intermingled throughout the text; and Amanda Anderson extends Gallagher's analysis by looking more closely at the intersection of realism and romance in the specific figure of the prostitute.[6] All these approaches significantly and importantly complicate Williams's assumptions about realism and its exclusive claim to truth and authenticity. In the process they also foreground the issue of form in the novel by focusing on the political work that the sentimental mode—as well as other nonrealist narrative modes—performs, thereby countering Williams's quick dismissal of sentimentalism as a retreat from the (assumed) political mode of realism.

As useful as these recent perspectives of *Mary Barton* are, they all replicate, ironically, the move away from the representation of work that Williams identifies as the novel's weakness. To be sure, they do so in the name of understanding how domestic narrative(s) in *Mary Barton* function, but nonetheless the issue of the representation of work all but disappears from these accounts. In this chapter, I want to suggest that reading *Mary Barton* in this way elides a crucial component of Gaskell's project. In order to show how this is so, we need first to return briefly to the oft-commented-on preface to the novel.

Much has been made of the fact that Gaskell begins *Mary Barton* with the disclaimer that she knows nothing about political economy. Instead, she has "tried to write truthfully; and if [her] accounts agree or clash with any system, the agreement or disagreement is unintentional" (4). Just as Gaskell distances herself from theories of trade, then, she also distances theories of trade from the truth, suggesting that perhaps her disclaimer is a bit less humbling than it might first appear.[7] On one level, the move from the political to the moral sphere implied by the shift from trade to truth is unsurprising given that the moral domain was deemed the proper sphere of influence for women writers in the nineteenth century. Terry Lovell highlights the force of this writerly female provenance in her discussion of Gaskell's feminine persona: "She has a recurrent refrain, her disclaimer of any knowledge of political economy. As author, she claims the right to speak not from knowledge of 'the facts' but from an identification with the feelings of an oppressed and suffering workforce. In so doing, she claims a woman's privilege."[8] As Lovell goes on to argue, Gaskell certainly had read many works of political economy, but "it would be presumptuous in a woman to speak authoritatively in a woman's voice of such matters. Where she could legitimately speak was of course from sympathetic feeling, and this is what she chose to do, at the cost of playing down her intellect."[9]

On another level, though, the matter of female authority in the novel has other, more pervasive ramifications as well. The separation Lovell refers to—between the economic, the social, and the moral—is itself part of a larger, newly emerging social formation. In *Making a Social Body: British Cultural Formation, 1830–1864*, Mary Poovey identifies this process as one of modern disaggregation. Modern disaggregation involves the gradual separation and institutionalization of different domains of knowledge and social practices on the basis of specific rationalities. So, for example, the Poor Law of 1834 newly distinguishes between *pauperism* and *poverty* in terms of separate domains: the former becomes a moral and physical designation (the components of which later come to encompass the social domain), the latter an economic category. In the process, issues of morality and health are dissociated from one's economic situation, at the same time that they continue to exist in a relationship of relative autonomy, maintaining traces of their originary affiliation. As Poovey argues, when novelists, specifically, entered the "Condition of England" debate, "they were implicitly arguing that a feminized genre that individualized distress and aroused sympathy was more appropriate to the delineation of contemporary problems than were the rationalizing abstractions of a masculine genre like political economy."[10] Of course, paradoxically, this very separation of domains reflects the rationalizing discourse of political economy, and, more generally, the formal rationality of capitalist market relations. Nonetheless, the force of Gaskell's appeal involves resituating issues of work and poverty in a realm of "feeling" seemingly outside of or uncorrupted by the quantitative, statistical epistemologies of either the economic or the political realm.

Whether her opening proviso is read finally as a weak or a strong move, its presence at all registers the peculiar constraints under which Gaskell found herself as a result of *Mary Barton*'s subject matter. By the time even of *North and South* (1855) such cautionary notes apparently were unnecessary. Certainly, too, the whole issue of the preface is vexed by the fact that her publisher, Edward Chapman's request for it left Gaskell completely at a loss. Perplexed and irritated, she wrote to Chapman, "I hardly know what you mean by an 'explanatory preface.' The only thing I should like to make clear is that it is no catch-penny run up since the events on the Continent have directed public attention to the consideration of the state of affairs between the Employers, & their work-people. If you think the book requires such a preface I will try to concoct it; but at present, I have no idea what to say."[11] Clearly, if Gaskell had any concerns about the novel, they stemmed from it being perceived as lowbrow and sensationalist, written quickly to capitalize cheaply on public interest—a far cry from Chapman's concerns.

While the preface as it was finally published does not register Gaskell's concerns in the form given in her letter, it does, however, offer a more complex apologia than the turn away from political economy would suggest. For the preface begins with Gaskell's motivation for writing the novel in the first place, namely, her sympathy for working people and her sense of "how deep might be the romance in the lives of some of those who elbowed me daily in the busy streets of the town in which I resided" (3). She then goes on to note their anguish at the "lottery-like nature" of their lives and the consequent animosity they feel toward the rich, a sentiment that Gaskell ultimately refuses to judge: "Whether the bitter complaints made by them of the neglect which they experienced from the prosperous—especially from the masters whose fortunes they had helped to build up—were well-founded or no, it is not for me to judge. It is enough for me to say, that this belief of the injustice and unkindness which they endure from their fellow-creatures taints what might be resignation to God's will, and turns it to revenge in many of the poor uneducated factory workers of Manchester" (3). The coupling of sympathy with the refusal to judge is significant in two respects: first, it is Gaskell's sympathy that necessitates her disclaimer. Without the ability to feel for the workers, and to represent that concern, her publishers probably would not have had to worry about her representation of them being misunderstood. Second, the ability to see through the workers' eyes, as it were, and to do so without (or at least before) enforcing judgment on them delineates a narratorial voice desirous of more than the moralizing stance implied by Gaskell's abnegation of political economy. Indeed, it is the very coupling of these two impulses (feeling and seeing) that continually challenges the oppositional structure—romance versus politics, morality versus political economy—Gaskell explicitly articulates in her disclaimer. For want of a better term, Gaskell's "sentimental realism" allows her both to feel for the workers and their plight and to detail their workaday existence, both in the domestic and the political realm. *Contra* Williams, it is not a question of Gaskell's sentimentalism jeopardizing her realism or vice versa or of the two being at odds with one another but rather of each mode enabling the other—and to such an extent that the resulting text warrants a disclaimer. To feel is to see and vice versa.[12]

But these prefatory comments also expose an ambivalence on Gaskell's part toward her subject matter that persists throughout the narrative and ultimately defines the novel's conflicted "structure of feeling." Ostensibly, the novel is about work and the working class. Yet, like its generic compatriots, it summarily avoids any direct representation of work itself. Given this absence, one might be tempted to conclude that any focus on work in the novel is a fruitless attempt to find something that does not even exist.[13] But, as Gaskell's own statements suggest and the narrative of *Mary Barton* confirms, the presence of work is inseparable from the novel's attempt to sympathize with the working class. Even as Gaskell claims in her preface to the novel that she is not going to judge whether the workers' complaints are legitimate or not, the fact of their work intrudes on her nonjudgmental stance: "Whether the bitter complaints made by them of the neglect which they experienced from the prosperous—*especially from the masters whose fortunes they had helped to build up*—were well-founded or no, it is not for me to judge" (3, emphasis added). Rising up, parenthetically, is a clear statement of the working poor's responsibility for the wealth of the rich; they have literally made the rich rich. Similarly, later in the preface, the "common interests" unifying factory workers and factory owners are defined in terms of their work relations, as "employers and the employed." As much as the novel does not, then, directly confront labor per se, its presence forms the guilty conscience of the text.

This "knowledge," of the centrality of labor to the social relationships which unfold in the novel, defines what is most unusual about *Mary Barton* and necessitates the narrative's move into the domestic realm. By itself, this latter displacement is not particularly unusual. Nancy Armstrong, along with other critics of the industrial novel, has shown convincingly how the domestic realm reroutes the political through the sexual. But what marks Gaskell's project as special is the presence of the productive sphere at all. Its representation, I will argue, both makes visible the kind of strategic rerouting Armstrong identifies and ultimately blocks its successful completion. The unifying domestic politics of the novel, that is to say, cannot finally neutralize its fractious class politics, precisely because they are shown to be rooted in work. Like the acknowledgment of how workers have made their masters' fortunes, the narrative's brief foray into the productive relations between masters and men as seen through John Barton's eyes manages, despite Gaskell's claims otherwise, to articulate a class divide between workers and employers defined by their radically different relationship, respectively, to work and the sphere of production. In the space of this divide the narrative gestures toward the makings of a proletarian public sphere. Marking the inability of *Mary Barton*'s text to fully incorporate and defuse this alternative public sphere in its vision of Christian brotherhood is a question at the center of the novel, posed provocatively and repeatedly by John Barton: "How comes it they're rich, and we're poor?" (65).[14] Attention to how this question functions in the novel as a whole, I contend, will restore the text's political unconscious, and, in turn, establish why this question can never be answered by the text and why its unanswerability testifies to the singular achievement of *Mary Barton*.

The Work of Domesticity

If earlier criticism of the industrial novel emphasized the political efficacy of the sphere of production over the sphere of consumption, and more recent criticism has reversed this trend, this chapter has as its goal bringing the two together. In order to do this, it is imperative, first of all, to be particularly attentive to the varieties of cultural work each of these spheres engages in, and to what purpose. For this reason, the following reading will be a close one, so as to carefully demarcate the boundaries of production and consumption and to suggest what might be gained from listening to the (revolutionary) story Gaskell's juxtaposition of these two spheres relates. As I want to argue, finally, by way of comparing the specific work secrets perform in the domestic as opposed to the productive sphere, there is only one secret that the text founders on. Although the economic and sexual realms are shown to be deeply imbricated in one another throughout the novel, it is only when the text enters the productive sphere that it turns away from its own economics. In this first section, then, I aim to show how complex but nonetheless resolvable the novel's sexual politics are within its own symbolic economy.

Mary Barton's aunt Esther forms the focus of a secondary plot seemingly far removed from the realm of industrial labor. A tale of romance gone bad, Esther, distinguished from the other Manchester factory girls by her "fresh beauty of the agricultural districts," falls in love with a man above her in class, moves from Manchester with him, and is subsequently abandoned and left to fend alone with their child. Unable to support her ailing baby, Esther turns to the streets to make money. Despite her efforts, the baby dies and Esther, now a fallen woman, becomes an outcast, lurking on the margins of *Mary Barton*'s social world and the novel itself. From the margins, however, Esther occupies anything but a secondary role in the plot. In fact, she figures finally as the cause of almost everything that happens. Fully illustrative of the deep paradoxes which reside in Esther's position within the text, the centrality of her marginal status marks the limits of *Mary Barton*'s world — of what it can entertain with respect to class and gender relations — and reveals its irrevocable relationship to relations of production. These connections reveal themselves through a narrative structure of secrets and surprises buttressed by an ideological frame of "true love."

Markedly absent from the opening pages of the novel, it is the mystery of Esther's disappearance that disrupts its one pastoral scene. In the first dialogue, as the Wilsons and Bartons picnic at Green Hays Fields, George Wilson, in a low aside, "while a sudden look of sympathy [dims] his gladsome face" (8), asks John Barton whether he has received any news of Esther yet. In response, John Barton speaks of Esther's beauty, declaring it to be a "sad snare" (9); indicative of her seductive powers, the very mention of Esther's name must be shielded from the young Mary's ears.

In a parallel scene, when the Bartons and Wilsons return home to have tea, it is Alice Wilson who inadvertently brings up the unmentionable subject of Esther in her toast to "absent friends" (18). The mere intimation of Esther's absence casts a pall over the meal as "every one thought of Esther, the absent Esther; and Mrs. Barton put down her food, and could not hide the fast dropping tears. Alice could have bitten her tongue out" (18). The episode serves as a model ideological event: Alice says one thing, "absent friends," and "everybody" understands what is meant; this common understanding defines and unifies the group from which Esther is excluded. From the outset, she is thus established as an absent presence disruptive to and yet simultaneously constitutive of the community.

The potency of Esther's threat to the community is definitively established when the elder Mary Barton dies giving birth. The cause of death is given as "some shock to the system," which John instantly attributes to Esther's sudden and mysterious disappearance: "His feeling towards Esther amounted to curses. It was she who had brought on all this sorrow. Her giddiness, her lightness of conduct, had wrought this woe. His previous thoughts about her had been tinged with wonder and pity, but now he hardened his heart against her for ever" (23). Spirit, giddiness, lightness of conduct, wonder and pity: these epithets initiate a series of later descriptions of Esther in which the notion of excess predominates. Indeed, she becomes the site of a complex nexus of imagery suggestive of uncontrollable expansion and contamination: she is "the old leaven" fermenting in Mary's "little bosom" (81); the "polluted outcast" (235); the "leper-sin" from which "all stand aloof dreading to be counted unclean" (159); the stain of sexuality "for the very bodily likeness [between her and Mary] seemed to suggest a possibility of a similar likeness in their fate" (127). So insinuating is her influence that, in the end, Esther is directly or indirectly linked to every major event in the novel: in addition to bringing on the moral and psychological dementia leading John Barton to murder Carson, Esther prompts Mary's romance with Harry Carson; makes her attraction to Carson known to Jem; and inadvertently reveals to Mary that John Barton is Carson's murderer. Condemned for wanting to be a "do-nothing lady" (10), she becomes instead a distorted deus ex machina of sorts, who wreaks moral havoc whenever she appears and without whom the narrative itself would seemingly "do nothing."

Lurking behind this vision of moral bankruptcy lies the scourge of prostitution. As John openly predicts: " 'Esther, I see what you'll end at with your artificials, and your fly-away veils, and stopping out when honest women are in their beds; you'll be a street-walker, Esther' " (9). While the directness of John's statement may be surprising, it is the reasons behind it that indicate the overdetermined nature of Esther's presence in the novel. Oddly enough, John Barton attributes this danger to Esther's work in a factory—not, as one might expect, because factory work is morally injurious but rather because women with independent incomes, and the ability to support themselves, are: " 'That's the worst of factory work, for girls. They can earn so much when work is plenty, that they can maintain themselves any how"

(9).[15] Besides not taking into account the nature of the work itself—either factory work or prostitution—this explanation curiously inverts cause and effect: prostitution results not from economic hardship, as was the case with most women who turned to prostitution, but from economic freedom; the fear prostitution elicits comes from women being in a position to "maintain themselves any how." [16] In the process, economic deprivation is rewritten as an excess of means (money) and mobility (individual/sexual freedom), the dual nature of which is perfectly captured in a later description of Esther's nature as "violent and unregulated" (290).[17]

The generalized nature of this fear becomes clear when various Manchester workers and their women relate their grievances to John Barton. A digressive debate ensues over how Prince Albert would feel if his wife worked outside the home. Reeling off a list of the trials of a man returning to a home not properly overseen by his woman, with such irksome tribulations as having "his meals all hugger-mugger, and comfortless," Alice ends by declaiming that "[she'd] be bound, prince as he is, if [Prince Albert's] missis served him so, he'd be off to a gin-palace, or summut o' that kind. So why can't he make a law again poor folks' wives working in factories?" (121). Mary, countering Alice, ventures that the Queen and Prince cannot make laws in any case. By parodying working-class ideas about how government works and raising the pervasive threat of women's economic and sexual freedom, this passage both admits and denies the importance of class divisions in its reworking of them along gender lines. For here the threat of freedom honors no class boundaries. Prince Albert is as susceptible to gin-palaces and the prostitutes who frequent them as John Barton if women are allowed to work outside the home. Esther's fate thus condenses a wide constellation of fears and anxieties, from specific concerns about working-class political legitimacy to the trans-class issue of domestic ideology and its corresponding gendered division of labor. As the specter of prostitution, Esther becomes a site where labor and pleasure seem to collapse into one another, or, at least, appear too close for comfort's sake: given the convoluted reasonings above, it matters less that we understand the intricacies of these relationships than that we begin to lose sight of cause and effect altogether (an issue to which I will return in the final section of the chapter). Significantly, though, these fears are expressed through something akin to an open secret. Throughout the text, Esther's disappearance or absence signals her presence and its ill effects; she is at once always not there and everywhere. If the text's "openness" to prostitution is not at issue, as the debate over Prince Albert would suggest it is not, what exactly necessitates such secrecy? Is there perhaps some deeper secret lying behind Esther's fallenness? The clue to this mystery, I want to suggest, lies in Esther's alter ego Mary. For Mary, so like Esther that they are always being compared, and yet ultimately saved from Esther's fate, seemingly offers the "lesson" of the text, choosing correctly where Esther faltered.

Like Esther, Mary desires a man above her in class. Both of them, moreover, act on their desires. Esther, as we have seen, does so to her demise. In contrast, Mary spends the bulk of the novel atoning for her desire, after only the briefest glimpse of it being allowed detection in the first place. Yet the briefness of this glimpse in no way diminishes its profound effects. Quite the contrary, the abruptness of its quelling speaks volumes about the potency and danger her expression of desire holds. Thickening the mystery-driven plot, her desire is initially kept secret, known only to the reader and Sally Leadbitter, Mary's romance-reading confidante and matchmaker, and only revealed once it no longer exists.

Almost before readers even have a chance to register Mary's flirtatious pleasures with the mill-owner's son, Harry Carson, Mary begins to bemoan her susceptibility to his charms and her fantasies about him: "Oh, why did she ever listen to the tempter? Why did she ever give ear to her own suggestions, and cravings after wealth and grandeur? Why had she thought it a fine thing to have a rich lover?" (230). Coded in terms of class, Mary's cravings are for "wealth and grandeur," and the temptations of having a "rich lover." Further emphasizing the class dimensions of desire, the text constructs Mary's sexuality in relation to her two lovers, Harry Carson and Jem Wilson, the one rich, and the other poor.[18] When Mary unequivocally rejects Jem Wilson's marriage proposal it is because she secretly dreams of marrying Harry Carson: "There was one cherished weakness still concealed from every one. It concerned a lover, not beloved, but favoured by fancy. A gallant, handsome young man; but not beloved. Yet Mary hoped to meet him every day in her walks, blushed when she heard his name, and tried to think of him as her future husband, and above all, tried to think of herself as his future wife" (43).

While Mary wants to view her romantic interest as properly leading toward marriage, the narrative intimates that this is a stretch since Harry is simply "a lover, not beloved," "a gallant, handsome young man; but not beloved." The repetition of "not beloved," combined with Gaskell's emphasis on the fact that Mary actively works to fit her desire within the confines of marriage (she *tries* to think of him as her future husband and herself as his future wife), suggests that there are two radically different species of desire at odds with one another: one which is transgressive, because its object is sexual; the other, appropriate because its object is "beloved."

As opposing sentiments, fancy and love determine the appropriateness of Harry Carson as an object of desire. Whereas Mary merely favors Carson "by fancy," she ultimately realizes her love for Jem. In a remarkable reversal of sentiment, Mary comes to this realization immediately after she has rejected Jem's first proposal of marriage: "Her plan had been, as we well know, to marry Mr. Carson, and the occurrence an hour ago was only a preliminary step. True; but it had unveiled her heart to her; it had convinced her, she loved Jem above all persons or things." Suddenly, the creature comforts that Harry could provide her appear as "hollow vanities," "now [that] she had discovered the passionate secret of her soul" (131).

What is the meaning, then, of this "passionate secret" Mary suddenly discovers? Interestingly, this secret, disclosed and spoken rather than left to conjecture (as in the case of Esther), exposes the negation of desire rather than its expression. While Mary worries about how she can win back Jem's affections, fearing that she may now have lost him forever, she takes solace in the fact that she is at least finally safe from harm: "She had hitherto been walking in grope-light towards a precipice; but in the clear revelation of that past hour, she saw her danger, and turned away, resolutely, and for ever. That was some comfort: I mean her clear perception of what she ought not to do; of what no luring temptations should ever again induce her to hearken to" (132). It is not so much that Mary now knows what she desires—Jem as opposed to Harry—but that she relinquishes the pleasures of desire altogether, knowing "what she ought not to do." The moral imperative "ought" involves a closing off of sensations—sexual or otherwise—that makes possible her eventual entrance into marriage.[19] Jem is not only substituted for Harry but the very sensual pleasures, the "luring temptations," that Harry afforded too are foreclosed irredeemably, disallowed by a regulative moral code whose defining characteristic is its clearness, its lack of susceptibility to obscured, projected, or ambivalent expression.

Pleasure is defined in relation to how one *chooses* one's object of choice, where that "choice" is based on "true love" rather than distinctions of class; interest toward the object chosen—love versus fancy—rather than the object itself determines the value of one's choice. Within this regime of sexual politics, reaching beyond one's class is rewritten in terms of a generalized form of transgressive desire that has no class determinants. Like Mary's feelings for Carson, the intimate link between desire and economics is rendered "fanciful." Put simply, Mary's initial preference for Carson is presented as misplaced not because he is the mill-owner's son but because her feelings for him are driven by the same kind of "unregulated" passion that drove Esther eventually to prostitution. But, not coincidentally, this same politics effectively maintains working-class and middle-class identities as distinct from one another. The discovery of the "passionate secret of her soul" leads Mary "naturally" back to Jem, who happens fortuitously to be a member of her own class, thereby conveniently bypassing the whole question of cross-class desire and alleviating the potential conflict raised by it, without ever having to acknowledge it as a real conflict.

Under cover of Mary's relinquishment of her sexual desires, her fantasy of economic and class power, of the kind of consumer she could be if married to Harry Carson, is denied; Mary does not simply enter into any marriage but, specifically, a working-class marriage. The secret enclosed in this sleight of hand is, at bottom, an economic one, not a sexual one: what Mary "discovers" but which remains unspoken is that she does not even want the goods that a higher class position would give her; she belongs with her own class and, best of all, this identification is actively chosen rather than imposed from above. Unlike the open sexual secret of Esther's prostitution, and the excess it implied, this economic or class secret is better kept by the narrative and actually reverses its terms: if Esther's "fall" rewrites deprivation as excess, Mary's "success" reads in excess deprivation. Financial comfort is thus exchanged for moral comfort, with the extent of their incompatibility underscored by the relief Mary feels when she learns of Harry Carson's death: "Then, again, she reproached herself a little for the feeling of pleasure she experienced, in thinking that he whom she dreaded could never more beset her path; in the security with which she could pass each street corner—each shop, where he used to lie in ambush" (225). As this newly found sense of security suggests, the very space of Manchester has been radically altered in order to make room for this new vision of pleasure. Within this mode of pleasure, moreover, Esther can remain the exception rather than the rule.

But even as the narrative attempts to erase class determination, it continually resurfaces. While Mary's desire for Carson is reconfigured in terms of morality, the class difference between them is never entirely effaced. Jem speaks of Harry as "the lover above [Mary] in rank" (162) and Esther claims that "Mary is innocent, except for the great error of loving one above her in situation" (164). Underlining the gravity of such an error, Esther allows that it would be far better to kill Mary than to let her consummate her desire for Carson. Admittedly, Jem and Mary only explicitly voice these acknowledgments of class difference once the potential threat motivating them has been removed. Already at this point in the novel, Mary, unbeknown to either Jem or Esther, has declared her love for Jem to the reader. With the fear of this potentially transgressive desire alleviated for the reader, its socially disruptive force, too, is thus apparently recontained.[20] Yet the text is less unequivocal in its "strategies of containment" than this reading would seem to allow. In short, such "timing" can be read in contradictory ways: as a successful containment of class difference in the interest of some vision of classless universalism (be it bourgeois or Christian or both), or as a revealing instance of that self-same class difference and the strategies necessary to contain it.

Rather than forcing one reading over the other, *Mary Barton*, I want to suggest, refuses such an either/or choice. Instead, its narrative structure of secrets at once obscures and reveals the class distinctions underlying its romance. The conceit of the secret, that is, unwittingly allows for the kind of slippage between cause and symptom that marks Gaskell's text and ideological apparatuses more generally. A return to the example with which we began—Esther's exclusion from the opening "pastoral" community—highlights the contradictory, almost seesaw-like effect this narrative structure creates. To begin with, Esther's disappearance and the secrecy surrounding it prompts questioning: Wilson asks for news of Esther; Alice unthinkingly toasts to "absent friends," and as quickly wishes she "could have bitten her tongue out" (18), immediately raising questions about just what kind of actions on Esther's part would necessitate such dramatic silencing and secrecy. Later, as Esther's circumstances become known, these questions lead to even larger questions of causality: Is Esther excluded from the novel because she has fallen, that is, chosen immorally, or does she fall because the larger structures of class and gender determine the limits of her choices? To these questions, paradoxically, *Mary Barton* answers yes, and yes, again. The text, that is to say, uncannily presents both of these cases, and, like the refusal to judge which Gaskell claims for herself in the preface, resists nullifying the effects of a class-based perspective even as its investments lie in seeing individuals as "architects of their own fortunes" (167). While Mary becomes a "lady by right of nature" (167) and thus confirms the myth of universal subjecthood, the (literal) remains of Esther live on as a concrete reminder of the mythic nature of such subjecthood. As Amanda Anderson describes Esther's presence at the end of the novel, "the text insists on a material residue, even as it enforces Esther's final punishment"—her exile from the community and her eventual death, after collapsing like a "crushed Butterfly" under Mary Barton's window.[21]

As in the preface, the combination of feeling and seeing that structures Gaskell's response overall to the working class enables this double vision. The novel can *see* both of these perspectives precisely because it *feels* both of them and vice versa. If, for example, the masters can say of the workers, "they're more like wild beasts than human beings," the narrator counters with "(Well, who might have made them different?)" (182). Offsetting the socially ungrounded moralism of the masters, the narrator's interjection forces the return of a certain, if limited, vision of social determination to the masters' assessment: "you have made them what they are." Similarly, with respect to Esther directly, even as the narrative figures her as the cause of its trajectory of death and tragedy, it simultaneously positions her within a larger causal chain of social effects. When she claims responsibility for Jem's alleged shooting of Carson, for instance, knowing that she was the one who told Jem of Mary's flirtation with Carson, the narrator follows her self-reprisal with "Poor, diseased mind! And there was none to minister to thee!" (235). Defining moments such as these expose the sentimental register's force in *Mary Barton*: its ability to complicate and indeed engender its "realism." Time and time again, the sentimental realm of romance is shown to be fully imbued with political meaning; notions of "true love," figured as the means to symbolically resolve class tensions in the political sphere, end up reproducing those very tensions.

Nonetheless, taken by themselves, these tensions do not strain the narrative to the point of collapse. While they certainly mark class difference in the text, they leave open viable avenues for reconciliation. The symbiotic relationship between masters and workers ("you have made them what they are")—when viewed in the light of the meeting hall—leaves the masters fully in control, as producers rather than products of their workers' labor. Thus while these interjections might seem to uncannily resonate with Gaskell's parenthetical acknowledgment in the preface of the workers' contribution to their masters' riches, they actually cast employers and their workers in directly inverse relations: whereas the narrative suggests that the masters have made the workers what they are, the preface slips into quite the opposite, intimating that the workers have made the masters what they are. As long as the narrative stays outside the productive realm, this latter possibility remains hidden or invisible, indeed virtually unthinkable. Similarly, as long as class difference is shaken from its economic moorings, it can circulate without causing irreparable damage. Mary escapes the melodramatic script of the libertine seducing the working-class girl and in the process frees the narrative from its potential for cross-class conflict once the script itself is rewritten in terms of a sexual preference not an economic one.[22]

At the most basic level, then, treating the working class and its attendant threat of class conflict as serious subject matter for literature makes transparent what becomes more covert in domestic fiction: the intimate relationship between politics and courtship. As Ruth Yeazell characterizes this distinction, considering later domestic novels, "[even] in novels that seem to have little to say about class conflict or the threat of revolution, the courtship of the heroine may cover a political story—though both the story and the act of covering it over have themselves been concealed."[23] But there is also something unique about *Mary Barton* and the manner in which its domestic resolution relates to its "political story." Unlike other industrial or domestic fiction, it attempts to confront the problem of industrial labor and its relations of production *in the productive sphere*. This attempt generates a story at odds with Gaskell's representations of family life and the sphere of consumption. If domesticity fashions a resolution to the problems raised by Esther and Mary, the same is not true when it comes to the productive sphere. Far from providing any sense of closure to its problems of production, the novel instead reveals the irresolvable nature of the conflict between "masters and men" under capitalism. John Barton forms the locus of this problematic and it is to him that we must now turn.

The Scene of Production, or, "We Made Them What They Are"

Few would dispute that John Barton represents the working man's perspective in *Mary Barton*. Despite such consensus, or perhaps because of it, little critical attention has been paid to the specifics of John's perspective. Instead, it is simply assumed that his views are commonly understood ones and left at that. A closer look at the nature of Barton's arguments, however, unearths a far richer debate taking place, and one that, Gaskell's disclaimers notwithstanding, evokes a deep knowledge of political economy.

In one of many arguments with his fellow workers, John Barton challenges, "You'll say (at least many a one does) they'n getten capital an' we'n getten none. I'll say, our labour's our capital and we ought to draw interest on that" (66). Despite his less than orthodox understanding of the relation of labor to capital, Barton defines the conflict between laborer and capitalist in economic terms. If the capitalist has capital to draw interest on, he wagers, so too should the worker—with the clear implication that currently the two exist in an unequal relationship vis-à-vis capital. Drawing out the consequences of this difference, Barton, throughout the early part of the novel, exposes inequalities of class on both the social and the economic level: he argues that no wealthy person can be seen helping a child dying for want of food, or sharing provisions with an out-of-work laborer; when economic crises hit, it is never the "gentlefolk" who contract scarlet fever from poor, dank living conditions or die of starvation; and no matter how bad the economy gets, it never seems to stop the rich from consuming at comfortable rates.

Barton's observations obliquely address the issue of ownership and the relations of production. In contrast to one line of the narrative—that *does* read labor as capital for the working class and, in that way, constructs a vision of the laborer and capitalist existing in a system of free and equal exchange—John's "naive" formulation of their relationship emphasizes the obfuscations making possible such an equation. Given that the laborer cannot draw interest on his labor, as the images of want and starvation in times of economic crises underscore, and that laborer and capitalist exist in radically different relations to the means of production, any notion of free and equal exchange is a virtual impossibility. The crucial difference between laborer and capitalist, as Marx formulated it, rests on what each is able to sell in the marketplace: "The possessor of labour-power, instead of being able to sell commodities in which his labour has been objectified, must rather be compelled to offer for sale as a commodity that very labour-power which exists only in his living body."[24] This condition of the worker makes the concept of a "free laborer," exchanging labor with the capitalist on equal terms, spurious, for as Marx sardonically points out, the laborer is "free in the double sense that as a free individual he can dispose of his labour-power as his own commodity, and that, on the other hand, he has no other commodity for sale, i.e., he is rid of them, he is free of all the objects needed for the realization [*Verwirklichung*] of his labour-power."[25] This discrepancy is the structural underpinning for John's observation of what happens during an economic depression: the laborer, with nothing to exchange but his labor-power, is left with no commodity to take to market when the mills close. That the working class possesses only its labor and therefore must sell it in order to survive is attested to all too vividly in the nine deaths from illness and starvation witnessed in *Mary Barton* and John's exasperated "I don't want money, child! I want work, and it is my right. I want work" (115).

While John may want work, and even have work at times, the nature of that work is never represented concretely. Like labor under capitalism, it functions simply as *abstract labor*: labor, which by its nature, is alienated and estranged. Thus, while Gaskell claims to know nothing of political economy, her text, in essence, reenacts its precepts and explanatory structure. As Marx describes political economy, it "proceeds from the fact of private property. It does not explain it. It grasps the *material* process of private property, the process through which it actually passes, in general and abstract formulae which it then takes as *laws*. It does not *comprehend* these laws, i.e., it does not show how they arise from the nature of private property. Political economy fails to explain the reason for the division between labour and capital, between capital and land."[26] In the novel, private property itself is never addressed and nor is its relationship to the division between labor and capital. Likewise, the question of what labor is or the possibility of a potentially different relationship to one's labor is never raised. In short, the capitalist system of production is never an object of scrutiny: estranged and alienated labor and its organization under capitalism—the division of labor and its particular gendered nature under patriarchy—is a given for Gaskell.[27]

Despite the limitations of these assumptions (with respect to the kind of social change they can imagine), they do not prevent Gaskell from voicing her real concern, expressed in the preface: the "state of feeling" among "too many" of the Manchester workers and the discord it provokes between employees and employers. Moreover, as P. J. Keating observes, Gaskell depicts the unequal partnership against which John Barton rebels so compellingly that ultimately she has to retreat from her own representation of his views with apologies for being too realistic.[28] Immediately after presenting the weaver's perception of the mill-owners' wealth and minimal discomforts during economically slack periods (regardless of hard times, concerts are still crowded and stores continue to overflow with luxury goods), Gaskell flatly denies its veracity: "I know that this is not really the case; and I know what is the truth in such matters: but what I wish to impress is what the workman feels and thinks" (24).[29] The problem is that her narrative impresses on us so well what John Barton feels that our sympathies do indeed lie with him; his feelings and response to them carry far more emotional and narrative weight than the narrator's claims otherwise. In other words, the narrator's explicit statements about the "truth in such matters" are contradicted by the narrative's implicit representations of that "truth"—and so much so that the sympathetic outpouring Gaskell desires from her readers finds its object in John Barton.

Admittedly, these sympathies are of a particular nature. They draw on a form of identification whose dynamic is primarily driven by moral concerns rather than concerns of social inequality; by reform rather than the supersession of capitalist relations. Thus, when the narrator claims that John Barton's feelings do not accurately reflect the real relations between masters and men, it is because John is not looking in the right place. Where he looks to his own labor and what the narrator deems as overly concrete economic distinctions, Gaskell redirects our attention to the supposedly less fractious realm of Christian morality—a realm presumably less prone to miscalculation because based on universal feelings rather than particularistic facts.

To depict the effects of industrialism, then, Gaskell turns not to the factory but to the home. The novel moves from the opening scene in which the Bartons share tea with the Wilsons in a communion of families toward the gradual disintegration of both families and their homes. In our first visit to the Barton home, much narrative attention is given to describing the actual items they own. This description reads as a model of the ideal domestic scene, from the warm glowing fire in the fireplace, to the cupboards full of crockery and glassware, the potted geraniums, the japanned tea-tray, the crimson tea-caddy, and the requisite blue-and-white checked curtains, "now drawn, to shut in the friends met to enjoy themselves" (15). As the novel progresses and the Bartons' already meager subsistence disappears when John loses work, this room is progressively denuded of its "many conveniences" as each item is sold to obtain food.

Certainly it is hard to sit back and watch this decline into poverty without twinges of middle-class guilt and pity for the wretched state of the poor. Moreover, this concern for the personal individual effects of poverty is not in and of itself misplaced. Yet, within the symbolic economy of the text, the ultimate focus on the destruction of the domestic economy serves to mask the productive relations making possible this destruction; the critique of industrialism rests on redressing the symptoms rather than the cause of the "illness." After all, it is only to these symptoms—the depletion of consumer goods and the basic want of necessities—that the widow's alms Gaskell hopes to elicit can be applied effectively.

The effect of this "charity of consumption" rather than production is perhaps best seen in Gaskell's treatment of collective struggle in the political sphere and the manner in which she characterizes the Chartist petition of 1839.[30] Historically, the catalyst for the petition was the unparalleled deprivations suffered by the working class in the manufacturing districts because of a severe economic depression in the cotton trade. (1839 was, in fact, only one in a succession of bad years extending from 1837 up through 1842.)[31]

The demand for the "People's Charter" consisted of six points: (1) annual parliaments; (2) universal male suffrage; (3) equal electoral districts; (4) the removal of the property qualification for MPs; (5) the secret ballot; and (6) payment of MPs.[32] In her treatment of the Charter, Gaskell presents its political demands equivocally, especially when it comes to the Chartists' desire to present these grievances to the government. On the one hand, she allows that their present state of destitution would naturally lead to resentment and alienation. On the other hand, she labels their actual politics "rabid" (85), suggesting that the Chartists are acting with misdirected and "ferocious precipitation" (85). Moreover, she frames the whole issue in such a way to imply that the purpose of the Charter is naive because the government is of course already aware of the suffering of the poor: "[The Chartists] could not believe that the government knew of their misery; they rather chose to think it possible that men could voluntarily assume the office of legislators for a nation, ignorant of its real state" (85–86).

This response is particularly striking since on the face of it the impetus behind the Charter shares much with Gaskell's own project in *Mary Barton*. While the Chartists draft their petition to inform the government of their suffering, *Mary Barton* aims to inform its middle-class readership of the miserable conditions of the working class.

The turning away in Gaskell's narrative from what is perceived now as the "rabid" radicalism of the working class mirrors the historical response of the British middle class to working-class demands following the passage of the First Reform Bill. After an initial period of support for continued reforms, liberal enthusiasm dampened and activity on the part of working-class revolutionaries was considerably tempered. In response to the Chartists, in particular, many of those who had advocated the Reform Bill were in no way supportive of the Charter. As Eric Hobsbawm describes the breakdown of the earlier alliance, "radicals, republicans, and the new proletarian movements therefore moved out of alignment with the liberals; the moderates, when still in opposition, were haunted by the 'democratic and social republic' which now became the slogan of the left."[33] In *Mary Barton*, this realignment is signaled by the implicit equation of the workers and the Trades Union's demands for change in the political realm (the Charter) with the extreme (read "rabid" and "ferocious") act of murder.[34] As a result, political agency on the part of the working class is all but nullified; the "brotherhood" of the Union disqualified by the "brotherhood" of man.

The contradiction between the two visions of charity contained in these notions of "brotherhood" would seem to be effaced when John as spokesperson for the working class murders Carson and subsequently all but disappears from Gaskell's text (he leaves on page 198 and does not return until page 353). Once the working class has been discredited politically by the immoral act of murder, in other words, their claims for political equality are seemingly no longer of interest. But, as I want to suggest, the contradiction, in fact, intractably remains—the more so because John must so definitively be ushered off stage, implying that the issues he has raised are not easily resolved within the space of the novel. His marked departure, therefore, undercuts Gaskell's argument for a charity of consumption only. John may be sent to his grave, but his representation of the economic, political, and class divide separating laborers from capitalists lives on to haunt his gravedigger's text.

Indeed, John Barton as representative of the working class not only lives on but is, as Gaskell's own narrative acknowledges, a creation of the middle class that would disavow it.[35] Gaskell likens this relationship to that of Frankenstein (in the process, tellingly mixing up the monster and his maker): "The actions of the uneducated seem to me typified in those of Frankenstein, that monster of many human qualities, ungifted with a soul, a knowledge of the difference between good and evil. Why have we made them what they are; a powerful monster, yet without the inner means for peace and happiness?" (170). The specter of Frankenstein resonates not only with the novel's fears about class but also about gender.[36] As a metaphor for the uneducated worker, the monster embodies the ambivalent dialectical relationship that connects capital to wage-labor: "we made them what they are." It also betrays Gaskell's ambivalent relationship to this "monstrous" working class created in her own narrative: what if the working class refuses its position as a product of the middle-class and instead asserts itself as a producer in its own right? What if, contrary to her wishes, it actually incites class against class? Discomfited by the unleashing of this monster, Gaskell attempts to recontain it within familiar ideological terrain, appealing to morality, to the basic difference between good and evil, thereby once again obscuring the economic and political forces undergirding its creation. Even so, the fear actualized in the figure of the monster cannot be entirely explained in historical and economic terms; rather, it is inexplicably implicated in a sexual politics and dynamic. At the center of this politics lies the fear of a form of pleasure able to cross class lines; a pleasure whose full expression, in fact, can only come about once class divisions and the inequalities in the realm of labor which produce them are overcome. The novel's trial—ostensibly to determine the guilt or innocence of Jem Wilson in the murder of Harry Carson—fittingly puts both these fears on display and highlights, in particular, the value of melodrama as a means to quell the threat of a boundless pleasure intimately tied to labor and replace it with a less threatening version of both labor and pleasure.

A Charity of Consumption, or, "They Know Not What They Do"

After a series of melodramatic events leading up to Jem Wilson's trial, Mary Barton finds herself on the witness stand and seemingly "on trial" herself. Asked by the judge to disclose her "heart's secrets," Mary Barton is placed in the humiliating position of declaring her love publicly in the midst of a political/theatrical spectacle: "And who was he, the questioner, that he should dare so lightly to ask of her heart's secrets? That he should dare to ask her to tell, before that multitude assembled there, what woman usually whispers with blushes and tears, and many hesitations, to one ear alone?" (324). Forced by the look of agony convulsing Jem Wilson's face in response to this question, Mary determines to reveal her true feelings for Jem. The fact that this painfully revelatory testimony has no bearing on the question of whether Jem did or did not murder Harry Carson appears to be a moot point, since it forms Mary's central scene in the novel, and allows her, as Sally Leadbitter so tellingly remarks, to "set up heroine on [her] own account" (358). Indeed such a revelation need not have had any bearing at all in the trial had Mary not kept her original secret: her love for Jem, "the passionate secret of her soul," discovered immediately after rejecting his proposal of marriage.

As it turns out, this is not, however, the only or the most important secret housed in Mary's soul. Throughout her testimony she struggles more fundamentally to preserve her grasp on reality, her sanity threatened by the knowledge that her father murdered Harry Carson: "But, in dread of herself, with the tremendous secret imprisoned within her, she exerted every power she had to keep in the full understanding of what was going on, of what she was asked, and of what she answered" (324). Later, she repeatedly intones to herself, "I must not go mad. I must not, indeed" (328). Like Mary's mind, reeling in the effort to maintain these two secrets as distinct, the narrative becomes a whirl of secrets in which the two plots—the so-called romance plot and political plot—become giddily indistinct.[37] Even after the trial, this slippage continues, as Jem debates for himself the nature of Mary's secret: "Sometimes he thought that John had discovered, and thus bloodily resented, the attentions which Mr Carson had paid to his daughter; at others, he believed the motive to exist in the bitter feuds between the masters and their workpeople, in which Barton was known to take so keen an interest. But if he had felt himself pledged to preserve this secret, even when his own life was the probable penalty, and he believed he should fall execrated by Mary as the guilty destroyer of her lover, how much more was he bound now to labour to prevent any word of hers from inculpating her father, now that she was his own; now that she had braved so much to rescue him; and now that her poor brain had lost all guiding and controlling power over her words" (336). The inconclusiveness about the motive for John Barton's actions blurs the two secrets organizing the trial and the larger narrative. Most importantly, it is precisely because Barton's motive for the murder remains a secret to all but a select few (Barton shares the nature of his crime with Carson's father and the naturalist and anti-unionist Job Legh, but significantly not with Mary or Jem, who arrive immediately *after* John Barton finishes his confession) that it can circulate and acquire multiple meanings. The properties of the secret, that is to say, ease circulation and promote a politically efficacious indeterminacy.

As floating signifier, the secret is filled by different content, depending on its context. While Mary, for instance, is allowed the knowledge that Jem did not murder Harry Carson, she is never disabused of the belief that her "infidelity" with Carson caused her father to murder him. Alternately, Jem wavers between two possible motives. Finally, the two characters in the text most opposed to John Barton's politics—Mr. Carson and Job Legh—hear the political version of Barton's story. The secret behind the murder thus performs double duty: it not only serves to undermine and discredit the Chartists as a viable political organization for working-class representation (since we as readers are in on the secret) but it remains a warning of what happens when desire crosses class lines.[38]

The extent of this latter warning is hardly inconsequential. Mary is not only punished for her initial desires; her body too must be disciplined and transformed beyond recognition. What was external and socially grounded —her attraction to Harry Carson, her knowledge of her father's murderous crime—is turned inward: Mary is "in dread of herself," "with the secret imprisoned within her."[39] As this language suggests, the emphasis shifts from an abstract "madness" to a material force physically housed in Mary's body. Immediately after the trial ends, and Jem is acquitted, Mary falls into a delirium that lasts for several days. Her recovery leaves her a changed subject, as "she, for her part, was softer and gentler than she had ever been in her gentlest mood; since her illness, her motions, her glances, her voice were all tender in their languor" (350). Not only is she now kinder and gentler, but she is thoroughly infantilized and desexualized, with her mind returning to the "tender state of a lately-born infant's" (348); upon awakening, "she smiled gently, as a baby does when it sees its mother tending its little cot; and continued her innocent infantine gaze into his face, as if the sight gave her much unconscious pleasure" (349). With this transformation complete, Mary is deemed "cured" and ready to enter into marriage with Jem.

The proliferation of meanings around the text's secrets ultimately casts doubt on causal analyses altogether. The narrator describes the motive for Barton's actions as "in some measure a mystery" (336); Mary forgoes thinking about their cause whatsoever, feeling that "in his sufferings, whatever their cause," he was "more dearly loved than ever before" (354); John Barton yearns for some excuse to explain his reasoning and produces a lack of agency as cause, whispering to Job Legh, " 'I did not know what I was doing, Job Legh; God knows I didn't" (367); the text echoes Barton when Mr. Carson finds solace in the Bible's pleading, "They know not what they do" (370). All these formulations renounce any strict logic of causality, preferring instead to defer such judgments or simply displace them to a different setting where causality itself is radically transformed, along with any notion of individual or collective agency.[40] This lack of a "solution" to the text's mystery signals the impasse *Mary Barton* reaches more broadly: ultimately unable to answer John Barton's question, the text experiments with different narrative modes with which to tackle the problem he represents, in the midst of an ever-increasing indeterminacy about the possibility for answering such questions in the first place. In other words, if Barton's question is allowed expression in the productive sphere its answer will hinge inevitably on economic distinctions: some men are rich and others poor because of their disparate relations to the means of production; or, in Barton's own terminology, because workers' labor finally is not the same as their owners' capital. In this register, the text comes face to face with *structural* violence and exploitation and, consequently, the need for structural change in order to resolve the current crisis. By contrast, as Mary's narrative attests, sexual conflicts can be mended within the current structure of social relations; as long as Barton's question can be resituated and redefined in broader moral terms, it loses its potency as an indicator of structural inequality. The shunting of questions of causality altogether thus has the affect of disarming working-class agency and, with it, the economics of agency in the interests of an apparently more inclusive vision of universal morality.

In this light, the narrative's use of melodrama makes perfect sense.

In Peter Brooks's theory in *The Melodramatic Imagination*, melodrama historically "becomes the principal mode for uncovering, demonstrating, and making operative the essential moral universe in a post-sacred era."[41] Brooks locates the origins of melodrama in the French Revolution: a symbolic and literal desacralization that simultaneously ushers in a new world—the world of modernity. In response, the melodramatic mode desires "to express all" (4): a surface-depth model in which spiritual value is unearthed from surface detail, it relies on a "metaphoricity of gesture" (10) that imbues the everyday or the ordinary with interest and deep meaning. For this reason, too, it is a mode of excess. Moreover, Brooks argues for a fundamental individualistic basis to melodrama, as "the entity making the strongest claim to sacred status tends more and more to be personality itself" (16). That is, the twin functions of melodrama—the desacralization and sentimentalization of ethics—lead us toward basic ethical and psychic truths and, in the process, lead us back to ourselves. Melodrama thus provides for and functions as a new alternative basis for an ethical community, one rooted in moral sureties at a time when such certainties are becoming historically obsolete.

If Brooks's analysis highlights what are considered now to be the classic features of melodrama—its tendency to personify absolutes such as good and evil, its use of excessive, exaggerated modes of expression and emotion, its providential plotting, and so forth—recent critics have unearthed with more historical specificity the centrality of melodrama (or what Elaine Hadley refers to as the "melodramatic mode") to nineteenth-century British culture.[42] Most interesting for our purposes is the strong historical connection between melodrama, prostitution, and working-class or "popular" politics. Patrick Joyce argues that melodrama offers a "singularly revealing way" into the social and political imaginary of Victorian England precisely because of its broad utilization and the particular kinds of "stories" or narratives it provided.[43] Melodrama not only spoke to a socially mixed audience in England in its appeal to moral law as opposed to contractual law but it also made a special appeal to the lower classes, those most in need of the symbolic assurance melodrama offered and those most able to "prove" the victories of virtue which were melodrama's mainstay. If the lowliest of the low could be shown morally triumphant, such triumph was within everyone's reach. (Conversely, the mighty were often brought low, again proving the worth of virtue over money.) In this way, melodrama both participated in the construction of categories that cut across class ("the people," "the audience," the theater "public") and appealed specifically to the powerless, be they the "poor" who were redefined as a result of the New Poor Law of 1834, women such as Caroline Norton fighting against her husband's proprietary treatment of her, prostitutes and reformers such as Josephine Butler campaigning against the Contagious Diseases Acts, or the working class responding to the transition from domestic to factory production. The melodramatic mode, that is to say, was centrally involved in the construction of a collective sense of community and social identity during the nineteenth century.

The nature of the community and the social identity forming and formed by the melodramatic mode, however, was nothing if not contradictory. On the one hand, melodrama's narratives offered a sense of agency and power to the excluded and powerless. On the other hand, those self-same narratives tended to produce "victims"—the helpless prostitute, the superseded handloom weaver, the outcast wife, the bereft mother—who lacked agency and were "saved" more often than not by chance or providence or inserted into a lost "golden-age" narrative which mythologized the past and its system of deferential social relations vis-à-vis class or gender or both. In an analysis of the agitation surrounding the Contagious Diseases Acts, for example, Judith Walkowitz shows how the rhetoric of melodrama both enabled female resistance to the state regulation of prostitutes proposed by the Acts and reinstated workingmen as the proper custodians of working-class women. "In this and other ways," Walkowitz concludes, "recourse to melodrama was a contradictory political strategy for feminists. Melodrama offered a powerful cultural resource for female political expression, but it set limitations on what could be said, particularly in relation to female agency and desire."[44] Similarly, Elaine Hadley illustrates how the melodramatic mode, in its challenge to new classificatory systems and laws, served as a powerful tactic of resistance to the consolidation of market practices while it also adopted aspects and values of institutionalized capitalism: "Continually complicated and compromised by the market in which it labored, and yet continually complicating and compromising that market, the melodramatic mode was, as its earliest critics detected, a truly heterogeneous form."[45]

The heterogeneity or "portable rhetoric" (Hadley's phrase) of melodrama is fully on display in *Mary Barton* and, moreover, it is crucial to understanding the contradictory nature of the novel's attempt to come to terms with the vagaries of industrial society and a modern market culture. The impetus behind Gaskell's writing of *Mary Barton* partakes of the melodramatic mode in its desire to delve beneath the surface of working-class life (what is visible, in passing, on the street) and recover its "deep romance." Within *Mary Barton*, melodrama both promises resolution (the trial will solve the mystery) and highlights the impossibility of melodrama's ability finally to achieve it (Jem is exonerated but the "who" and especially the "why" of the crime are left indeterminate by the trial's end). Put simply, melodrama does not and, most importantly, cannot satisfy John's search for the *source* of the divide between rich and poor.[46] Where melodrama works to individualize actions and unify through its construction of an undifferentiated audience (everyone watching the trial and Mary's testimony feels united in sympathy for her and her virtue, regardless of their status), the text stubbornly maintains the social forces—in this case, the economic differences produced by the conditions of labor—circumscribing the individual and the possibilities for community. The resulting balancing act leaves both "causes" in play with no clear verdict reached.

What melodrama can provide is a variety of pleasures whose effects might possibly be strong enough to help us to forget the central question with which the novel is concerned. Melodrama is at once an outlet for readerly pleasure; a substitute for the loss of community formed in and around labor and the sphere of production; an interpretive mode of certainty amid a narrative consumed by confusions and secrets; a vision of shared sympathy where "the poor" can be redefined in individual, affective terms rather than in purely economic ones and "class" too can be similarly refashioned along affective bonds.

Indeed, if the cautionary tale embedded in *Mary Barton* warns against unregulated expressions of desire, "sympathy" becomes the operative catchword for proper affective relations. An exemplary illustration of sympathy's parlance occurs early in the text when Mary's friend Margaret sings the Lancashire ditty "The Oldham Weaver." The song, presciently foreshadowing the fate of the Bartons, describes the sufferings of a weaver who loses work and gradually loses everything he owns. At the end of the song, the weaver's "Marget" declares that she will go up to London "an talk to th' greet mon" about their plight. When Margaret sings this song she transfixes her audience. But, more importantly, she herself is transfixed: "Margaret, with fixed eye, and earnest, dreamy look, seemed to become more and more absorbed in realising to herself the woe she had been describing, and which she felt might at that very moment be suffering and hopeless within a short distance of their comparative comfort" (37). The transporting effects of sympathy at once mirror the results Gaskell desires for her own readership and point out its problematic aspects. Such moments are defined simultaneously by an outpouring of feeling and a troublesome introspection that does not elicit positive action on the part of the sympathizer but rather passive inaction and an aestheticized relation to reform.[47] This "wasting" of emotion also perhaps speaks more broadly to the limits of an aesthetic of empathy, which, as Bertolt Brecht so famously criticized, leaves its audience equally wasted.

The effect of Margaret's singing and the fact that she sings a working-class ballad rehearses the larger contradictions contained in Gaskell's use of melodrama. With respect to "audience," Margaret's "performance" centers her as a melodramatic heroine, an agent worthy of the spotlight (completing the script, the blind Margaret miraculously regains her sight by the end of the novel), and yet simultaneously her role is undermined by the passive inaction it inspires in others and in herself. (In this context, it is not insignificant that Margaret advises Mary—once Mary has confided to her that she has rejected Jem's marriage offer but does indeed love him—*not* to act, but rather to wait and be patient.) The choice of a ballad for this performance seems highly suggestive, given the place of ballads within radical popular politics. As Patrick Joyce and others have shown, the ballad, and especially ballads about handloom weavers, shared much with modes of emplotment characteristic of melodrama, namely, "golden-age" motifs which figured utopia not as a desired future so much as a return to a better past. The "golden-age" form, according to Joyce, "had a special salience for the poor and powerless. Its drama of dispossession, lost virtue, struggle and eventual victory spoke most urgently to those who had felt loss and dispossession." As a result, "early nineteenth-century popular radical politics fed on this narrative."[48] Sung by Margaret, the ballad of the Oldham Weaver thus condenses the many layers of *Mary Barton*'s narrative: gender and class, romance and politics come together in its performance and in its form.[49] At the same time, however, the ballad highlights the narrative's dilemma with respect to the amount of agency the working class can be seen to have. As with the text as a whole, agency here is both given and taken away, fully subject, as it is, to a form of sympathy that essentially renders any sense of meaningful working-class agency suspect. We both hear the voice of the people, as it were, and witness its silencing.

Equally problematic is the vision of pleasure that replaces desire. Margaret, once again, offers an emblematic embodiment of desire's obverse, right and proper conduct. Her behavior and code of ethics is directly contrasted to Mary's susceptibility to the wiles of desire: "Margaret had no sympathy with the temptations to which loveliness, vanity, ambition, or the desire of being admired, exposes so many; no sympathy with flirting girls, in short. Then, she had no idea of the strength of the conflict between will and principle in some who were differently constituted from herself. With her, to be convinced that an action was wrong, was tantamount to a determination not to do so again; and she had little or no difficulty in carrying out her determination" (249). In essence, Margaret is immune to temptation and thus circumvents the problematic of desire altogether. Her immunity, however, still leaves open the question of what kind of pleasure can be culled from such a tightly regulated and certain moral schema.

Mary Barton offers two answers to this dilemma. On the one hand, it looks to maternal figures as a site for the joining of sympathy and pleasure. Mothers, as Hilary Schor argues, offer a nurturing kind of supervision, of "watchful love and loving watchfulness" which counteracts the factory overlookers' modes of surveillance; where mothers and maternal authority represent an alternative new order, overlookers literally overlook conditions in the factory (broken machinery, dangerous work practices) which actively harm the workers.[50] As she notes, however, the compass of maternal authority in the text remains limited. Moreover, most of these mothers are either dead or ineffectual and thus hardly compelling figures in whom to capture any meaningful practice of pleasure. Mrs. Wilson's sister, Alice, epitomizes this ineffectuality in her remembrances of her mother. Unable to return home to visit her mother, she remains fixated by her image, capable only of conjuring her out of her delirium.[51]

On the other hand, and this is the crucial move in the text, genre itself fills the place of pleasure. Faced with the difficulty of locating pleasure in any individual character (given the susceptibilities of individuals to desire), *Mary Barton* finds in melodrama a provisional space for the experience of pleasure. As the opening epigraph attests "there is always a pleasure in unravelling a mystery, in catching at the gossamer clue which will guide to certainty" (219). In answer to the mysteries posed by the working class, melodrama offers a form in which to combine an expression of pleasure with assurances of certainty, thus avoiding the pitfalls of desire. To do so, however, is also to consign pleasure to a realm divorced from labor, since melodrama functions as the mechanism that displaces labor and production to the domestic sphere—in the hopes of reconciling its contradictions and invocations of class/economic difference. In *Mary Barton*, this reconciliation takes place at John Barton's deathbed, as he and Mr. Carson are joined finally, in mutual sympathy, as fathers.[52]

As a result of the immense weight this displacement carries, holding out, as it does, an antidote to John Barton's narrative of class conflict, it is imperative for Gaskell to preserve the inviolability of the domestic sphere. Since, as we have seen, Esther becomes the means by which the narrative defines and maintains boundaries (even as she threatens to collapse them), it should come as no surprise that she is turned to for this task. By positioning Esther outside the domestic sphere, Gaskell attempts to transform the squalid working-class home she has detailed so painstakingly in the early parts of the novel into a virtually Edenic abode. The only time Esther visits Mary in the novel, she first goes to a thrift store to exchange her street clothes for more appropriately working-class garb. To the "outcast" prostitute these tattered clothes take on a "sort of sanctity" because of their connection to that "happy class to which she could never, never more belong" (236). Because of Esther's position, that happy class also appears to have a happy home. The living conditions that are the subject of the "most direct" representations are reworked by this shift in perspective: "[Esther] thought how easy were the duties of that Eden of innocence from which she was shut out: how she would work, and toil, and starve, and die, if necessary, for a husband, a home,—for children" (236).

This sanguine picture of domestic working-class existence cannot help but ring falsely when read against the conflicting representations of the home buttressing this vision of domesticity. The image of the Edenic working-class Manchester home so glaringly jars with its historical reality and Gaskell's representations of it that Gaskell's narrative finally moves its surviving protagonists, Mary and Jem, to Canada. The imperial project thus usurps the earlier place of pastoral, its collective national vision unifying the community around a new set of exclusions. Once threateningly discordant to the harmony of middle-class industry, Jem and Mary, as happily resigned members of the working class, now become fully part of the English nation as they head off in the service of the British Commonwealth.

The last words of the text highlight this shift in allegiances. Mary, receiving news from Jem as he returns home with letters from England, sighs, "Dear Job Legh! . . . softly and seriously" (393). Not insignificantly, Job is the novel's anti-Union spokesperson. Early on in the novel he complains bitterly that John Barton and his Union are usurping his freedoms as an Englishman: " 'I were obliged to become a member for peace; else I don't go along with 'em. Yo see they think themselves wise, and me silly, for differing with them; well! there's no harm in that. But then they won't let me be silly in peace and quietness, but will force me to be as wise as they are; now that's not British liberty, I say. I'm forced to be wise according to their notions, else they parsecute me, and sarve me out'" (197). Moreover, as an amateur naturalist with a lawyerly penchant, he represents a taxonomic approach to knowledge, dramatically at odds with the narrative's own valuing of feelings. Job's relationship to writing, for instance, is "little more than an auxiliary to natural history; a way of ticketing specimens, not of expressing thoughts" (340). Yet, despite these differences, the narrative equates Job with Gaskell herself, when Job echoes Gaskell's own statements about her knowledge of political economy, abjuring in almost identical language, "I'm not given to Political Economy" (384). Job thus occupies a dual role in the resolution to *Mary Barton*'s narrative conflicts: he registers the extent to which the narrative must shift gears in order to bring about a satisfactory conclusion and bears witness to how reduced Gaskell's own project becomes when faced with resolving the problems of representing the working class. Like the text as a whole, the doubleness of Job's position attests to the contradictory nature of Gaskell's novel: at once expansive and narrow in its treatment of the ideological terrain defining the working class, it simultaneously provides resolution and just as compellingly takes it away. Keeping the oscillating effect of the text in motion until its final lines, the ticketing, officious Job cannot entirely displace the "wild and visionary" John Barton.[53]

....

With the removal of Mary and Jem to Canada, England is left in the hands of the converted captain of industry, Mr. Harry Carson, whose deepest wish is "that a perfect understanding, and complete confidence and love might exist between masters and men; that the truth might be recognized that the interests of one were the interests of all; and as such, required the consideration and deliberation of all; that hence it was most desirable to have educated workers, capable of judging, not mere machines of ignorant men; and to have them bound to their employers by the ties of respect and affection, not by mere money bargains alone; in short to acknowledge the Spirit of Christ as the regulating law between both parties" (388). Obviously, the compact between masters and men that Mr. Carson envisions in no way mitigates the differences between them—and is remarkable, as well, for its exclusion of workingwomen. It proposes no substantive changes in the structural relationship defining workers and owners but rather appeals to a changed attitude toward these relations. In place of mistrust, anger, and violence, it asks for confidence, love, respect, and affection. Out of the same situation that the novel as a whole narrates, then, it promises a different result: an outcome in which now money alone will not determine how workers are "bound" to their employers.

There is nothing terribly exceptional here. If this resolution were all that *Mary Barton* had to offer, it would qualify under standard fare for industrial novels of the period: a paternalistic, conciliatory strategy toward workers overlooks class divisions and neatly unites workers and employers alike — on the employers' terms. But there is more to *Mary Barton* than this. Although it clearly participates in this hegemonic narrative, it also produces a counternarrative that calls into question the whole basis for such a vision of class hegemony. The defining feature of this counternarrative is its representation of what Oskar Negt and Alexander Kluge term the "proletarian public sphere." In contrast to the bourgeois public sphere enforced by Carson, the proletarian public sphere embodies the self-experience of the masses, recognizing and giving voice to the presence of work and productive relations in the public sphere. As Negt and Kluge envision it, the "[p]roletarian public sphere is the name for a social, collective process of production that has as its object the human senses in their interrelatedness." [54]

Despite the overriding ideology of *Mary Barton*, which functions to discredit its workers as a viable social force with a political consciousness of its own, Gaskell's narrative allows for a certain expression of this alternative public sphere in its attempt to fortify the bourgeois public sphere against class conflict. Preemptively, Gaskell makes a point of dissociating John Barton's views from those of the Owenites. Near the end of the novel, Mr. Carson, in an attempt to understand Barton's politics, equates them with Owenism: " 'You mean he was an Owenite; all for equality, and community of goods, and that kind of absurdity.' " This assumption is immediately countered with " 'No, no! John Barton was no fool. No need to tell him that were all men equal to-night, some would get the start by rising an hour earlier to-morrow' " (384). Any notion of an alternative social organization of labor and experience is summarily invalidated; a dismissal facilitated by the earlier evacuation of any notion of political agency on the part of the working class. Not only does John Barton finally see his political crime arising from misguided, "perverted reasonings" but Mr. Carson's desire for vengeance against Barton for killing his son is finally quelled by the Gospel teaching "They know not what they do" (370). [55]

Yet, in the one moment of the novel when Gaskell apologizes for her representation of John Barton's feelings, the narrative entertains, albeit only momentarily, the idea that there is a potentially different, collective experience of the public sphere: "what I wish to impress is what the workman feels and thinks" (24). Gaskell's retreat from her own representation, or, rather, the need for a retreat at all, remains as a mark of the exclusions necessary to constitute the nation as a whole. But, simultaneously, her depiction of those feelings provides a glimpse of a realm of experience excluded from the public sphere; the beginnings of a proletarian public sphere that would realize the emotions and sympathies and experiences Gaskell's narrative briefly identifies with as alternative. (In the process, too, it undercuts the claimed unity of working-class and middle-class interests which underwrote the First Reform Bill; and which came back to haunt the middle class during the crisis of the Second Reform Bill, as we will see in chapter 2.) Perhaps this "too real" possibility led Gaskell's contemporary readers to read into *Mary Barton* an incitement of "class against class." In other words, the class differences exposed in the novel's initial identification with John Barton remain to trouble its proffered vision of class conciliation. The power of this disruption, moreover, lies in its positive embodiment of a collective relationship to labor and pleasure, even as this relationship is felt primarily as a loss. After all, John Barton was "*the* person with whom all [Gaskell's] sympathies went,"[56] his "visionary" appeal founded on the fact that he "stood by" his "class, his order . . . not the rights of his own paltry self" (170). Finally, this possibility as well harbors the democratizing energies which Erich Auerbach sees residing in realism itself, insofar as realism "had to embrace the whole reality of contemporary civilization, in which to be sure the bourgeoisie played a dominant role, but in which the masses were beginning to press threateningly ahead, as they became ever more conscious of their own function and power."[57]

CHAPTER 2

A MODERN ODYSSEY

....

Felix Holt's Education

for the Masses

What they upbraid the bourgeoisie with is not so much that it creates a proletariat as that it creates a revolutionary proletariat. — Karl Marx, *The Communist Manifesto*

George Eliot's *Felix Holt* promises perhaps too much. Beginning in the memorable year 1832, it immodestly sets as its task the tracing of change in the English industrial landscape and the effects of this change on the fictional town of Treby Magna. The opening passage takes us back in time to the period immediately preceding the novel's setting, when "the glory had not yet departed from the old coach roads."[1] Eliot compares the sights, sounds, and fullness of immediately apprehensible experience offered by the long, slow journey by coach to a future where travel will more likely resemble a "bullet" being "shot through a tube" (75). Speed becomes the new determining force; it alters not only the landscape but our ability to relate to it as well.[2] For Eliot, the high-speed "tube-journey's" limitations are twofold. First, it is disruptive to memory. Second, and perhaps most importantly for the task at hand, it defies representation: "The tube-journey can never lend much to picture and narrative; it is as barren as an exclamatory O!" (75). Such a crisis of representation would seem to put Eliot's own role as writer in danger, if indeed she is to relate to us the changes in Treby Magna effected by industrialization. By setting the novel in 1832, however (although it was written in 1866), Eliot seems to want to avoid this representational impasse. By returning to this earlier period she will describe the process of this change, but not the experiences of it which are yet to come, foreseeable yet unrepresentable some time in the still-indefinite future (which was actually Eliot's own present).[3]

Eliot does, however, in a sense flesh out the barren O! of this future, of how it might be experienced, by telling us what it will not be, by showing us what the coach journey is and what it offers. Taking us along with her on a hypothetical trip from Avon to Kent, Eliot gives us a vision of the English countryside verdant with over-blossoming nature and a pace of life consonant with the rhythms of rural existence; the shepherd here moves in sync with the slow pace of his grazing cattle. Twined and tendrilled with wild convolvulus, many-tubed honeysuckle, scarlet haws, deep-crimson hips, blackberry branches, pale pink dog roses, and ruby-berried nightshade, it is a landscape demarcated by the "unmarketable beauty" of traditional English hedgerows. Were one to catch a glimpse of the people contentedly ensconced behind these hedgerows, one would see faces be-grimed with dirt; yet, lest this suggest a lack of moral uprightness, of wanton uncleanliness, the narrator clarifies that this is not your ordinary dirt but Protestant dirt, the kind of dirt that makes its possessors clean. These Protestants in particular are doubly scrubbed, saved as they are "from the excesses of Protestantism by not knowing how to read" (77). These are the glory days: the days before the rick-burners, the riots, and the encroachment of handlooms and mines—and with them Dissenters—on this pastoral cornucopia.

As the coach continues on its way, however, this scene passes, and the villages and hamlets with their coal-pits and manufacture draw near. At this juncture, a schism is registered. Whereas those inhabitants peopling the rural countryside are "sure that England was the best of all possible countries" (78), this manufacturing midlands' population is not so easily convinced. Indeed, the connection between the town and the country becomes hard if not impossible to discern; the traveler has literally passed from "one phase of English life to another" (79)—where dirt is no longer imbued with any great moral rectitude but is simply dirty. In this new landscape, it becomes difficult to read the signs so transparent in the agricultural regions. Whereas rural life apparently hides nothing valuable beneath its tendrils—"If there were any facts which had not fallen under their observation, they were facts not worth observing" (78)—such transparency between vision and object becomes unsettled and disrupted once one enters the new landscape of the town. Representation itself becomes indeterminate, precariously and dangerously up for grabs by a variety of different and contradictory interpretations. Here the parson preaches a sermon invoking his parishioners to "plough up the fallow-ground of your hearts" and its meaning is so opaque and so susceptible to being divergently interpreted that one group sees in it an argument for fallows and yet another sees it as an argument against them. Shaken by this highly unstable state of affairs, the parson expires in a fit of apoplexy.

Even within this potentially disruptive framework of change, however, there is a unifying force for Eliot, embodied in the figure of the coachman. That force is narrative, for what he can do—and the modern train conductor cannot—is gather stories. Because of the slow pace with which he, unlike the train, moves through the landscape, the old coachman is able to gather knowledge of its places and people, and this, for Eliot, is the raw material of "fine stories" (83). Indeed, as Eliot assures us, there are enough stories of English life, "enough of English labours in town and country, enough aspects of earth and sky, to make episodes for a modern Odyssey" (76).

Yet already within the space of Eliot's introduction, the threat to this kind of integrated storytelling is all too evident, creeping into even the coachman's relationship to the landscape. Embittered by the railroad's invasive presence on the landscape—materialized in a vision of the countryside "strewn with shattered limbs"—the coachman lapses momentarily into his own form of apoplexy; he is rendered speechless: "[he] looked before him with the blank gaze of one who had driven his coach to the outermost edge of the universe, and saw his leaders plunging into the abyss" (81). Where once there was something to relate, now there is momentarily only blankness and silence, the inability to narrate: the "high prophetic strain" briefly takes the place of the "familiar one of narrative" (81). This "prophetic strain" is both potent and cataclysmic, foretelling a certain future of shattered limbs and destroyed inns, which leads our coachman to the brink of the abyss and, significantly, the end of narrative. Represented by the railroad and its sure path of destruction, the prophetic mode is intimately connected to modernity itself. It figures for Eliot as all that is counter to narrative, and like the coachman's stories, Eliot's own narrative is susceptible to its powers. Threatened as it is by new forms of technology and the new social forces coming into being along with that technology, Eliot's story is precariously located in the interstices between two modes of storytelling: the prophetic and the narrative. As I will argue later, when Eliot, in the face of the destructive forces of industrialism, invokes her recuperative vision of national unity she ironically succumbs to the very mode of prophecy she is at such pains to forestall.

Within the context of this fast-disappearing "old-fashioned" storytelling Eliot will attempt to tell us the story of Felix Holt. Like the coach journey, Felix's story is already on the cusp, located somewhere between an old-fashioned narratability and an increasingly destabilized state of modern indeterminacy and speed. On the one hand, this is not new terrain for Eliot. Throughout her oeuvre she grapples with how to recover and draw the right connections between the past and the present; to understand the present as unfolding and evolving from the past in order to adequately see the relationship of each minute part to the whole, no matter how obscure each individual part may at first seem. On the other hand, *Felix Holt* breaks new ground precisely because the industrial novel's project necessarily requires the introduction of new forces existing in the *present*: the newly created phenomena of industrial workers and their labor.

The Conditions of Modern Life

Early on in the novel, Eliot identifies the forces of disruption altering the previously tranquil life of Treby Magna:

> Such was the old-fashioned, grazing, brewing, wool-packing, cheese-loading life of Treby Magna, until there befell new conditions, complicating its relating with the rest of the world, and gradually awakening in it that higher consciousness which is known to bring higher pains. First came the canal; next, the working of the coal-mines at Sproxton, two miles off the town; and, thirdly, the discovery of a saline spring, which suggested to a too constructive brain the possibility of turning Treby Magna into a fashionable watering-place. So daring an idea was not originated by a native Trebian, but by a young lawyer who came from a distance, knew the dictionary by heart, and was probably an illegitimate son of somebody or other. (124)

Most striking about this passage is the oddly passive quality of the "new conditions." They have befallen the town, unpeopled or disembodied, so it seems, brought on by canals, coal mines, and saline springs, and done to Treby Magna rather than by anyone. If there were to be a culprit in all this, it would be a combination of distance, book knowledge rather than experience, and illegitimacy, all residing in the person of the young lawyer and all of which together suggest a lack of connection or rootedness to place, a severing of the individual from the landscape which at one time, as Eliot suggests, were co-extensive with one another.[4] This distance threatens immediate experience, not only complicating Treby Magna's relations with the "rest of the world" but also the individual's relation to him/herself, in its awakening of "that higher consciousness which is known to bring higher pains." As the narrative of the book will attest, much of that pain for Eliot comes from a lack of transparency: the meaning of experience itself is undermined by modern life.

One way of dealing with such a lack will be to extend the framework of social experience beyond the confines of individual life to a much more expansive context, determined not by the individual but by the larger purview of what Eliot calls the "world's forces." After Felix is jailed for inciting the mob to riot, for instance, the problem at the heart of his conversation with Rufus Lyon is the absence of clearly definable motives for Felix's actions, which cause him to be misapprehended as the leader of the mob. In the face of this absence, Rufus and Felix talk about "the perplexed condition of human things, whereby even right action seems to bring evil consequences, if we have respect only to our own brief lives, and not to that larger rule whereby we are stewards of the eternal dealings, and not contrivers of our own success' " (467–68). Like Eliot's earlier description of Treby Magna's landscape, a similar sense of passivity inflects this view of change and history. Not only are the processes of change transforming the landscape brought on by conditions rather than people but those affected by these changes must themselves remain passive recipients of them, stewards not contrivers.

Even for Eliot's narrator, this enlargement of one's perspective seems fraught with problems. The breadth of such expansive terrain threatens to jeopardize, at the same time it enables, the act of representation. As Eliot's narrator would have it, the "truth" cannot be found in this terrain. In the same scene calling for the "larger rule," the narrator gives us some insight into Lyon's own perplexity about the matter: "[Rufus Lyon] cared intensely for his opinions, and would have liked events to speak for them in a sort of picture-writing that everybody could understand. The enthusiasms of the world are not to be stimulated by a commentary in small and subtle characters which alone can tell the whole truth; and the picture-writing in Felix Holt's troubles was of an entirely puzzling kind: if he were a martyr, neither side wanted to claim him" (466). On the one hand, there is the practical problem that people are seemingly not inspired by "small and subtle characters" but rather need the stimulus of a grand narrative. On the other hand, that grand narrative lacks full access to the truth; it is finally unable to "tell the whole truth." A desire for "picture-writing," an attempt to rescue an "immediate" perception, exists that is simultaneously denied by the nature of the material at hand: the representation of Felix as martyr is left unclaimed; the word "martyr" operates as a dangerously free-floating signifier adrift from its signified. This gap marks a relation of nonidentity between subject and object: what slips through, so to speak, is the possibility of an immediately readable present, a present that is simultaneously desired and denied.[5]

Moreover, as an earlier scene between Lyon and Harold Transome illustrates, while the narrator on one level positions Lyon as the brunt of others' jokes because of his naive yearnings for a direct correspondence between objects and their representation (276–77), on another level the narrator is clearly in sympathy with our "rusty old Puritan" whose "illusions" under closer inspection represent simply a different and better way of looking at things:

> but I never smiled at Mr. Lyon's trustful energy without falling to penitence and veneration immediately after. For what we call illusions are often, in truth, a wider vision of past and present realities—a willing movement of a man's soul with the larger sweep of the world's forces—a movement towards a more assured end than the chances of a single life. We see human heroism broken into units and say, this unit did little—might as well not have been. But in this way we might break up the sunlight into fragments, and think that this and the other might be cheaply parted with. Let us rather raise a monument to the soldiers whose brave hearts only kept the ranks unbroken, and met death—a monument to the faithful who were not famous, and who are precious as the continuity of the sunbeams is precious, though some of them fall unseen and on barrenness. (277)

The catchwords here are "a wider vision of past and present realities" and the "continuity" such a vision provides against the fragmented, incomplete picture of the individual life, a goal in keeping with the realist commitment to capture the interpenetration of the collective and the individual. The temptation to mock Rufus Lyon is thus offset by the more dangerous desire to escape history altogether.[6] Although the narrative as a whole will ultimately side with Lyon against Harold Transome, the temptation toward mockery for which the narrator chastises herself dramatizes the tension between the possible modes of narration Eliot has at her disposal. While the appeal for continuity is made in the name of adequacy, of a notion of representation whose primary goal is a fuller and "more assured" representation of reality, this realist criterion is jeopardized by its object of study: all that is new and not yet history in the wider sense to which Eliot is harkening.

Certainly this contradictory position of Eliot's is not confined to *Felix Holt*: on the contrary, it is vintage Eliot. But as I want to argue, it is Eliot with a twist. The questions of representation riddling Eliot's work as a whole are here radically overdetermined by the new presence on her landscape of industrial workers and industrial labor.[7] First, as we saw from Eliot's introduction to the novel, they are intimately tied to her own project as a writer: how to represent the processes of modernization when those processes seem by their nature—disembodied speed, the destruction of memory—to defy representation? Second, at the level of content, even the call to the past cannot stem the present forces at work on Treby Magna, forces that continually disrupt any comfortable connection or transparent relationship between the past and the present. The young "illegitimate" lawyer exemplifies this dislocation: he comes from afar, his knowledge is learned, not inherited, and his parentage is unknown. Cut off from the continuity of a traceable past, he embodies the potential threat of misrepresentation in his desire to urbanize the countryside and turn it into a commodified tourist attraction by marketing its natural resources. Finally, these questions on the level of the text are linked to their larger social context, the broader crisis of political representation raised by the debates over the Reform Bills of 1832 and 1867, debates whose essence lies not only in the question of who is entitled to representation but also what form that representation should take. At the heart of these polyvalent and overlapping crises lies the question of how to represent work.

All Play and No Work

Within *Felix Holt* one is hard-pressed to find any direct representation of work. What little is learned about work is learned through negation: by looking at what the workers do when they are not on the job, the reader is presumably to glean some sense of who they are and what they do at work. Thus Eliot takes us not into the factory or the mine but into the pub.

It is the pub that provides a sense of the workers' lives and their "miseries," and the relationship between the two: "One way of getting an idea of our fellow-countrymen's miseries is to go and look at their pleasures" (373). The scene is the Cross-Keys, the local pub where the working class enjoys its leisuretime. A "fungus-featured landlord" and a "yellow sickly landlady" pour "doctored ale," in a room reeking of "an odour of bad tobacco, and remarkably strong cheese" (373). Surely, if this dank, fetid atmosphere—by all accounts more suitable for the cultivation of mushrooms and mold than people's pleasures—provides the space for the workers' leisure, then the workers' miseries must be dreadful indeed. To drive home this point the narrator suggests that in comparison to other watering-holes the Cross-Keys actually presents a "high standard of pleasure" (374).

Talk in the pub revolves around the political issues occupying the minds of Trebians, specifically the impending election and more generally the question of representation on which it centers. Not surprisingly, there are plenty of political opportunists enlisted by each side ready to bend the ears of these working men in order to gain support for their particular candidate. One such man is Mr. Johnson, who visits the Sproxton pub with the express purpose of rallying the workers to the Radical cause of Harold Transome. In the course of buying rounds and sponging for Radical support, Mr. Johnson informs the workers of their no less than national role and importance in the upcoming elections:

> "No, no: I say, as this country prospers it has more and more need of you, sirs. It can do without a pack of lazy lords and ladies, but it can never do without brave colliers. And the country *will* prosper. I pledge you my word, sirs, this country will rise to the tip-top of every-thing, and there isn't a man in it but what shall have his joint in the pot, and his spare money jingling in his pocket, if we only exert our-selves to send the right men to parliament—men who will speak for the collier, and the stone-cutter, and the navvy" (Mr. Johnson waved his hand liberally), "and will stand no nonsense. This is a crisis, and we must exert ourselves. We've got Reform, gentlemen, but now the thing is to make Reform work. It's a crisis—I pledge you my word it's a crisis." (225–26)

From the venerable Mr. Johnson's speech it would appear that the inter-ests of working men occupy a central role in the election. But as with all political prevarications it is but another example of how words do not nec-essarily speak the truth.[8] The levels of deception are numerous. To begin with, Mr. Johnson delivers himself in the service of Harold Transome, who has taken on the false mantle of a Radical simply by *calling* himself one. Moreover, the colliers and miners themselves do not yet have the vote; their role therefore, according to Mr. Johnson, is rather to amass themselves for

Harold Transome by making their presence felt on election day and, when the opportunity arises, attacking Transome's opponents. This appeal falls on willing ears. One worker, aptly named Dredge, overzealously takes up the pugilistic aspects of the cause and has to be rebuked, gently reminded that actual hard knocks are out of the question—although the slinging of soft muddy things would be well within bounds. In contrast to the enthusiasm the workers as a whole show for Johnson's slick speech and reasoning, Felix Holt, witnessing this bravado performance, leaves the pub in disgust, loathe to hear his own heartfelt convictions (about the importance of working men, not their enlistment as potential disrupters of the election process) travestied by such a political charlatan.

One might read this scene as a straightforward condemnation of men like Johnson who play willy-nilly with the sympathies of the working class. Certainly opportunists are one focus of the narrative's critique. But it is a double-edged critique: the ease with which Johnson can manipulate the miners' sentiments says just as much about the marked absence of political acuity in the working class as it does about Johnson's opportunism. Their sympathies are to be played with so cavalierly because they lack a proper education in political know-how. They hang on the last word of Johnson's speech ("crisis"), for instance, not because they understand what this word means—they most surely do not—but precisely because they do not know its meaning and for this reason (or lack of reason) are thoroughly persuaded. His words convince by their incomprehensibility. This caricature of working-class sensibility is crucial to explaining the effect the absence of industrial work has on the structure of the novel as a whole. By parodying the workers, the narrative provocatively casts suspicion on their political abilities. In the process, the question of their representation moves from the issue of their natural right to self-representation as working members of English society to an evaluation of whether, given their political immaturity, they are in a position to be able to represent themselves.[9] At stake becomes a valuation of political knowledge, a valuation in which the collier and miner come up woefully short. From the issue of knowledge it is then but a small step to the question of culture itself. As Eliot makes explicit in the "Address to Working Men" (a speech appended to the end of the novel and delivered in the fictive voice of Felix Holt), "degrading, barbarous pleasures" such as those of the working class are nothing less than a sign of cultural privation, of the lack of those "precious benefits" which she calls the "common estate of society."[10] This "common estate," which Eliot, via the pub, shows no mere expansion of the franchise can provide, is "that treasure of knowledge, science, poetry, refinement of thought, feeling, and manners, great memories and the interpretation of great records, which is carried on from the minds of one generation to the minds of another" (621). The literary quandary of how to represent modern labor has been translated into an issue of political representation, which in turn rests on who the rightful heirs of such a conveyed tradition of culture can and should be.

Such a shift is integrally connected to the actual debates about reform in England beginning in the 1830s and continuing into the 1860s with the passing of the Second Reform Bill in 1867, just one year after Eliot wrote *Felix Holt*. The nature of this period of reform has been characterized by critics such as Raymond Williams and Patrick Brantlinger as one involving two distinct phases: the first, the middle-class reform of the 1830s through the mid-1850s in which political reformist action was believed to be the mechanism through which to alleviate social problems (grouped under the umbrella term the "Condition of England"), and the second, in which the optimism and energy of this earlier period of reform is replaced by the "cult of progress," that is, the belief in the inevitability of historical progress, of "laws" of evolution and organic growth that displace human agency as the motor of change.[11] These two phases are divided along class lines. Whereas the First Reform Bill centered on the issue of enfranchising the middle class, with the 1867 Bill the middle class found itself in a decidedly different position, possibly having to cede rather than gain power through the extension of the franchise to the working class. With the middle class in a position potentially to lose power, the political ground of reform radically shifted; the hegemony of the middle class was threatened. At this point broad issues of culture began to play a significantly larger part in English political life. Culture and its related terms—education, responsibility, moral and intellectual fitness, obligation, trust, and so on—slowly came to displace questions of natural right; these cultural criteria took precedence over what properly constituted an individual's right to representation.[12] As Patrick Brantlinger notes, "one stood for or against a new reform bill, depending partly on one's definition of culture and on one's belief as to whether those who were to be enfranchised had enough of it or not."[13]

Curiously enough, it is this latter phase of reform that *Felix Holt* narrates. As the pub scenes illustrate, what is of central concern is whether the workers have the cultural capital to warrant a *political* right to representation. If the caricature of their political and intellectual ineptitude were not evidence enough, the depiction of their mob violence on election day resulting, as it does, in an anarchic, seemingly politically unmotivated riot definitively answers this concern with a resounding no.[14] Thus, while *Felix Holt* is set in the period of crisis of the First Reform Bill of 1832, ideationally the crisis it confronts and attempts to reconcile is that of the Second Reform Bill, contemporaneous with the actual period in which Eliot was writing the novel. In the narrative's own practice, then, the present is not written as a continuation of the past but rather is projected back onto the past. The collapse of present into past conflates two distinct historical moments into one moment, a moment, moreover, that as the result of the fusion must always remain an ideal.

This metaleptic return has direct consequences for Eliot's representations of work. Since the ultimate basis for political judgment rests on cultural capital, neither work nor the workplace are necessary sites for political claims to representation. Production is repressed, excluded from the status of reality. In a sense, then, it becomes not so much a question of being unable to represent work but of its seeming irrelevance to the "present" 1860s politics of culture. In the process, thirty-odd years of history are conflated, years that include, significantly, the working-class militancy of the 1840s when, from a middle-class British perspective, workers' struggle in the political form of Chartism reared its ugly head and threatened to divide the nation along class lines. The active forgetting of that which has not yet happened—given the historical setting of *Felix Holt*—eliminates with it the memory of class conflict.

It is precisely this attempt to purge the past of its fractious discontinuities that is necessary to constitute the nation. It is the *absent* space of work that will be filled by the concept of "nation," which, unlike work, serves to unite the heterogeneous workers and middle-class citizens populating *Felix Holt*. In essence, the "Condition of England" question is "answered" through its supersession by culture: the nation becomes synonymous with culture, specifically English culture, which in turn provides the ideological cement necessary to symbolically unite worker and capitalist in their mutual *national* identification as English.[15] Much like our coachman, whose narrative was temporarily interrupted by the penetration of urban capital (manifest in the railroad) into the countryside, the narrative of *Felix Holt*, faced with the presence of industrial labor, moves into a prophetic register which foretells the steady, progressive realization of a national destiny.

A second look at Mr. Johnson's speech bears out this shift in political terrain. Framed by an unquestioned belief in history as progress—"as this country prospers," he begins—Johnson's speech mirrors the movement of reform just described and diverts attention from labor politics per se to a national politics: "the country *will* prosper . . . will rise to the tip-top of everything." As the future tense of his discourse appropriately emphasizes, he moves into the prophetic mode, virtually *prophesying* the nation and its fortunes. This prophetic mode, as with the coachman, leaves the realm of descriptive, realistic narrative, and indeed must: it constructs a political space divorced from political action and devoid of any conflicts that would hamper national unity. The only form of action entertained is the workers' rioting which results from a misguided and wholly unpolitical mob mentality, a mentality, it is underscored, "animated by no real political passion" (428). To the extent that the workers are reduced to a "mad crowd," their collective subjectivity is limited to passive receivership (possibly) of England's great cultural heritage. In Arnoldian fashion, culture and its expression in the "nation" come to stand virtually in opposition to history: like Arnold's understanding of "anarchy," history within *Felix Holt* is too embedded in the thick of things, too susceptible to divisions of class and ideology. Reaching across this divide, culture functions as a protective enclosure, a space where the social practices of labor are suspended. Within the domain of culture, social relations and the abstract form of social domination intrinsic to them are severed from their sociohistorical constitution in determinate, structured forms of practice.

The politics of culture in which *Felix Holt* is engaged, as discussed above, more properly represents the period of reform of the 1860s following the Chartist struggles of the 1840s, a period which contains within it the defeat of the first wave of working-class militancy: action on the workers' part has already been effectively quelled and overcome. When attempting to confront industrial labor, then, the narrative shifts into a register that already precludes it from social consideration. Within the text, Chartism and the alternative vision of work it carries with it is represented as a historical impossibility—though ostensibly the novel is situated in 1832.

Yet Eliot does attempt to narrate a form of labor complementary to her mobilization of culture. To do so she must turn back to the past. In an attempt to reconnect figuratively the brain and the hands, to offer an alternative to the nonrepresentability of the hands alone, Eliot leaves the domain of the industrialized working class and returns to the residual socioeconomic mode of artisanal production. Mental and manual labor are combined in the figure of Felix as artisan and organic intellectual. This return can be read generally as a desire to maintain social positions that are the creation of obsolete modes of production.[16] Within the context of the novel, it serves to carve out an extra-economic realm seemingly independent of industrial production.

The strangeness of Felix's economic markings is acknowledged in the text: "Felix was known personally, and vaguely believed to be a man who meant many queer things, not at all of an every-day kind" (427). Part of this "queerness" results from Felix's marginal position outside the economy of exchange: "He had put a stop to the making of saleable drugs, *contrary to the nature of buying and selling*" (465, emphasis added). From his newly created role as lower-middle-class artisan, Felix putatively escapes the snares of modernization—market relations and the instrumentality they express. On the one hand, there is a utopian element in Eliot's move back to quasi-artisanal production; a desire somehow to reestablish the fast-disappearing connection between manual and mental labor, to slow down the pace of change and resist the fragmentation of space threatening the cohesiveness of the rural community. Herein lies the creative performative capacity utterly denied the industrial worker. On the other hand, caught as he is in a historically outmoded economic structure and cultural form, Felix represents a regressive resistance to "modernity" itself. Like Eliot's disembodied notion of culture, he is "not at all of an every-day kind" (427).

In essence, the narrative's investment in him lies to a large extent in the contrast he provides to the modern worker. As the fictive author of the "Address to Working Men," he advises the workers to recognize the organic, evolutionary nature of things, and therefore to "take the world as it is"; to accept the superiority of the "masters" who hold the keys to this cultural treasure "which is the life of the nation" (621–22). In this sense, Felix Holt hovers didactically over the text as a model—of resistance to the penetration of capital and of acquiescence to a politics of class conciliation premised on a unifying vision of cultural nationalism. To expose the ideologies and discourses of modern nationalism and its construction within bourgeois culture is to discover the traces of the repressed history contained in (the absence of) industrial labor.

Love's Labors

Just as the division between work and culture presupposed a reconfiguration of the relation between external and internal (the workers, potentially external forces of disruption, are "internalized" within the boundaries of English culture), the relation of England to its other Others—the Orientalized East—operates through the construction of internal/external boundaries of mutual exclusivity. The Orient enters *Felix Holt* in the guise of Harold Transome, who arrives back on England's shores at the beginning of the novel. The novel says little about Harold's exploits while he has been away in Greece save for the fact that he has accumulated large sums of money and an heir. While the actual source of Harold's money is left unspecified, his experience abroad has reshaped his views on the processes of modernization at home. The apparent (and grossly stereotypical) slothfulness of the Easterner justifies the self-interested practices of competitive *English* commerce: "If you had lived in the East, as I have, you would be more tolerant. More tolerant, for example, of an active industrious selfishness, such as we have here, though it may not always be quite scrupulous: you would see how much better it is than an idle selfishness. I have heard it said, a bridge is a good thing—worth helping to make, though half the men who worked at it were rogues" (275). The "industrious selfishness" that Harold espouses is sharply contrasted to Felix's resistance to market forces. Indeed the dichotomous positions they hold mark the alternative visions of work that organize *Felix Holt*. These alternatives, like those represented by the shift from production to pleasure when dealing with the workers, are mapped appetitively by the opposite pleasures each affords. If *Felix Holt* turns to the pub to explore workers' pleasures, when looking for bourgeois pleasures its haunt is (figuratively) the bedroom, the realm of sexual desire. The figure of Esther Lyon, in particular, offers the means for evaluating the different pleasures identified with Harold and Felix and the alternative social visions manifest in them.[17]

Throughout the novel Esther functions as a liminal figure. In terms of her class identification, she can be read as the representative petit bourgeois. The product of an aristocrat and a sailor, she operates from within an indeterminate class position, liable to be as easily swayed by the class interests of the aristocracy (in the figure of Harold Transome) as by those of the working class (identified falsely, as we have seen, with Felix Holt). Esther's sexual desires and her eventual capitulation to Felix serve as cautionary political allegory. Torn between Felix and Harold, Esther's ultimate acceptance of Felix mirrors the transformation desired by the text for the working class. They, like Esther, should accept their proper *function* within the body politic: accommodation to current social conditions in the interests of the health of the nation as a whole.

The mechanics whereby the gendered body of Esther is made part of this "organic" national body reveals the violence and domination underlying the seemingly benign picture of accommodation. Specifically, the romantic plot of *Felix Holt* makes explicit the link between culture and power, a link obfuscated in the realm of work and production. By looking, then, at how power circulates through the figure of Esther we can recover the missing link, the (repressed) body, on which culture and imperial power is written.

Esther spends the greater part of the novel in a condition of conflicted indecisiveness, at a juncture where she must choose between the initially illusive pleasures and privileges of the aristocratic "queenly" life and the hardworking, self-sacrificing ethic of Felix's artisanal "vocation." Thanks to the convoluted legal subplot of entail which cedes to Esther legitimate rights to the Transome estate, and therefore negates the potential for cross-class sexual conflict, Esther can make what looks like a voluntary choice between her two lovers. It is crucial that this is a voluntary choice; what is at stake is the principle of self-regulation.

On one level, Esther's education, her private journey through successive stages of personal development, can be read as a microcosm of the modern narrative of "inevitable progress" as she learns to discard the Romantic texts she initially identifies with in favor of the "realism" Felix Holt embodies —a process built on a necessary disillusionment, and moving toward the "disinterested objectivity" of scientific rationality: "The favourite Byronic heroes were beginning to look something like last night's decorations seen in the sober dawn . . . if Felix Holt were to love her, her life would be exalted into something quite new—into a sort of difficult blessedness, such as one may imagine in beings who are conscious of painfully growing into the possession of higher powers" (327).[18] Romanticism is clearly not the suitable genre for this awakening. The final death knell to any sort of Romantic utopia comes when Esther's vision of Oriental love is shattered by Harold's informing her that his Greek wife had been a slave: "Hitherto Esther's acquaintance with Oriental love was derived chiefly from Byronic poems, and this had not sufficed to adjust her mind to a new story, where the Giaour concerned was giving her his arm. She was unable to speak" (541). The identification of Harold as Giaour is an odd one. At once it both situates him within an Oriental narrative—as Christian, no doubt, but labeled as such from within a non-Christian, Muslim perspective—and radically severs Esther's identification with that narrative.

We, as readers, certainly know enough about Harold to realize there is no fear of him "going native." Early on in the novel, in fact, Harold's character and ambitions are described in these terms: "He was addicted at once to rebellion and to conformity, and only an intimate personal knowledge could enable any one to predict where his conformity would begin. The limit was not defined by theory, but was drawn in an irregular zigzag by early disposition and association; and his resolution, of which he had never lost hold, to be a thorough Englishman again some day, had kept up the habit of considering all his conclusions with reference to English politics and English social conditions" (197). Nonetheless, the moment the Orient, even if only metaphorically, takes on flesh and blood, the pleasures it seemed to afford Esther lose their allure. So much so that when Harold names Esther "the empress of [her] own fortunes—and more besides," a rather befuddled Esther replies: "Dear me . . . I don't think I know very well what to do with my empire" (501).

While Esther will ultimately reject the role of empress, Harold's relationship to her maps the novel's vision of East/West relations.[19] As the revelation that Harold's wife was a slave makes clear, the validation of the English woman comes through the dehumanization of the non-European woman. The contrast is meant to show Esther that "her own place was peculiar and supreme" (541). At the same time, however, the situating of Harold's Eastern experience in Greece, as opposed to India or Africa, falsely separates Harold's venture from the British imperial enterprise. Harold is figured more as an adventurer than a colonist or imperial administrator, thereby separating the work of empire from its socioeconomic moorings. What these two figurations suggest is a subtle distinction between different operations of cultural and economic power. When such force is meted out genteelly in the interests of its larger (legitimizing) cultural project, then it appears to lose its nasty repressive edge and regain its status as lofty "cultured" ideal. As Esther remarks about Harold Transome's mode of governance on his own estate, what is so impressive is the naturalness—owing to his gender—of his domination, "the masculine ease with which he governed everybody and administered everything about him, without the least harshness, and with a facile good-nature which yet was not weak" (524). Any show of brute force or direct repression, however, must remain invisible. In other words, Harold's attempts simultaneously to devalue the worth of his Eastern wife and increase Esther's value backfire precisely because of the directness of exchange they expose.

The economic underpinnings of Harold's "work" in the East do, however, have a domestic corollary in his courtship of Esther. This exchange takes place at the same time that Harold is in the process of wooing Esther, a possibility that only even arises once Harold learns that Esther is the legitimate heir to the Transome estate. Indeed when he first discovers that the heir is in fact an heiress, he weighs the possibility of success with her in purely legalistic terms, referring to her as a claimant whose "legal" right can (and should) be united with what he sees as his "rational" claim. While the mechanism for acquiring an English wife may not seem as direct as that of simply buying her, the economics underlying the "exchange" are essentially the same.[20] The entrance of money, and with it, an openly exploitative exercise of power, demystifies the more finely veiled traffic in women.

Moreover, as we learn later about Harold, he prefers what the narrative deems "Oriental" relationships: "Having Harry as an heir, he preferred freedom. Western women were not to his taste: they showed a transition from the feebly animal to the thinking being, which was simply troublesome. Harold preferred a slow-witted large-eyed woman, silent and affectionate, with a load of black hair weighing much more heavily than her brains. He had seen no such woman in England, except one whom he had brought with him from the East" (454–55). This kind of freedom, bought as it is through individual pleasure-seeking, marks Harold Transome as an egoist, something which, within Eliot's narrative world, always spells moral and social bankruptcy.

Against the individual and opportunistic pleasures driving Harold's sexual pursuits, the text invites us to see Esther's final union with Felix as the opting for an "authentic" culture, unsullied by the crude and instrumental market forces of buying and selling. Yet the mechanics of their union, rather than providing any real alternative to such forces, simply dresses up the workings of cultural domination in a finer, more veiled frippery—as Esther chooses in Felix nothing short of the law: "He was like no one else to her: he had seemed to bring at once a law, and the love that gave strength to obey the law . . . the first religious experience of her life—the first self-questioning, the first *voluntary subjection*, the first longing to acquire the strength of greater motives and *obey the more strenuous rule*—had come to her through Felix Holt. No wonder that she felt as if the loss of him were inevitable backsliding" (369, emphasis added). Esther is successively "stung," "shaken in her self-contentment," filled with mortification and anger, and the "sense of a terrible power over her that Felix seemed to have as his angry words vibrated through her"—feelings that become "almost too much for her self-control" (212). Ultimately, this mortification feeds her sense of gratification: "she revolted against his assumption of superiority, yet she felt herself in a new kind of subjection to him. He was ill-bred, he was rude, he had taken an unwarrantable liberty; yet his indignant words were a tribute to her: he thought she was worth more pains than the women of whom he took no notice" (213). In short, Felix, as pedagogue and master, causes Esther to embrace her own subjection. Crucial to our reading of Esther's education and its relation to the culture of imperialism is the way in which this process of personal subjection is internal, regulated by the self, and involving a choice or perhaps more accurately a recognition on Esther's part that she is indeed inferior to Felix and thus subject to his superior powers. Such internal regulation conveniently alleviates the necessity of external repression altogether as the "colonizer"—in this case, Felix—is thoroughly absorbed into the consciousness of the "colonized." As Gilles Deleuze and Félix Guattari argue, Oedipus is the figurehead of a psychology that corresponds well to this kind of domestic imperialism. It is "colonization pursued by other means, it is the interior colony, and we shall see that even at home . . . it is our intimate colonial education."[21] In a word, Oedipus is what teaches us to desire our own repression.[22] The culmination of this colonial mentality is achieved when Esther finally relates to Felix's words as if they were her own, realizing that they "at last seemed strangely to fit her own experience" (556).

The powerlessness inherent in such a recognition is clearly marked in the novel as a condition specific to women. We have only to remember Mrs. Transome, who functions as Esther's foil, and who, like her, is subjugated by her own desires; her downfall caused not only by her sexual infidelity but also by the sheer fact that she is a woman who loves to rule bereft of a province in which to exercise her will.[23] In this respect, Eliot is often heralded by critics for her protofeminist representations of the plight of women in patriarchal society.[24] But her understanding of the desires denied women is itself problematic. That is, for Eliot, there is a fundamental connection between power and culture that remains unquestioned: the desire to rule or to dominate is never in and of itself critiqued; instead it is always a question of how that rule is exercised. When that rule is suitably cloaked in a domesticated, naturalized hierarchy of duties or functions, it masks any relation to the naked power relations underlying its operation. Indeed, at the end of the novel, Eliot recreates Esther's and Felix's past for us, to the extent that all of Esther's feelings of subjection and humiliation become but pleasant lover's pleasures: "They smiled at each other, with the old sense of amusement they had so often had together" (557). It is just such pleasure, entailed in Eliot's version of "authentic" culture, that greases the machinery of domination, both on England's shores and beyond. This vision of domestic pleasure, so clearly meant to offset that other image of pleasure which *Felix Holt* gives us, that of the miners and their pubs, more potently underscores the way in which pleasure itself, and with it labor—whether in the direct form of economic domination or the more mediated domain of culture—is severed from reality, excluded from the public sphere, by the mechanisms of power fueling England's cultural project of nationhood.

Prophesying the Nation

In his study of the *Bildungsroman*, Franco Moretti reads *Felix Holt* as symptomatic of the end of this symbolic form, a casualty, as it were, of history in the making.[25] This form, now insufficient to the new project at hand— the representation of the masses or the "collective"—is superseded by one in which the individual figures merely as a part of the whole. Within such a framework, Felix's vocation is seen as originating from an "ethnic or social partiality." Once the biography of the individual can no longer capture history, the narrative opts for the building of enclaves or subcultures that preserve "communal" values at odds with the larger dynamics of the "great world." This transition occurs as an effect of larger historical processes, namely, the sacrifice of individuality that typifies the "age of the masses." For Moretti, then, the failure of *Felix Holt* as a novel rests in the conflict between these two structures: Eliot, by attempting to tell her tale of the masses, yet with only the worn-out, historically outdated narrative form of the *Bildungsroman* at her disposal, is unable ultimately to represent her "collective" subject. Her novel, flawed not from lack of writerly skill but because it lies on the cusp of a historical transition, marks this transition that has not yet found a form adequate to its representation.

But what this analysis fails to take into account is the way in which Eliot sets the partiality of Felix's view and the domain of his actions within the larger social dynamic of change and progress. As the "Address to Working Men" stipulates, it is precisely in the interests of society, of *Gesellschaft* as *Gemeinschaft*, that "revolutionary" views such as those identified with an organized working class must be domesticated within the confines of a national English culture. In order to ensure the survival of the social organism, to use Eliot's own metaphors of organicism, each part must recognize and perform its function in relation to the body as a whole. Within such an organic view of the nation, there can be no cultivation of subcultures, for each part of necessity is always integral to and inseparable from the whole. Rather, in the interests of this national body the validation of what Moretti reads as the subculture of Felix's position must remain sub.

One final indication of the shift from a regional communal identification to a broadly British nationalist one is evident in the inscription with which Eliot opens *Felix Holt*:

Upon the Midlands now the industrious muse doth fall,
The shires which we the heart of England well may call.

. . . . .

My native country those, which so brave spirits hast bred,
If there be virtues yet remaining in thy Earth,
Or any good of thine thou bred'st into my birth,
Accept it as thine own, whilst now I sing of thee,
Of all thy later brood the unworthiest though I be. (74)

This poem, a slightly altered version of a passage from *The Thirteenth Song* of Drayton's *Poly-Olbion*, contains a significant revision. Whereas Drayton speaks of only one "shire"—Warwickshire—Eliot harks to a plurality of shires; these shires together comprise her "native country" of England. In essence, Eliot remakes this poem about regional pride into something akin to a national anthem. Much like the narrative of *Felix Holt* as a whole, the present is rewritten in the past with all traces of difference or conflict essentially erased.

In a sense, then, nationalism, or the identification of oneself as part of a nation, is the linchpin between (the dissolution of) community and the modern state, between history and change. In place of the ruptures and discontinuities of self and community, national identification reinscribes a notion of wholeness and continuity. As such, nationalism mediates between the seemingly knowable past and an unknowable present and future. It bridges the representational gap in *Felix Holt*, the tension between the prophetic and the narrative.

In the novel, as we have seen, this mediation takes two forms: the one, represented by Felix Holt, functions through the creation of a historically obsolete figure who seamlessly occupies a realm removed from daily life. The other, represented by Esther, and by extension the working class, acknowledges the existence of chaotic desires, of a *dis*continuous sense of self, of the nonidentity of reason and reality, subjects and objects, of the internal splits and ruptures that make Esther feel as if her thoughts and her life were a "heap of fragments" (264). It is this possibility that the prophetic register of *Felix Holt* shuts down; the force of Eliot's text works to bind these fragments together into a unified form. Hence the crucial role of education in the novel: Esther and the working class require education precisely in order to make their experiences match those of Felix Holt, in order to bring them within the national fold. In the face of an unnarratable, unrepresentable present, Eliot slips into the prophetic mode; she must prophesy the unity of a nation to be created. Thus, whereas the prophetic mode in which Felix Holt functions writes an uninterrupted history of progress in the guise of culture, the narrative process of integration—of both the workers as a class and Esther as a woman—into that history reveals a residue of labors and pleasures yet to be redeemed. While at some level Eliot's *Felix Holt* registers this uncomfortable fit—between labor and pleasure, between the narrative and the prophetic—it ultimately resolves such discomfort by rendering invisible that which does not "fit." In this sense, *Felix Holt* truly is a *modern* Odyssey: like the dialectic of Enlightenment in Adorno's and Horkheimer's analysis, *Felix Holt* enacts a narrative of instrumental rationality in which labor only finds expression in its narrowest sense as the antithesis of pleasure.

PART II

Coming of Age in a World Economy

....

If, as Franco Moretti claims, the age of the masses signals the end of the *Bildungsroman*'s reign, a return to its last decades of preeminence highlights its intimate connection to the expansion of industrial capitalism into a genuine world economy. As the British historian Eric Hobsbawm characterizes what he calls the age of capital (1848–75), the globe was essentially "transformed from a geographical expression into a constant operational reality. History from now on became world history."[1] Spurred on by the railway, whose import George Eliot intuited so perceptively as the motor of modernity, and followed by the subsequent inventions of the steamer and the telegraph, capitalist development had found by midcentury the means to match its need to expand and colonize ever greater realms with its ability, practically, to disperse itself across the globe.

In the whirl of the heady boom economy that lasted until the crash of

1873, free trade became the catchword for continued progress. With the repeal of the Corn Laws in 1846, protectionism was abandoned completely in England, opening the way for the free flow of goods, raw materials, and foodstuffs, in exports and imports. As Richard Cobden, a fervent proponent of free trade, claimed grandiloquently, "commerce is the grand panacea, which, like a beneficent medical discovery, will serve to innoculate with the healthy and saving taste for civilization all the nations of the world. Not a bale of merchandise leaves our shores, but it bears the seeds of intelligence and fruitful thought to the members of some less enlightened community; not a merchant visits our seats of manufacturing industry, but he returns to his country the missionary of freedom, peace, and good government—while our steam boats, that now visit every port of Europe, and our miraculous railroads, that are the talk of all nations, are the advertisements and vouchers for the value of our enlightened institutions."[2] While certainly less bombastic, other accounts of the day reinforce how pervasive Cobden's optimism about free trade was.

Amid the ascendancy of commercial values, however, strident voices of dissent criticized the transformation of morality into "money values." Deeming the current order philistine in its emphasis on the acquisition of wealth above all else, Matthew Arnold attacked the confusion of means with ends as the defining characteristic of the "age of machinery." "Machinery" was being mistaken as an end in itself rather than a means toward what Arnold termed "perfection," or its disinterested pursuit in "culture": culture, in contradistinction to the misplaced faith in machinery, and its attachment to a "mechanical and material civilization,"[3] properly combined what Raymond Williams refers to as right knowing with right doing. Culture, for Arnold, thus became an antidote to the prevailing political winds of Utilitarianism as well as the threatening agitation (in Arnold's eyes) of the working class; it functioned as the potential glue to hold together an emergent social order in the face of an "old routine" which had "wonderfully yielded."[4] In his articulation of these principles, however, Arnold's emphasis on process—on right doing, on "becoming" rather than "having"—itself yields to the dangers of abstraction, allowing culture, as Williams has argued, to become almost a fetish.[5] "Right doing" is superseded by "right knowing"; the notion of culture as "becoming" is replaced by culture as an absolute: "Culture became the final critic of institutions, and the process of replacement and betterment, yet it was also, at root, beyond institutions."[6]

The devaluation of "right doing" has its material analogue in the disparagement of the working class, who tend toward "anarchy" in their blind faith in "doing as one likes." Against their pursuit of personal liberty, Arnold holds up "settled order and security," as the battlements necessary to prevent "social disintegration."[7] While the kind of fear the working class invokes in Arnold is directly tied to their doings—their marches and public demonstrations for shorter working hours and better wages and so forth, labeled by Arnold as "rowdyism"—their "rawness" as political subjects is buttressed by a deeper dismissal of the productive sphere altogether. Directly linked to Arnold's argument against "external civilization," production constitutes one more false value of an overly utilitarian worldview, and, therefore, something which has no place in a proper valuation of culture. Assessing Mr. Bright's (the voice of middle-class Liberalism) commendations about the franchise and the working class's contribution to the "greatness of England,"—"See what you have done! I look over this country and see the cities you have built, the railroads you have made, the manufactures you have produced . . . I see that you have converted by your labours what was once a wilderness, these islands, into a fruitful garden; I know that you have created this wealth, and are a nation whose name is a word of power throughout all the world"—Arnold sees only philistines attempting to proselytize in the name of industrial performance as an end in itself. As he concludes, "It is the same fashion of teaching a man to value himself not on what he *is*, not on his progress in sweetness and light, but on the number of the railroads he has constructed, or the bigness of the tabernacle he has built."[8] As a result, work, production, or really any material acting on the world—any real sense of *doing*—is severed from the world of culture.

The relationship between Arnold's plea for a certain kind of culture and the consequent ushering of labor off the social stage clearly completes the project of the industrial novel, as argued powerfully by Catherine Gallagher. As I want to suggest, however, the presence of industrial labor and its social and political consequences does not disappear from later texts (outside the rubric of the "industrial novel"), although it certainly takes new forms. Indeed, as I will argue in the following chapter, the problematic of labor after the "industrial novel" finds its form in a new but integrally related problematic: how to represent capitalism, which, as Fredric Jameson has shown in another context, fully involves the issue of "how to express the economic—or, even better, the peculiar realities and dynamics of money as such—in and through literary narrative."[9]

For a number of reasons, the *Bildungsroman* provides an ideal site for negotiating this problematic. As the "symbolic form of modernity" (and here I follow Franco Moretti's analysis), the *Bildungsroman* had as its task acculturating the modern individual to his (it was almost always a "he") modern existence and vice versa; in short, as a form, it makes meaning out of modernity.[10] A process rife with contradiction, the *Bildungsroman* is at once dynamic and unstable, restless and in search of an ending. Perfectly captured in the experience of "youth," these contradictions are not so much worked out or "solved" as they are juggled and absorbed. As Moretti pithily notes, the "I do" which seals the marriages at the ends of *Bildungsromane* equally marks a consent between the individual and the world: the willingness to compromise, to forgo the lures of freedom for the benefits of socialization and, possibly, happiness. This negotiation is, of course, inseparable from the development of capitalism which gives to modernity its peculiar character. Moreover, the very figure of "youth" is nothing if not an allegory for the unfolding of history more generally. As such, the *Bildungsroman* registers the particular stresses and strains of modernity as well as its overall sense of history.

Extending Moretti's argument, I want to push the analysis of modernity in a slightly different direction: by focusing on the radical change in geography which Hobsbawm identifies, I want to suggest that the developments—individual, social, political, economic—which the *Bildungsroman* emplots in its latter decades contain both linear/narrative histories as well as spatial ones. In their attempt to deal with the realities of a world economy, that is, these novels not only narrate individual biographies but also map world geographies. An attentiveness to this spatial history in conjunction with the more explicit narrative or biographical history we expect from these texts reveals the embeddedness of modernity in imperialism and, furthermore, locates this embeddedness in the vexed presence of a work regimen that stubbornly disallows the enforced and/or desired separation of these social formations. In other words, although these novels are at pains to maintain the so-called core and periphery of the British Empire as separate from one another, the imperial work they narrate continually threatens these self-same boundaries. In this context, it is not so much that labor disappears, as has been commonly understood, but that it, like the world economy of which it is a part, begins to be radically transformed. No longer quite so easily located, labor finds its literary expression in the traffic the late *Bildungsroman* directs between "home" and "abroad."

CHAPTER 3

SEEING THE INVISIBLE

....

The *Bildungsroman* and

the Narration of a New Regime

of Accumulation

Seeing the invisible is exhausting. —Jean-Luc Godard, *Hélas pour moi*

Considered now to be the "high-water mark of industrial values," the Crystal Palace Exhibition of 1851 symbolized the "visibility of human progress."[1] Under the patronage of Prince Albert, its aim was nothing short of "[conquering] nature to [man's] uses."[2] The exhibition, along with other subsequent ones in Vienna, Paris, and even Philadelphia (the largest of them all, in 1867), represented triumphant capitalism celebrating its own achievements at a moment of spectacular and accelerated economic expansion. The mood was so high in the 1850s and 1860s that there appeared to be no end in sight to the possibilities of progress. Capturing the sense of discovery entailed in this moment of unprecedented growth, the Victorian businessman and Marxist H. M. Hyndman went so far as to liken the period from 1847 to 1857 to the era of the geographical discoveries and conquests of Columbus, Vasco da Gama, Cortez, and Pizarro.[3]

Yet a mere twenty years later, by the 1870s, it was already clear that capitalism would be more of a roller-coast ride than earlier anticipated. Instead of a continually ascending arc of growth and expansion, capitalism was better described as a series of booms and busts. In an increasingly global economy, moreover, slumps would be global as markets became more closely integrated.

This profound shift in how the globe functioned and was conceived and experienced speaks directly to the project of realism and novelists' attempts, during this period, to represent the economic and social changes occurring as a result of an increasingly global economy. When geography itself becomes an active participant in Britain's social formation, how exactly does one represent that "constant operational reality" in the novel?[4] Until recently, matters of global geography and empire have been assumed to inhabit primarily the margins of nineteenth-century texts, visible, if at all, in eclipsed or repressed references to Caribbean plantations, the East India Company, or colonial madwomen in the attic. Edward Said argues that it really takes until the end of the nineteenth century for the empire to become a central area of concern in literature; earlier, the empire is either a "shadowy presence" or "embodied merely in the unwelcome appearance of a fugitive convict."[5] Clearly, however, these shadowy presences or unwelcome appearances occupy a fair amount of novelistic space, as criticism, following the lead of Said, has shown.[6] How then is one to reconcile the apparent marginal place of imperial matters in these texts with the pervasiveness of such marginalia?

This chapter focuses on two *Bildungsromane* written during the dramatic period from the 1850s to the 1870s, in order to argue that the "operational reality" that is empire finds its way centrally into these texts via their respective attempts to represent an increasingly cosmopolitan world and the moneyed economy defining it. Written in 1860–61, Charles Dickens's *Great Expectations* provides an ideal moment in which to begin to explore these changes. Tracing Pip's development from an apprentice at a forge to a clerk in an imperial trading company, the novel essentially narrates, through the figure of Pip, the larger socioeconomic forces shaping Britain's development: the shift from a rural to an urban culture, the growth of the middle class, and the increasing penetration of commodity logic into ever greater spheres of everyday life. These forces are all felt "at home" in the lived experience of Britons and have tended to be the ones focused on in analyses of the novel. But, as I will argue, matters of empire are equally central both to the larger issue of Britain's development and to Pip's development as an individual. They have not been seen or, at best, have remained marginal because we have been looking in the wrong place for them: instead of focusing only on material that directly references imperial localities, circumstances, and events, we need to examine how the novel, in its effort to grapple with a newly evolving moneyed economy, represents the organization of labor as a whole. Doing so will reveal a "domestic" existence thoroughly defined by a world economy and the imperial relations sustaining it.

This change in focus also prompts important rethinking about the *Bildungsroman* itself as the symbolic form for modernity. As I will show, the changed historical reality of imperialism required for its narrative representation the use of both temporal and spatial histories. Narratives of individual development, that is, remain incomplete without the narratives of spatial development within which they operate. In *Great Expectations*, the spatial history mapped by Britain's relationship to its penal colony, Australia, and figured in Magwitch's relationship to Pip completes the temporal history of Pip's Great Expectations: by positioning imperial labor as central to the text, this spatial history enlarges the linear biography of Pip's development and thus substantially rewrites Pip's history and the history of modernity more generally.

George Eliot's *Daniel Deronda* is also concerned with geography and its new operational reality. Written in 1876, Eliot's last novel is the first of her oeuvre to grapple directly with the new urban culture and the kinds of literal and figural dislocations—of land, bodies, work, and community—manufactured by it. In its attempt to create an alternative sense of community to counter the alienating effects of modernity, *Daniel Deronda* turns to Judaism as a site for imagining a productive vision of national unity. Seemingly unencumbered by the imperialist mentality pervading dominant British culture, the shared history defining the Diaspora figures as both a product of and alternative to modernity's rootlessness and displacements. But, like *Great Expectations*, the spatial history of which this shared history is a part complicates the narrative's search for a nonexploitative, democratic expression of nationalism able to organize people's desires both individually and collectively. While in *Great Expectations* it is the literal presence of Magwitch and his money that charts the global movement of capital and its reliance on imperial labor, in *Daniel Deronda* it is the absence of the East that delimits its international frame. As I argue, the nature of the impasse Eliot's narrative reaches is less about the individual failings of the novel than it is symptomatic of the contradictions which define modernity and which begin to be felt with the growth of a world economy. These contradictions, I conclude, write themselves into both the content and the form of Eliot's last novel.

As the title of this chapter indicates, I see *Great Expectations* and *Daniel Deronda* sharing a common project in their respective attempts to narrate a new regime of accumulation. I take the phrase "regime of accumulation" from David Harvey, who draws on the "regulation school" of economic thought in his use of the term. As he suggests, the notion of a regime of accumulation can help explain the nature of social change during a transitional historical moment because it takes into account both the production and reproduction of capital, or what Harvey refers to as the "total package of relations and arrangements that contribute to the stabilization of output growth and aggregate distribution of income and consumption in a particular historical period and place."[7] Quoting from Alain Lipietz, Harvey clarifies what the "total package" entails: "A particular system of accumulation can exist because 'its schema of reproduction is coherent.' The problem, however, is to bring the behaviours of all kinds of individuals—capitalists, workers, state employees, financiers, and all manner of other political-economic agents—into some kind of configuration that will keep the regime of accumulation functioning. There must exist, therefore, 'a materialization of the regime of accumulation taking the form of norms, habits, laws, regulating networks and so on that ensure the unity of the process, i.e. the appropriate consistency of individual behaviours with the schema of reproduction. This body of interiorized rules and social processes is called *the mode of regulation.*'"[8] This latter notion of a "mode of regulation" working in conjunction with a particular schema of reproduction offers what I take to be an extremely useful way of conceptualizing the kind of work Dickens's and Eliot's *Bildungsromane* perform. This kind of model enlarges the customary analysis of norms, habits, and individual behaviors in *Bildungsromane* by placing them within a larger system of accumulation. It offers as well a way of reading the period from the 1850s to the 1870s as a historically specific moment of capitalist cultural development and, as such, a unique challenge to novelists attempting to represent its realities. In this way, these novels can be said to take on, in their time, the same kind of challenge Fredric Jameson sees Bertolt Brecht, in his time, engaging in their respective attempts to represent or personify capitalism itself. As with Brecht, such a project necessarily involves "attempting to personify something too complex for representation, because it involves not only so many distinct lives and points of view, but also a world of things—technical processes as well as raw materials, and final products to be sold and used: the three great branches of production, distribution and consumption, which scarcely intersect at all, and on which there can be no unifying viewpoint."[9]

Both *Great Expectations* and *Daniel Deronda* produce and are produced by a new regime of accumulation accompanying the expansion of capitalism worldwide. By dint of this expansion, a fundamental paradox arises. As the economy expands, the need to understand it as a whole becomes at once more necessary and more difficult: more necessary because to understand the system is to understand its global operation; more difficult because the system's sheer size complicates such an understanding. This challenge is further complicated as labor and its place in the global economy become more difficult to represent directly given both the increasingly complex relations between domestic and imperial markets and the abstract nature of labor processes themselves as work becomes fully mechanized and workers' labor divided or Taylorized to individual, specialized, and fragmented tasks. To speak of this problem in philosophical terms, the relationship between the particular and the universal, the concrete and the abstract takes on a special urgency at this historical moment, inflected as it is with the task of organizing national parts into an international whole. This problematic is especially present in Eliot's novel, where the narrative is concerned both with how all the "parts" go together and what happens when the "whole" no longer grounds the individual in his or her everyday experience.

In *Great Expectations* and *Daniel Deronda* increasing abstraction in a variety of social arenas and guises becomes a problem of sight or visibility. Pip must continually operate within a system whose rules he cannot entirely decipher because they function beneath the surface of social interactions and involve a complex network of social forces and agents. The mysteries of origins, inheritance, and sources of income consuming Pip's existence are mysterious precisely insofar as they embody abstract processes that resist representation. In *Daniel Deronda* learning how to see *through* these kinds of concealments defines the process of *Bildung* itself, as both Daniel and Gwendolen, in their respective coming of age stories, struggle with the logic of commodity culture. Even more than *Great Expectations*, *Daniel Deronda* is already so fully in the thick of a global economy that any kind of immediacy is shown to be nothing more than a chimera. Whereas, in the 1860s, the fragmentation produced by abstraction and globalization can still be contained within a coherent whole of narrative relations, by the end of the 1870s, this containment is becoming more and more tenuous, as the form of Eliot's *Bildungsroman* bears the traces of the fragmentation it has worked so hard to overcome. Both novels thus comment finally on the "visibility of human progress," an idea so seemingly incontrovertible when Britons exhibited their global wares in 1851. By the end of the 1870s not only is "progress" a highly contested term but the question of "visibility" itself has been complicated by the same processes celebrated at the Exhibition; no longer simply visible evidence of Britain's sway in the world, the global realities embodied in the imperial booty exhibited in London become for Dickens and Eliot problems of narrative representation, the crux of which lies in a new world economy whose structures of organization remain largely invisible.

Great Expectations

A most beastly place. Mudbank, mist, swamp and work; work, swamp, mist and mud-bank. — Charles Dickens, *Great Expectations*

At the moment when Abel Magwitch reveals himself to be the man behind Pip's money, he gives his account of why he undertook this project. Thinking he is providing a reassuring narrative for his actions to Pip as well as to us presumably as readers, he confirms that "yes, Pip, dear boy, I've made a gentleman on you! It's me wot has done it! I swore that time, sure as ever I earned a guinea, that guinea should go to you. I swore arterwards, sure as ever I spec'lated and got rich, you should get rich. I lived rough, that you should live smooth; I worked hard, that you should be above work."[10] Needless to say, this news is not good news to Pip, the reasons for which critics have been quick to explain. Not really broached at all, however, is the nature of Magwitch's actions themselves. Why would a man in Magwitch's position, helped by little Pip to secure food and the means to cut off his leg-irons, determine at that moment of rescue that turns out not to be a rescue after all to dedicate his life to making Pip a gentleman? Why, in other words, does Magwitch become the instantiation of Great Expectations and the mystery plot surrounding him the means for uncovering its processes? Finally, why is this plot enclosed in the larger form of a *Bildungsroman*?

To start with the last question first: In his diagnosis of the English as opposed to the continental *Bildungsroman*, Franco Moretti offers a bleak picture of its value for the literary critic. As he claims, the literary critic will find "but one long fairy-tale with a happy ending, far more elementary and limited than its continental counterparts."[11] Fortunately for the historian of culture, as Moretti argues, the prospects are not so dire: from this viewpoint these novels illustrate for us the basic tenets of liberal-democratic civilization. If the continental *Bildungsroman*, that is, really is about what *Bildungsromane* are supposed to be about—wild youth, restless yearnings, a trumping of necessity by freedom, the willingness to say I'd rather die than succumb to the status quo, in short, a refusal to bow to the constraints of bourgeois culture—its poor English variant easily cedes to necessity, preferring bread alone to freedom's prospect of no bread at all. In the place of freedom's dynamism, the English *Bildungsroman* installs a stable juridical framework dispensing justice, fairy tale–like, and productive of a universal notion of the law, that is, the belief not only that everyone " 'has a right' to justice" but that "everyone, in fact, *receives* justice."[12]

While the shift Moretti advocates, generally, to an analysis of "political culture" seems crucial to an understanding of *Great Expectations*, his reading of the novel specifically seems to bear the burden of the poor relative too heavily: it can just never equal up to its continental brethren. Yet, where is the "long fairy-tale" in *Great Expectations*? Where are the simplistic distinctions between good and evil, the absolutes that foreclose angst, the childlike attitudes and resolutions?

By my reading, the novel gives us a sordid tale of endless shame and self-abasement, mediated by acute moments of degradation, fear, and the threat of bodily harm. Hands in this novel are almost always poised to strike or to strangle and Ticklers, far from their nominal meaning, never produce joyful squeals or giggles. Likewise, servants become Avengers, schoolmates Spiders, benefactors convicts. One might be tempted to say it's a tale where everything is turned willy-nilly topsy-turvy, where no one appears to be what they are—save for the fact that there is a logic to the "turning" and its revelations of "lowness" and deception. Since, as Moretti claims in his larger political frame, the form of the *Bildungsroman* "held fast to the notion that *the biography of a young individual was the most meaningful point for the understanding and the evaluation of history*," and since work was the single most changed aspect of nineteenth-century culture, then it follows that somehow work itself, in some form or another, must be at the heart of *Great Expectations*, the novel, as well as Great Expectations, the concept.[13] Indeed, I will argue that work so pervades every aspect of the novel that it is simply not seen as work as such. In this way, predictably, the novel participates in the seductions of an emergent middle-class culture premised on the invisibility of the body, work, and class—in short, a culture that exults the banal.

But this is only half the story and the reason why Magwitch is crucial to the text: he is the only character in the novel engaged in the literal work of empire and its processes of primitive accumulation. Without him, that is to say, the novel/British culture lacks its engine of production; hence the "coincidence" that all the major plots in the novel intersect in some way with Magwitch's. He has to fuel Pip's Great Expectations because this is how Great Expectations are fueled. The dialectic, then, between the visible and the invisible, work and the disappearance of work that Dickens's novel stages provides us with the underside of a liberal-democratic culture: a world created and sustained by a global regime of accumulation, in which everything is increasingly subject to the dictates of the market, and hence nothing finally is "off the clock" or free from work.

Mining the Quarry

Just before Pip realizes that his Great Expectations are simply "poor dreams," after all, and just after he learns that the aim of Estella's charms is to deceive and entrap men, he relates a curious "Eastern tale" called "The Enchanters, or, Misnar, the Sultan of India." The tale, told in the manner of the Arabian Nights, reads like this: "In the Eastern story, the heavy slab that was to fall on the bed of state in the flush of conquest was slowly wrought out of the quarry, the tunnel for the rope to hold it in place was slowly carried through the leagues of rock, the slab was slowly raised and fitted in the roof, the rope was rove to it and slowly taken through the miles of hollow to the great iron ring. All being made ready with much labour, and the hour come, the sultan was aroused in the dead of the night, and the sharpened axe that was to sever the rope from the great iron ring was put into his hand, and he struck with it, and the rope parted and rushed away, and the ceiling fell" (312). Lest we wonder why Pip pauses at this fateful moment in his own life to recount this story, he makes clear the direct connection between them: "So, in my case; all the work, near and afar, that tended to the end, had been accomplished; and in an instant the blow was struck, and the roof of my stronghold dropped upon me" (312).

The tale is remarkable on a number of levels. First, its telling implies a direct parallel between Pip's "Western story" and its "Eastern" counterpart. Even more than this, the story of the East reveals the meaning of Pip's story; the Eastern tale becomes a necessary complement to and even indispensable part of understanding Pip's narrative. Second, the care with which Pip narrates the sultan's triumph emphasizes the contradictory aspects of its making. "Slowly" is reiterated four times in the space of one sentence to describe the preparations for the murderous deed, whereas the deed itself requires but one swift swing of the axe. Simultaneously a laborious task and one seemingly devoid of labor, all the apparati required for its completion remain hidden: the slab is invisibly fitted in the roof, the rope wends through a long tunnel, and the sultan himself, far from the scene, severs the rope. Finally, aside from the agency assigned to the sultan, all the other activities mentioned lack a subject doing them. This latter fact is especially telling when transposed to Pip's narrative: work has been accomplished both "near and afar" but left indeterminate *by whom* and *under what conditions*.

As an allegory for Pip's own predicament, the emphasis in the sultan's tale on labor would seem to be misplaced. As any group of undergraduates reading the novel love to moralize, the problem with Pip's aspirations is that he doesn't want to work for them. Less noticed but equally prevalent, it turns out, almost no one in the novel seems to really want to work at all. The business conduct Pip observes at Pumblechook's consists mainly in each tradesman, in a domino effect, watching one another, so that Pumblechook looks across the street at the saddler, who eyes the coachmaker, who contemplates the grocer, and so forth, with the cycle finally ending, fittingly, with the watchmaker whose trade uniquely absorbs his attention; Herbert Pocket famously "looks about him" for capital, which appears and disappears, depending on the time of day and his mood; Orlick longs for and murderously resents the "ease" he sees Pip enjoying as a small boy; Wemmick relies on "portable property" to make his way; Compeyson practices the art of forgery; Pip is described, after his rise in fortune, by the local newspaper as a "young artificer in iron," perfectly capturing the tension around work in the novel, in the double meaning of "artificer" as both a skilled or artistic worker or craftsman and a deviser, contriver, or ingenious schemer.[14] Throughout, characters either look to be "made" by someone else or are "made" that way, as in Estella's pointed rejoinder to Miss Havisham, "I am what you have made me" (304).[15] How, then, is this the great novel of middle-class virtue and the benefits to be gained by hard work and industry?

Again, the sultan's story provides important clues to this question. As noted earlier, only one "agent" is identified in the tale: the sultan himself. He pulls the strings, as it were, and from a position of invisibility. Recall, too, that this passage immediately precedes the chapter in which Magwitch appears on Pip's doorstep and reveals himself to be his benefactor. Clearly, following the allegorical ties being drawn, Pip must occupy the role of the sultan's poor enemy felled in the double-entendred "flush of conquest," while Magwitch can be none other than the sultan—he who causes the ceiling to fall on Pip. But equally, given what Magwitch will reveal about his investments in Pip, he stands in for the invisible workers whose agency he supplies. Within such an equivalence, the place of work in the novel takes on new meaning, invested now, as it is, both invisibly throughout the text and in a particular person and site. "All the work, near and afar" which Pip identifies as going into his own "making" logically coheres when we can locate work partly in Magwitch's labor and, specifically, colonial convict labor. In short, it makes sense that Pip's livelihood comes directly from the work of empire—not his work but others' work performed "near and afar," in England and in her far-flung colonial dominions, among them, of course, Australia. Matters of empire, generally considered to be visible only on the margins of nineteenth-century texts, appear to be more central when viewed in terms of the organization of labor.

In this respect, the terms and conditions of convict labor too deserve attention for the traffic they direct between domestic and imperial labor. As Robert Hughes has shown, there are intimate links between domestic labor issues and the whole project of transportation and Australia's "founding." From its inception as an idea, the transportation system was driven by the need to deal with the increasing number of felons for whom there was literally no space in England. In a first attempt to deal with this problem, the English government began using offshore hulks as temporary holding places for convicts (the same kind of hulks that Magwitch and Compeyson escape from at the opening of *Great Expectations*). However, as the means for apprehending criminals got better (primarily with the institution of a police force under Robert Peel in 1829), the number of convicts increased to such an extent that they could not all be handled by the hulks. It wasn't so much that there actually was more crime, as Hughes points out, but simply that more crimes were being detected. Given these problems, "transportation had undeniable merits." It not only removed prisoners and prisons from England altogether but "supplied Britain with a large labor force consisting entirely of people who, having forfeited their rights, could be sent to distant colonies of a growing Empire to work at jobs that no free settler would do."[16]

Importantly, most of the crimes committed were "offenses against property" and, accordingly, 80 percent of all transportation was for these offenses. In the midst of the processes of industrialization—the growth of towns, rising birthrates, mass unemployment, increasing mechanization, a saturated labor market, and falling wages and rising prices (especially in the period from 1811–30)—crimes of theft rose as did their terms of punishment.[17] A long list of the trades of those on transport ships from the convicts' own descriptions ranges from "amusers or puzzlers" (pickpockets' accomplices who distracted their victims by throwing dirt in their eyes) to pradnappers (horse-thieves) to skinners (women who deceived children and sailors in order to steal their clothes). While the minute specificity of these myriad kinds of thievery might fool us into assuming an equally varied set of causes for them, poverty most often was their driving force. Trial records chronicle thefts as petty as stealing the silverware from a former employer (in order to help a destitute wife whose newborn child had just died from starvation) being punished by seven years transport. The discrepancy between crime and punishment, according to Hughes, speaks to the overriding aim of transport: finally, it was less about punishing individual crimes and more about cleansing England of an entire enemy class by shipping it elsewhere, "where it would stay, providing slave labor for colonial development and undergoing such mutations toward respectability as whips and chains might induce. The main point was not what happened to it *there*, but that it would no longer be *here*."[18]

By locating imperial work in the figure of Magwitch, Dickens's narrative registers the literal dependency of England on her colonial possessions and slave labor, thereby undermining the kind of enforced separation between "there" and "here" that Hughes locates in the transportation system—and more generally within a colonial mentality. If none of the relationships in the novel escape ties of mutual dependency (think of the "web of connections" or the "family romance" commonly used to describe how everyone in Dickens's novels turns out to be related in some way to everyone else), Estella's "I am what you have made me" begins to look like a generalizable statement that extends across the text's network of social relations and across Britain's empire. Pip is what Magwitch has made him; likewise, Herbert is what Pip has made him, via what Magwitch has made Pip. The two markers of "youth" and, by extension, the new world order, that is to say, are inextricably linked to—in fact *created by*—the literal work of empire. In the process, the traditional rhetoric of empire—of the native's dependency on the colonial mother—comes crashing down, much like the sultan's ceiling. Despite the absence of miners mining, or Magwitches shown hard at work, not to mention the total elision of the Aborigines from the colonial equation, a faint foretaste of the revolutionary potential of relationships of dependency can be found, an acknowledgment that will find its realization, less than a century later, in Frantz Fanon's claim that "Europe is literally the creation of the Third World."[19]

Circulating the Goods

Of course, Dickens is no Frantz Fanon and *Great Expectations* is no postcolonial text but rather remains within an imperial logic designed to rewrite the concept of Great Expectations and the making of a gentleman in a socially palatable way, one that will loosen its bonds to a rigid class determinism and a defunct aristocratic ideal. It is here that the "invisible" workers come into play. As long as work remains invisible, Dickens's narrative seems to say, it can appear effortless and unexploitative. An exemplary case in point is Herbert Pocket's situation. Frank Capra-esque in its vision of success—small-time entrepreneurs can save or be exempt from the excesses of greedy, big-time capitalists—Herbert makes it in spite of himself. Unable to apply himself to much of anything except the occasional visionary descrying of capital in the afternoon, he is likable precisely to the extent that he is constitutionally unsuccessful. When Pip first meets him in London, and Herbert describes himself as a "capitalist—an Insurer of Ships," Pip observes: "I had grand ideas of the wealth and importance of Insurers of Ships in the City, and I began to think with awe, of having laid a young Insurer on his back, blackened his enterprising eye, and cut his responsible head open. But, again, there came upon me, for my relief, that odd impression that Herbert Pocket would never be very successful or rich" (183). Once Herbert actually becomes a partner in Clarriker's East Indies trading company, and Pip a clerk there, the size and stature of the business mitigates its success: as Pip clarifies, "I must not leave it to be supposed that we were ever a great House, or that we made mints of money. We were not in a grand way of business, but we had a good name, and worked for our profits, and did very well" (480).

Yet, as this passage demonstrates, the erasure of work entailed in Pip's early assessments of Herbert cannot be left to linger over and inflect the novel's resolution. Not only does work resurface ("we worked for our profits") but Herbert's whole character must be reinvented as well. The once pale slacker is transformed virtually into an employee of the month: "We owed so much to Herbert's ever cheerful industry and readiness, that I often wondered how I had conceived that old idea of his inaptitude, until I was one day enlightened by the reflection, that perhaps the inaptitude had never been in him at all, but had been in me" (480). Notably, Pip's rewriting of Herbert betrays a dramatic enough reversal that the text seems to know it cannot get away with it unremarked on. The clunky gears employed to engineer this shift suggest that there is more than one kind of work being done here. At once, Pip's assurance that they worked for their profits echoes Magwitch's claims about his work in Australia—"Wotever I done, is worked out and paid for" (345)—and is distinguished from it. Whereas Magwitch's work is written all over his body (hence his inability to disguise himself), and tainted always by crime, Pip's entire "education" has had as its goal stripping all marks of labor from his body, from the major turning point of his life, his first encounter with Estella, to a minor exchange with his rowing instructor where he claims that "[t]his practical authority confused me very much, by saying I had the arm of a blacksmith. If he could have known how nearly the compliment lost him his pupil, I doubt if he would have paid it" (195). In other words, Magwitch becomes identified with production and the corporeality of the criminal or working-class body (remember that Compeyson, because he can disguise himself as a middle-class gentleman, is able to finger Magwitch with his crimes) while Pip becomes schooled in the art of consumption. From the moment he arrives at the Temple and undergoes Herbert's gentle proddings about not putting his knife in his mouth "for fear of accidents," he learns how to consume properly. Ultimately, once ensconced in his new job at Clarriker's, Pip is fully established at the distribution end of imperial trade. Within this developmental narrative, production per se virtually disappears from the novel: we hear about Magwitch's time in Australia but not about the work itself and, of course, Magwitch himself cannot remain legally in England, given the deportation laws on return. The implied and desired separation between production and consumption/distribution would seem to suggest that they exist in different systems altogether, in radically distinct spaces even, with incompatible rules, as riven as the divide between the country and the city, the working and the middle classes, evidenced by Joe's awkward inability to navigate London.

Yet how distinct finally are these spaces in Dickens's narrative? Just as Pip's expectations cannot be understood without the sultan's tale, the developmental narrative's meaning is incomplete when viewed apart from the spatial organization of work and empire mapped by the novel. The relationship between these narratives—the one about biography, the other about space—finds its meaning in the dialectic between appearance and essence which structures *Great Expectations*.

From the beginning of Pip's biography, his challenge is to understand "the identity of things" (3). But time and time again, what constitutes that identity becomes muddled or disguised or obscured. Whereas in the opening pages "the identity of things" is directly connected to the appearance of the convict on the moor—Pip assigns his "first most vivid and broad impression of the identity of things" to the "memorable raw afternoon towards evening" (3) when he first meets Magwitch—the remainder of his childhood and the period of his Great Expectations is all about distancing himself from such a connection. Based on a series of misapprehensions or false appearances—being asked to play at Satis House, seeing Jaggers on the stairs there, being received by Estella—Pip conjures up a benefactress in Miss Havisham, a go-between in Jaggers, a lover/wife in Estella, and a genteel lifestyle in London. Once in London, Pip spends his time conspicuously consuming, be it in the purchase of goods like the furniture, clothing, and other accoutrement of the gentleman or services, the most notable being his servant, who so terrorizes both Pip and Herbert that they dub him the Avenger. He is so clearly but a sign of Pip's newfound wealth that he virtually disappears from the novel after his initial appearance.[20]

In this world of appearance money has a singularly valuable role, in the ease with which it, unlike shackled convicts, can move in the world, undetected, invisible, with no strings attached. Throughout Pip's transition to the gentleman's life, money greases the way. In his transactions, especially with Jaggers, money does not even have to change hands; it simply pays the bills (or doesn't, as Pip goes increasingly into debt) sight unseen. It also holds out the possibility of hiding or doing away with the kinds of shame identified with Pip's childhood experiences. When, much to Pip's mortification, Joe decides to visit London, Pip wishes only that money could prevent him from coming: "If I could have kept him away by paying money, I certainly would have paid money" (218). As a medium of exchange, money offers the means to convert qualitative difference into quantitative sameness, to operate, in Marx's definition, as the universal equivalent. This process is nowhere better on display than when Jaggers attempts to offer Joe money in exchange for the loss of Pip as his apprentice. Epitomizing the metropolitan world of quantitative compensation, and what the narrative ultimately will find critical about it, it is almost beyond Jaggers's comprehension that Joe would refuse such recompense. He simply sees one form of money (Pip's work) being replaced by another (cash). From Joe's perspective, however, they are irredeemably and qualitatively different: "'If you think as money—can make compensation to me—fur the loss of the little child—what come to the forge—and ever the best of friends!—'" (141). The mere suggestion of the equivalence drives Joe into an apoplectic fit, so out of the realm of possibility is it for him. Where Jaggers sees money, Joe sees a little child. While, retrospectively, Pip sees in this moment the worth of "dear good faithful tender Joe" (141), during his time in London Pip is far more swayed by the system of value Jaggers represents, precisely because of the disappearances (the elision of the child behind the money—which is also, although not in Joe's view, a cloaking of the work behind the money) it facilitates.

Even when these erasures are coded as "good" uses of money, their mediatory effects are similar, as when Pip provides for Herbert's partnership in Clarriker's. Above all, the beauty of Pip's gift to Herbert is how undetectable it is: "The whole business was so cleverly managed, that Herbert had not the least suspicion of my hand being in it. I never shall forget the radiant face with which he came home one afternoon, and told me, as a mighty piece of news, of his having fallen in with one Clarriker (the young merchant's name), and of Clarriker's having shown an extraordinary inclination towards him, and of his belief that the opening had come at last" (299). A relationship thoroughly produced by money can thus appear to have a human face. Clarriker shows an "extraordinary inclination" toward Herbert, Herbert's success comes with no effort on his part, and Pip's expectations can do "some good": "At length, the thing being done, and he having that day entered Clarriker's House, and he having talked to me for a whole evening in a flush of pleasure and success, I did really cry in good earnest when I went to bed, to think that my expectations had done some good to somebody" (299). A "good" version of the otherwise perverse and inhuman circulation of capital (the excesses and extremes of Jaggers with his lifeless reliance on evidence at the expense of feeling), Pip's gift, like money more generally, effaces its origin or source, first in the figurative "hand" Pip has in it, but more profoundly in the literal hand Magwitch has in it. But now appearance itself—masking the "invisible workings" behind it— restores the goodness to money.

In this light, the horror that Pip feels when he first sees Magwitch in London and learns that he is his benefactor might be said to arise from the recognition it forces on him, once again, of a connection he has been happy to forget. On the face of it, it is the connection between Pip the gentleman and Magwitch the convict that is so horrifying to him. Pip suffers physical aversion when he learns of Magwitch's identity: "The abhorrence in which I held the man, the dread I had of him, the repugnance with which I shrank from him, could not have been exceeded if he had been some terrible beast" (319–20). Later, this extreme repulsion is explained by the fact that Pip realizes he has deserted the best of men, Joe, for the worst of them, a convict, whose "hand might be stained with blood" (322). But, on a deeper level, Pip's horror over Magwitch's identity reminds us of that earlier "identity of things" whose identity up until this point has remained safely hidden. In short, it is a moment in the text where the larger structure making possible Pip's expectations is made brutally visible—and at a point when Pip is thoroughly invested in its refusal.[21] It should thus come as no surprise that at this same moment money loses its ability to smoothly exchange people for things. In the hopes of getting rid of Magwitch, and fearing the worst, Pip attempts to repay Magwitch (and hence any debt he might have to him) for the two pounds he sent (via Compeyson) when Pip was still a small boy. Replacing the dirty notes he then received with his now "clean and new ones," Pip watches as Magwitch cavalierly twists up the notes and sets fire to them. In the presence of the person for whom money substitutes, it would seem, the solvency of money is destroyed.

To be sure, the ruse is that Pip constantly confuses essence and appearance; a routine reading of the novel has it that what Pip really learns through his trials and travails is the value of essence over appearance. Again, too, this is a reading that the text encourages, so much so that it is hard to get students not to write papers about how Pip finally learns who he really is; moreover, in their readings he discovers an understanding of "human nature" that looks uncannily like the students' own. Far from acknowledging this extraordinary pull in the text in order to make fun of it (or of undergraduates), I introduce it rather to suggest both how seductive this strand is and why. In effect, it does what Pip fantasizes his Great Expectations will do: work all but disappears from such a narrative of development, replaced instead by a vision of universal subjectivity that turns out to be nothing more expansive than a distinctively bourgeois subjectivity. But this disappearing act also obscures an even more important underlying transformation: a shift from talking about essence to focusing on appearance. If Marx's lesson about commodity fetishism and the nature of capitalism is to be taken seriously, certainly one needs to be able to read disguises well, to distinguish essence from appearance, something with which Pip, too, obviously is gravely concerned. As Norman Geras summarizes the relationship between essences and appearances under capitalism, "the appearances that mystify and distort spontaneous perception of the capitalist order are real; they are objective social forms, simultaneously determined by and obscuring the underlying relations. This is how capitalism *presents itself*: in disguise."[22]

To read the disguise that *Great Expectations* presents us with, then, is to treat its appearances as real at the same time that we remember the work appearance accomplishes. To do so is to acknowledge the extent to which the world of *Great Expectations* is already thoroughly reified as well as the extent to which the narrative itself registers this profound alienation. It is commonplace to talk about the way in which objects are personified in Dickens, but the real "identity of things" Pip hopes to learn ends up working in the other direction: it is people that end up being things, the most extreme example of this being Estella, who is reduced to her sheer commodity status and put up for sale to the highest and most brutal bidder. But others too, less dramatically, occupy this same alienated state, from minor characters such as Pumblechook and Wopsle to Jaggers and Wemmick and Pip. Wemmick, perhaps most of all, personifies the coordinates for such alienation in his continual paeans to "portable property." Embedded in the notion of "portable property" is the fantasy that person and property can be separated from one another; that property can move and circulate independent of persons. When Wemmick fears that Magwitch will be caught by the authorities and/or Compeyson, he warns Pip to " 'avail [himself] of this evening to lay hold of his portable property. You don't know what may happen to him. Don't let anything happen to the portable property' " (372). After Magwitch has been taken, and Wemmick reviews the disastrous results of the attempted flight with Pip, he clarifies the principle behind "portable property": " 'The late Compeyson having been beforehand with him in intelligence of his return, and being so determined to bring him to book, I do not think he could have been saved. That's the difference between the property and the owner, don't you see?' " (452). In short, the separation between property and owner rehearses the process of commodity fetishism, insofar as relations between people are transformed into relations among things. The portability of property is enabled by its literal detachment from the person whose labor produced it. As Wemmick reinforces, the process of detachment frees up objects or portable property for circulation. Whereas Magwitch's capture forecloses his further circulation (between Australia and England, Pip and Herbert), his money need not suffer the same fate. In other words, when Magwitch's labor is turned into a thing (in this case, money) it can freely circulate and by all means should, according to Wemmick.

Given the conflicting valences that money can acquire, the novel is at pains to distinguish between good and bad forms of money. As noted earlier, Pip hopes to replace the tainted one-pound notes he receives as a child from Magwitch with his own crisp clean new bills. Unlike the new bills, the old notes cannot seem to shake their owner's criminal existence. The "fat sweltering one-pound notes . . . seemed to have been on terms of the warmest intimacy with all the cattle markets in the county," and their connection to their giver (at this point thought to be Compeyson) sets up a chain of connections in which Pip thinks about the "guiltily coarse and common thing it was, to be on secret terms of conspiracy with convicts—a feature in [his] low career that [he] had previously forgotten" (79). But the new notes, too, share the same source of origin. How then are they to be distinguished? Following the logic of the narrative and its plot twists, appearance alone is the only guide. Bad money, the kind that smells, too visibly reveals its source; good clean money maintains its disguise, at least until that disguise has nothing left to hide. The truth about Pip's role in Herbert's success is eventually revealed to Herbert but only many years later, long after Magwitch has died and Pip's respectability, as "third in the Firm," has been firmly established. In this way, *Great Expectations* would seem to be about the impossible task of simultaneously representing money (as the defining feature of the new economy and its new values) and keeping it invisible. But, equally, the novel keeps bringing us back to the source of that money: work. Pip does not ultimately take Wemmick's advice and "lay hold" of Magwitch's portable property but rather allows person and property to go down together, as it were. As a result, the money fittingly reverts to the state, bringing the product of Magwitch's labor full circle, as it returns to the English government that had appropriated Magwitch's labor in the first place when he was transported to Australia. A closer look at the fate of Pip's expectations reveals a similar prevalence of work—now in the form of a different kind of invisibility, the invisibility of middle-class work and its structures of consumption/pleasure—whose appearance has become so commonplace as to almost escape our notice altogether.

Consuming Pleasures

Within the great expectations that turn out to be nothing other than capitalism (perhaps this accounts for the thoroughly anticlimactic nature of the ending?), the fantasy of not working becomes the reality of always working—with the important proviso of liking it too. Following once again the invisible ropes wending their way through Dickens's narrative, the sultan's tale would have us believe that, if anything, work is repressed in the novel, with its return signaled in the figure of the East/Magwitch. But reading the sultan's tale only as the return of the repressed—in the form of imperial work—misses other forms of labor at work in the text. In other words, the "near" of work "near and afar" defining the meaning of the sultan's tale for Pip runs the danger of disappearing. Certainly, this disappearance is desired by Pip as much as his readers. It is here, after all, in the absence of work, that some space for pleasure surely is to be found. Yet, repeatedly, the novel forecloses this possibility. Not only do characters have to work continually at removing the signs of labor from their bodies, most obviously amplified in Jaggers's obsessive hand washing, but the space for pleasure is constantly being filled by nothing other than work, so much so that even play is turned into work.

Ordered to play at Miss Havisham's, Pip's "playing" there takes on the semblance of a regular job. When the offer first comes, work is held out as a punishment by Mrs. Joe should Pip not rise properly to the task: " '[Miss Havisham] wants this boy to go and play there. And of course he's going. And he had better play there,' said my sister, shaking her head at me as an encouragement to be extremely light and sportive, 'or I'll work him' " (51). Despite her threats, however, Pip finds himself unable to play once directed to do so by Miss Havisham. As the elder Pip looking back confides, "I think it will be conceded by my most disputatious reader, that she could hardly have directed an unfortunate boy to do anything in the wide world more difficult to be done under the circumstances" (59). The "playing to order" expected of Pip becomes so onerous that on Pip's next visit to Miss Havisham's she asks him whether he is willing to work instead. Unlike his response to Miss Havisham's "Are you ready to play?," Pip can "answer this inquiry with a better heart than [he] had been able to find for the other question, and [he] said that [he] was quite willing" (84).

Work thus becomes interchangeable with "playing to order" — a process not limited to Pip's experience with Miss Havisham but rather descriptive of the pattern of work for Pip's peers as well. Estella fulfills this same function in her wooing and entrapping of men; and Herbert, like Pip, must learn how to regulate or systematize his playing with capital. The company of Clarriker's — its very structure — gives order to the earlier play of Herbert's imperial fantasies. Rendered humorous initially because of their excess, these fantasies nonetheless mirror the work Herbert eventually ends up doing. Reeling off a list of his future accomplishments, he claims, with laughable grandiosity: " 'I shall not rest assured with merely employing my capital in insuring ships. I shall buy up some good Life Assurance shares, and cut into the Direction. I shall also do a little in the mining way. None of these things will interfere with my chartering a few tons on my own account. I think I shall trade,' said he, leaning back in his chair, 'to the East Indies, for silks, shawls, spices, dyes, drugs, and precious woods. It's an interesting trade . . . I think I shall trade, also,' said he, putting his thumbs in his waistcoat pockets, 'to the West Indies, for sugar, tobacco, and rum. Also to Ceylon, especially for elephants' tusks' " (183–84). This fantasy becomes the reality of working at a real trading company where the actual catalogue of trade is less grand than all this, but not significantly different in terms of its features. Indeed fantasy and reality switch places once the trading begins: the actual business of Herbert's job is left uncatalogued, replaced by "airy pictures" Herbert sketches "of himself conducting Clara Barley to the land of the Arabian Nights, and of [Pip] going out to join them (with a caravan of camels, [Pip] believes) and of [them] all going up the Nile and seeing wonders" (416). Rather than work becoming play, however, as this later fantasy might suggest is the case, it is instead simply aestheticized by being made invisible. Much like Herbert's renaming Pip "Handel" because of a piece of music written by Handel called *The Harmonious Blacksmith*, the image Herbert paints of a mythic land and caravans of camels cannot entirely efface the work—be it of the blacksmith or of empire—being thus aestheticized.[23] A kind of "now you see it, now you don't" performance thus gets played out with respect to how and when work gets represented.

If the novel holds out any promise of a real conversion of work into play, it comes through the relationship between Pip and Joe. As James Kincaid argues in the provocatively playful *Annoying the Victorians*, the merging or oneness that takes place between Pip and Joe offers one of many examples throughout Dickens's canon of an alternate, boundaryless conception of self. He sees this merging especially in the letter Pip writes to Joe when he is first learning how to read and write; repeating Joe's own quirky genteel-isms, Pip writes of the time when he'll be apprenticed to Joe, "WOT LARX." Seeing in this phrase the blending of Joe and Pip into one, Kincaid goes on to suggest that "perhaps we never witness any larks; perhaps they are never realized in the plot. But they exist all the same, exist even more powerfully because they are in the form of a promise that defies fulfillment, a sign that need point to no other place, that is realized in itself."[24] I think this reading of the larks Pip and Joe share can be extended to a vision of work as well. Certainly the larks that will follow Pip's apprenticeship reverse the order of things in the novel: instead of play being stifled into "playing to order," "playing to order" is liberated, freed from the bounds of work into the joys of play and the pleasure such larks announce. The extent to which this goes against the prevailing view is clear when compared to the dominant visions of Pip's apprenticeship, nowhere more evident than in the quintessential figure of "public opinion" in the novel, Uncle Pumblechook, who defini-tively declares, "This boy must be bound, out of hand. That's *my* way. Bound out of hand" (104). (In fine Pumblechookian fashion, this declaration is repeated no less than three times.) Now, while Pumblechook certainly is nothing if not the fool, he nonetheless verbalizes a theme running through-out the novel: the nature of the kinds of bonds holding people, both indi-vidually and to one another. The bond Kincaid articulates between Joe and

Pip clearly escapes the contractual and constraining bonds Pumblechook advocates; likewise, its vision of work escapes them. But, significantly, the comparison ends here. While Pip can find a language in "WOT LARX" able to be "realized in itself," the same is not true of work. Pip does not realize an alternate conception of work but instead is absorbed fully within the dominant model. Lest the possibility of returning to some older mode of work be anachronistically put forward, Pip's hopes of marrying Biddy and settling down at the forge are unequivocally dashed when he returns and finds Biddy already married to Joe. To Dickens's credit, Pip really cannot go back (it is a *Bildungsroman* after all) and, likewise, can find no alternate way forward (it is a realist novel after all): the structure of realization within which Pip works simply won't allow it.

In this view, Pip's enculturation into modern, that is, autonomous, bourgeois subjectivity and the regimen of modern work starts to look a lot more like an education in becoming a cog in the wheel, or better yet, a drone. Asked by Estella in their last meeting whether he does well, he replies, dispiritedly, "I work pretty hard for a sufficient living, and therefore—Yes, I do well" (484). The "do well" hesitatingly following the "therefore"'s pause disrupts the easy logic that would complete this sentence with a statement of Pip's happiness: "I do well and therefore I'm happy." To simply "do well" leaves ambivalent whether Pip is talking about his financial or his emotional well-being; the distinction between them has been confused or collapsed despite the narrative's best efforts to keep them separate. Like but also unlike the drone bee, Pip lives off the labor of others—Magwitch and the imperial relations he figures—and must labor continually himself, suggesting that the real fantasy in *Great Expectations* is that capitalist distribution and imperial production occur in remote social spaces and that those like Pip can somehow escape the degradations of an economic system built on production for profit by "working hard" for one's profits, not making too many of them, and keeping one's hands clean. "Working hard" elides the means for making profits, namely, the accumulation of surplus value; a sufficient living downplays the insufficient and inhumane conditions under which imperial workers labor.

As much as it desires to make this the case, the regime of accumulation *Great Expectations* maps spatially via Magwitch and relations of work tells another story altogether. In this one, "doing well" is always fraught with the memory of the living labor on which it depends; so much so that the one "good act" Pip considers himself to have done, setting Herbert up in business, rests squarely on colonial convict labor. Pip's and Herbert's "good fortunes" are so inextricably wedded to Magwitch's fortune that their being depends on it.

Instead, then, of carving out a space free from market relations, *Great Expectations* impresses with its new social geography: its mapping of the limitless encroachment engendered by an exploitative property system on all spaces of potential pleasure. Within this system, the meaning of space itself is transformed. The notion of an "outside" to the system, or of margins opposed to centers, collapses as all spaces become equally rife for the market. This does not mean, of course, that the inequalities between margin and center disappear; rather the desire to maintain strict boundaries between them, or, more accurately, to keep those existing on the margins or in the periphery at (Botany) bay, becomes increasingly impossible as "peripheral" spaces and populations become central to Britain's development. In the novel, this impossibility is registered most obviously in Magwitch but also in the other marginal figures—Orlick, Compeyson, Drummle—who refuse to remain on the sidelines and instead keep reemerging from the marshes and ooze and prisons and penal colonies to reassert their centrality in Pip's development.[25] The breaking down of any "safe" space free from convicts, the "criminal classes," or colonial realities has two significant effects. On the one hand, it denies a stable viewpoint from which a moralizing ethical commentary on modernity can be made. Dickens's use of the double narrative in *Bleak House*—his reliance on both a classically omniscient narrator and Esther—provides a place on the "outside," or at least a protected "inside" (Esther's narrative/domesticity/the home), from which to criticize the alienating processes of modernity and to preserve the humanitarian values and practices under threat by those processes.[26] By contrast, in *Great Expectations*, no such stable viewpoint exists.[27] As such, the novel is deeply symptomatic of capitalism itself, insinuating its structures into all "unoccupied" or uncolonized spaces. By the end of the novel, even the ground beneath the ruins of Satis House that Estella has tried to preserve above all else is being readied for development.

On the other hand, the novel's refusal to cede to its own fantasy of uncorrupted space paradoxically provides the leverage necessary to see beyond its own structures or conditions of possibility. Pip is not happy and no amount of new endings can make him so; but importantly the guilt that jeopardizes his happiness is hardly personal. As he despaired on his twenty-first birthday, "coming of age at all seemed hardly worth while in such a guarded and suspicious world as [Jaggers] made it" (292). By far the rule rather than the exception, Jaggers' "guarded and suspicious world" epitomizes the world of

Pip's/the novel's/Britain's development: subtended by the labor of empire, no one's hands may remain entirely clean. In this world, work in all its global manifestations is ever-present, and pleasures are literally consuming. Perhaps this is why, finally, *Great Expectations* simply cannot produce a satisfying vision of resolute happiness. For as long as the circulation of commodity logic and its contraband continues unimpeded, uncorrupted pleasures and the space within which to enjoy them are hard to come by.

Daniel Deronda

Men, like planets, have both a visible and an invisible history. — George Eliot, *Daniel Deronda*

If *Great Expectations* enacts the process of acculturation in an imperial age, *Daniel Deronda* constitutes a meditation on what such a model, ideally, should look like. Incorporating two related senses of acculturation, the novel is equally about the processes whereby Daniel and Gwendolen acquire the culture of dominant British society and about how that culture can and should be modified by or merged with other cultures and values. As in *Great Expectations*, the nature and meaning of relations — both familial and social, national and international — in a predominantly urban cosmopolitan culture forms the center of this investigation. But, unlike Dickens's *Bildungsroman*, George Eliot's is much more explicitly concerned with the limits of modernity: of how to structure social life in such a way to promote meaningful social interactions when the processes of modernity simultaneously enable and impede hitherto undreamt-of possibilities for "relatedness" and truly global communication. Searching for a figure of dispersal to counter the negative effects of modernity's dislocations, Eliot sees in Judaism and the Diaspora a connectedness that relies less on a rootedness to place (Eliot's catchphrase for the rudimentary criterion of identity), since that is quickly becoming historically obsolete, and more on the shared nature of histories, which are rendered meaningful in the lived experience of individuals and which are, importantly, able to travel. What was registered negatively — dispersal, dislocation, modern detachment — thus gains a positive valence when anchored imaginatively in a community whose ties are historically binding rather than literally grounded in a physical place.[28]

Since the time of *Daniel Deronda*'s publication, the success of Eliot's attempt to narrate this new vision of "relatedness" has been widely and hotly debated. Starting with Eliot herself, the issue of how the two plots of the novel do or do not go together has been the focus of critical attention. In response to contemporary reviews, Eliot famously took umbrage at her readers' inclination to "cut the book into scraps and talk of nothing in it but Gwendolen," claiming that she "meant everything in the book to be related to everything else there."[29] The history of criticism on *Daniel Deronda* seems for the most part, however, to take us in quite the opposite direction, following the lead of F. R. Leavis's pronouncement on the well-nigh ungodly split between the Gwendolen and Deronda plots. The latter, often referred to simply as the "Jewish portion" of the novel, is, in Leavis's view, nothing more than a blight on the rest of the book—there simply to be done away with; in his words, literally to be cut away.[30] When, *pace* Leavis, the two parts of the novel are read together, the Jewish portion is often interpreted as a corrective to the dehumanized personal relations defining the Gwendolen plot.[31] In other words, the Deronda story finds itself in the unusual position of being deemed either completely superfluous or utterly indispensable to the novel as a whole. In either case, the two plot lines are treated as separable from one another.

Added to this critical bugbear is the difficulty of situating *Daniel Deronda* within Eliot's oeuvre, given its especially weighty place as the last novel and also the only contemporary, urban novel. In a sense, the fear of the coachmen in *Felix Holt* (examined in chapter 2)—that the railroad, or the speed of modern technologies, will destroy the ground of storytelling—meets its match in *Daniel Deronda*, where the space of the novel expands to encompass the Continent and eventually, if only anticipatorily, the East. In her introduction to the novel, Barbara Hardy describes *Daniel Deronda* as a "kind of writing which was much more conspicuously ideological and symbolic than anything George Eliot had done before."[32] In a similar vein, Henry James accused Eliot of rendering a "diagram" rather than a "picture."[33] Instead of judging the merits of an ideological or diagrammatic novelistic structure, I want to suggest, however, that we look elsewhere in assessing *Daniel Deronda*: to an exploration of the reasons for this move toward abstraction, which, not coincidentally, I will contend, reproduces the increasingly abstract nature of social relations themselves. Exploring what I call the structure of "relationality" in *Daniel Deronda*, I aim to show how Eliot's attempt to reconstitute imaginatively some form of community free from the ravages of industrialization dovetails with emergent national discourse in Britain's "Age of Empire." But, rather than seeing this as an individual failing on Eliot's part, or as evidence of a bad novel, I want to argue that it is only by engaging the problematic of modernity so fully in all its contradictory aspects that Eliot's narrative reaches this impasse in the first place. Its so-called failings, that is to say, are what lend the novel its continuing *frisson*, especially in our immediate political climate, where Eliot's project is in large part still ours as well. As Eliot's novel attests, this project is finally as much about form as it is about content, about how to negotiate the mechanics of its/our own narratability.

Playing the Market

Early on in the novel, in response to her mother's claim that "marriage is the only happy state for a woman," Gwendolen Harleth peevishly retorts, "I will not put up with it if it is not a happy state. I am determined to be happy — at least not to go on muddling away my life as other people do, being and doing nothing remarkable. I have made up my mind not to let other people interfere with me as they have done" (58). This is but the first of many refusals on Gwendolen's part to succumb to the pressures of being a woman. Later, she will avow that she "was not going to renounce her freedom, or according to her favorite formula, 'not going to do as other women did'" (168). At another point she entertains the possibility that perhaps she need not even marry: "The questioning then [with respect to Grandcourt], was whether she should take a particular man as a husband. The inmost fold of her questioning now, was whether she need take a husband at all — whether she could not achieve substantiality for herself and know gratified ambition without bondage" (295). Once back with Grandcourt and actively being wooed by him, she again declares that "[she] will not be told that [she is] what women always are" (360).

As anyone familiar with *Daniel Deronda* knows, none of these claims or speculations remotely characterizes what actually happens to Gwendolen. Believing herself to have found the man whom she can master in Henleigh Grandcourt — and thus gain mastery over her own life — she finds herself, on the contrary, entirely under her husband's mastering thumb, her hopes for any kind of happiness or pleasure entirely destroyed, her existence reduced to suffering the tortures of his psychological terrorism. In all, it takes but seven weeks for this reversal of fortune, although the slow deliberateness and systematic cruelty of this process makes it seem infinitely longer. If one were looking for a yardstick to measure this change, Gwendolen herself offers a good one when she acknowledges, "I have always, ever since I was little, felt that mamma was not a happy woman; and now I daresay I shall be more unhappy than she has been" (335). Hardly the kind of competition one wants to win at, this measurement of individual shares of unhappiness provokes larger questions about Gwendolen's role within the narrative as a whole. Why is she so harshly treated? What is the relationship between her actions and her suffering? On the face of it, her treatment at the hands of the narrator seems almost as cruel as Grandcourt's, given how explicitly she is set up to fall. The painful disjuncture between her declarations and her actual experience and the disproportionate degree of irony leveled at her by the narrator would seem to have as its target something more than simply her narcissism. Even Rosamund Vincy, after all, is not punished so brutally.

To be sure, important critical legwork has been done on the ways in which the Gwendolen plot represents a microcosm of the larger system of imperialism, a system which Eliot implicitly criticizes through the trope of empire she uses to describe Gwendolen's relationship with Grandcourt.[34] "Empire" repeatedly defines their relationship: Gwendolen is the "princess in exile" lording over her "domestic empire" with "her power of inspiring fear";[35] whenever she might lose her confidence—as when she is shocked by the sudden appearance of the Spanish death mask during her dramatic debut at Offendene—she as quickly would recover and regain "the possibility of winning empire" (95); after she receives Grandcourt's note on her return from Leubronn, she "feels some triumph in a tribute to her power" as she "again seemed to be getting a sort of empire over her own life" (337), while Grandcourt, conversely, wishes "to be completely master of this creature" (346). Grandcourt's desire is multiplied by the anticipatory pleasure he receives from the challenge of mastery—with his pleasure, fittingly, all the more heightened by Gwendolen's resistance: "He meant to be master of a woman who would have liked to master him, and who perhaps would have been capable of mastering another man" (365).[36]

Like the colonial subject, rendered subservient and powerless by dominant English culture, Gwendolen will be quashed by the powers that be. Should we happen to miss this parallel, the narrative draws it for us, hypothetically imagining Grandcourt as a colonizer: "if this white-handed man with the perpendicular profile had been sent to govern a difficult colony, he might have won reputation among his contemporaries. He had certainly ability, would have understood that it was safer to exterminate than to cajole superseded proprietors, and would not have flinched from making things safe in that way" (655). The eerie foreshadowing of Kurtz's "Exterminate the brutes!" aside, this passage highlights the interrelatedness, if not interchangeability, of Grandcourt's domestic and imperial mentalities. From this perspective, Gwendolen's punishment, her subjection by Grandcourt, plays out an imperial drama in which empire and its structures of being have so permeated the "home country" that they have insinuated themselves into the most intimate recesses of individual relationships.

Yet somehow by itself this reading does not seem to quite plumb the question of "why Gwendolen?" and "why in this particularly cruel fashion?" Daniel Deronda's mother, for instance, like Gwendolen, desired mastery over her husband, but, unlike Gwendolen, actually gets it, suggesting at the least that there are husbands who can be ruled by their wives. Clearly with Gwendolen it is the method of mastery as much as the will to it that defines her particular fate: a method that finds its expression in the language of gambling. The novel opens with Gwendolen at the roulette table, winning famously until Daniel Deronda enters the room and causes a dramatic reversal of fortune; from the moment she feels Deronda's gaze on her, Gwendolen immediately begins to lose and to do so dramatically. In this introduction to Gwendolen, the milieu at Leubronn is as important as the action. Around her numerous Europeans mill about the gaming tables, all seemingly as displaced as Gwendolen, all driven by the desire to win — and most importantly, to win at someone else's expense.[37] The players comprise a serried mix of social classes, much like the crowd in the metropolis: "The white bejewelled fingers of an English countess were very near touching a bony, yellow, crab-like hand stretching a bared wrist to clutch a heap of coin — a hand easy to sort with the square, gaunt face, deep-set eyes, grizzled eyebrows, and ill-combed scanty hair which seemed a slight metamorphosis of the vulture" (36). Although they all appear superficially to be quite different, profound similarities exist among them: "But while every single player differed markedly from every other, there was a certain uniform negativeness of expression which had the effect of a mask — as if they had all eaten of some root that for the time compelled the brains of each to the same monotony of action" (37). A vision of leveling sameness, of a mind-numbing and automaton-like monotony, these players represent a Taylorization of the psyche that throughout the novel is typical of dominant English culture, and of the culture of the educated, metropolitan upper middle classes.[38] What they all "share" is a competitive self-interest that paradoxically renders the concept of a shared sociality meaningless.

Deronda's gaze delivers this critique of gambling. As he explains later, once he and Gwendolen are acquainted, " 'there is something revolting to me in raking a heap of money together, and internally chuckling over it, when others are feeling the loss of it. I should even call it base, if it were more than an exceptional lapse. There are enough inevitable turns of fortune which force us to see that our gain is another's loss: — that is one of the ugly aspects of life. One would like to reduce it as much as one could, not get amusement out of exaggerating it' " (383). Deronda's criticism centers on gaining at another's expense, and moreover, *desiring* to do so; the entire structure of such "play" involves benefiting from someone else's loss and knowing beforehand that that is the desired goal. As Deronda admonishes, gambling thus reproduces, by exaggerating, the more everyday instances of loss and "turns of fortune" that inevitably occur. In this way, gambling stands in as a figure for the larger economic system and its "ugly aspects"; hardly an isolated anomaly, it merely exaggerates the conditions of the status quo.

Deronda's gaze is definitive not only for its content but for its form. Long before Gwendolen hears Deronda's articulated criticisms of gambling, what makes her shrink from their encounter is the irony with which Deronda looks at her. He not only scrutinizes her, with the results of his scrutiny leading him "farther and farther away from the glow of mingled undefined sensibilities forming admiration," but to Gwendolen it feels as if he "was measuring her and looking down on her as an inferior . . . that he felt himself in a region outside and above her, and was examining her as a specimen of a lower order." All this looking "roused a tingling resentment which stretched the moment with conflict" (38). As she plays and loses her "last poor heap of napoleons" (39), Gwendolen finally faces Deronda directly, only to see a "smile of irony in his eyes as their glances met; but it was at least better that he should have kept his attention fixed on her than that he should have disregarded her as one of an insect swarm who had no individual physiognomy" (40). Any look that distinguishes Gwendolen individually is better than no look at all; but the measuring glances Deronda sends Gwendolen's way nonetheless reduce her to a "specimen of a lower order," just short of "an insect swarm" with "no individual physiognomy." In contrast to the gambling with which she is occupied, Deronda's kind of looking inscribes a hierarchy of orders that counters the leveling sameness and monotony characterizing the gamblers by demarcating individual physiognomies or differences — even if it does so negatively, by way of "superciliousness and irony" (40). Deronda's look marks the first time Gwendolen's mode of thinking receives a "disagreeable concussion" (40), when the basis for her thinking — "that she knew what was admirable and that she herself was admirable" (40) — is shaken (although not totally overthrown, at this point).

Deronda is not the only one who looks at Gwendolen in this way. The narrative, too, shares this ironic stance toward her; Deronda's gaze has its equivalent in the irony contained primarily (but not exclusively) in the epigraphs to each chapter. These are most pointed in the opening sections of the novel when Gwendolen is struggling with the thought of marrying Grandcourt and especially when she learns about the existence of Lydia Glasher. For instance, in Book Two, in the chapter (14) where Lydia confronts Gwendolen in the Whispering Stones and tells her of her relationship with Grandcourt, the epigraph reads:

> I will not clothe myself in wreck—wear gems
> Sawed from cramped finger-bones of women drowned;
> Feel chilly vapourous hands of ireful ghosts
> Clutching my necklace. Let your dead love
> Marry its dead. (181)

Obviously, Gwendolen both clothes herself "in wreck," and, in the wearing of Lydia's diamonds (forced on her by Grandcourt), feels the "hands of ireful ghosts" clutching at her. The diamonds become "poisoned gems" (407); the poison "enters" into Gwendolen; and Lydia's words, likened to an adder lying on the jewels (406), repeat themselves incessantly in Gwendolen's mind. The combination of Lydia's words and the diamonds so unhinges Gwendolen that she suffers a "nervous shock" (407) which leaves her screaming "with hysterical violence" (407) when Grandcourt enters the room.

A similar kind of shock (albeit tempered by twenty-first-century sensibilities), I want to suggest, accompanies our response as readers to the ironic distance framing Gwendolen's numerous comeuppances. Time and time again, the absolute divide between what an epigraph promises and what gets delivered (to Gwendolen) shocks with its harshness. Should an epigraph boast of how firm resolve loves nothing more than strong temptation in order all the better to "flout Enticement in the face," it is a strong bet that Gwendolen will wither beneath those self-same lures and fall prey to the enticements she meant to flout. The pointedness of these attacks speaks to the energy and incisiveness behind the novel's overall critique of the increasing commodification and reification of daily life. The gamble Gwendolen takes in her marriage to Grandcourt defines everything that is wrong with contemporary society. In her first conversation with Deronda after Grandcourt has drowned, this is made explicit in Gwendolen's confession: "I meant to get pleasure for myself, and it all turned to misery. I wanted to make my gain out of another's loss—you remember?—it was like roulette—and the money burnt into me. And I could not complain. It was as if I had prayed that another should lose and I should win. And I had won. I knew it all—I knew I was guilty" (757). Gwendolen's playing of the market, in both the specific context of marriage and the larger context of the economy as a whole, leaves her, before Grandcourt's death, as simply an object in Grandcourt's eyes and a complex object lesson in ours.

So much a figure for the ethos of the market, Gwendolen's "guilt" is hardly her own personal guilt. Instead, the continual flouting of her will by the narrative and her final object status make palpable the tenacity of the status quo and the dangers of trying to win at its own game. The irony directed at Gwendolen results in a sense of the inescapability or oppressiveness of the dominant institutional structures and the values they relentlessly reproduce. The voraciousness of these institutional pressures—certainly most in evidence with respect to women—tends to pull all things within their conventional orbit. The more Gwendolen protests, the more the institutions she is protesting against figuratively eat her up. Even as Gwendolen is composing an unconventional narrative for herself in a potential union with Grandcourt, one in which she will resist doing what other women do, her uncle, the Rector, Gascoigne is viewing their union as exemplary: "This match with Grandcourt presented itself to him as a sort of public affair; perhaps there were ways in which it might even strengthen the Establishment . . . Grandcourt, the almost certain baronet, the probable peer, was to be ranged with public personages, and was a match to be accepted on broad general grounds, national and ecclesiastical" (176-77). Where Gwendolen writes resistance, Gascoigne and public opinion, more generally, enforce conformity.

At the same time, the novel's recourse to irony in order to narrate this world highlights the larger problem Gwendolen and the epigraphs figure— and one which significantly impacts Eliot's role as storyteller: the attempt to narrate the new space of a world economy. Mapping the relationship between different genres and their historical moments, Fredric Jameson argues that the age of imperialism entails an increasing opposition between lived experience and the economic and social forms that govern that experience, as the national economy rapidly expands beyond its own frontiers. Of particular interest are the problems of figuration this contradiction poses: if, as Jameson posits, the phenomenological experience of the individual subject rests within a limited corner of the social world but the structurally determining coordinates of that experience lie elsewhere—"bound up with the whole colonial system" that comes to define the economic stage of imperialism—how does the artist go about representing such a state of affairs? In other words, how can novelists represent something invisible to but nonetheless determinant of the lived experience of their characters? As Jameson underscores, the problems for a work of art are "crippling"; a new situation arises "in which we can say that if individual experience is authentic, then it cannot be true; and that if a scientific or cognitive model of the same content is true, then it escapes individual experience."[39] It is precisely a version of this dilemma that I see Eliot grappling with in *Daniel Deronda*. In this light, criticisms such as Henry James's about the failure of the novel to be a "picture" as opposed to a "diagram" can be productively rearticulated to account for the changed nature of *Daniel Deronda*'s historical situation. Translating James's critique into Jameson's language, what James takes offense at is the fact that structure in the novel (the "diagram") has trumped experience (the "picture"). Instead of seeing this as a fault, however, we need to see it as a compelling and early attempt, formally, to deal with the vexing problematic of how to narrate the geographic, imperial realities of late-nineteenth-century history. To understand fully how *Daniel Deronda* engages this problematic, we need first to look further at the relationship between the novel's representation of empire and its formal use of irony.

Eliot's vision of empire, contained as it is within the Gwendolen plot, tells us something significant about the increasingly alienated relationship between private life and the public sphere in England's cultural representation of itself. As we saw in *Felix Holt*, the figure of the artisan represented an attempt to reassert the interconnectedness of private and public life in the form of a communal labor based on values other than that of profit. Now, in *Daniel Deronda*, the values of commerce have so thoroughly permeated social relations that the notion of value is disconnected from any larger sense of public morality. As Eliot, in the persona of Theophrastus Such, ruefully opens "Moral Swindlers," "It is a familiar example of irony in the degradation of words that 'what a man is worth' has to come to mean how much money he possesses; but there seems a deeper and more melancholy irony in the shrunken meaning that popular or polite speech assigns to 'morality' and 'morals.'"[40] The "shrunken meaning" to which Eliot refers is the kind of morality that can separate the private actions of an individual from public life.[41] What Gwendolen's fate as Grandcourt's wife so effectively illustrates is a generalizable state of dissociation between public and private realities: a state amounting, in Lukács's words, to a kind of "transcendental homelessness," which defines not only the particular fate of Gwendolen under Grandcourt's imperial thumb but the fate of the individual modern subject and British culture under monopoly capitalism, the economic stage of imperialism.[42]

At its worst, this ironic dissociation leads to outright cynicism. When, for instance, Gwendolen discusses her match with Grandcourt with Gascoigne, he is taken aback by her instrumental relationship to the whole affair. As their talk ends, Gwendolen concedes that she has been "foolish" to even think of *not* accepting Grandcourt: "'I know that I must be married some time—before it is too late. And I don't see how I could do better than marry Mr Grandcourt. I mean to accept him, if possible.'" As the narrator interjects, Gwendolen "felt as if she were reinforcing herself by speaking with this decisiveness to her uncle" (179). But what unsettles her uncle about Gwendolen's response is not her indecisiveness but "how bare a version of his own meaning" she reproduces. In short, the distance between Gwendolen's feelings and the proper feelings of a girl contemplating marriage startles him: "He wished that in her mind his advice should be taken in an infusion of sentiments proper to a girl, and such as are presupposed in the advice of a clergyman, although he may not consider them always appropriate to be put forward. He wished his niece parks, carriages, a title—everything that would make this world a pleasant abode; but he wished her not to be cynical—to be, on the contrary, religiously dutiful, and have warm domestic affections" (179–80). Just as "The Moral Swindlers" deplores the loss of a certain kind of moral value, the value of the match for Gwendolen rests exclusively on its literal worth to her.

The complexity of the narrative's relationship to Gwendolen and women, more generally, is fully captured here. While decrying the kind of instrumental relations Gwendolen embraces, the narrative, nonetheless, also underscores their particular resonance for women given their commodity status. Simply put, Gwendolen, in her cynical scheming, unsentimentally exposes the economic underpinnings of the institution of marriage and the powerless position assigned to women within this system of exchange. These "bare" facts upset the Rector because they refuse the cover of "warm domestic affections," themselves fully part of the *institution* of marriage, but envisioned otherwise through their naturalization. Gwendolen's cynicism thus enables a feminist critique of the objectification of women at the same time that her method of critique forms the main target of criticism by the narrative as a whole. Almost the same can be said for the other resistant woman in the text, Daniel Deronda's mother, the Contessa Alcharisi. Her transgressive act was to deny Daniel his inheritance as a Jew by concealing his paternity and keeping this concealment a secret from her own father. The act of concealment marks her transgression. Throughout the text, nothing is worse than trying to keep hidden the relations among individuals; hence the gravity of Gwendolen's attempt to deny Lydia's existence in her marriage to Grandcourt.[43] In the case of Daniel's mother, concealment appears to be the only strategy available to ensure her success. Describing the nature of her relationship with her father, and what it required in terms of her actions, Alcharisi asserts that "when a woman's will is as strong as the man's who wants to govern her, half her strength must be concealment. I meant to have my will in the end, but I could only have it by seeming to obey . . . I could not act it to myself that I should begin to defy my father openly and succeed. And I never would risk failure" (695). In contrast, everything about Daniel rebels against such strategizing, having come to "regard concealment as a bane of life, and the necessity of concealment as a mark by which lines of action were to be avoided" (435). When practical concerns threaten to shake his principles, as when he debates whether he can in good conscience keep the discovery of Mirah's family secret if the family turns out to be undesirable, he steadies himself by remembering his own history: "Was it not his secret complaint against the way in which others had ordered his life, that he had not open daylight on all its relations, so that he had not, like other men, the full guidance of primary duties?" (433). Concealment thus means differently for women than for men; it both hints at some maneuvering room within an oppressive system of gender relations and heralds a transgression for which women pay dearly. Whereas Grandcourt's "secret" about Lydia Glasher is an open one that becomes nothing more than a mere episode in his "anecdotic history" (458), Gwendolen's and Alcharisi's secrets determine that their respective histories will be consumed by suffering and (possibly) penance. Like the vision of social relations Gwendolen's cynicism affords her, Alcharisi's strategic use of concealment grants her a modicum of control over her life and simultaneously denies her control.[44]

Clearly, the narrative as a whole is trying to reestablish a richer and more tenable model of morality that would overcome the kinds of divisions that irony and cynicism and concealment (regardless of its gendered inflections) reflect. But like the methods at Gwendolen's and Alcharisi's disposal, the narrative turns to a form of critique that is part of rather than separate from its object of criticism. Working almost singularly through irony, the epigraphs framing Gwendolen's experience reflect an altered sense of narrative distance in that they "communicate" not so much through their representation of lived experience but by their undercutting of it. In other words, they reinscribe the gap the narrative desires to overcome. This distancing calls into question the conditions of narratability; the ground of narration itself is fundamentally shaken by what Walter Benjamin terms the diminishing "communicability of experience."[45] Daniel vocalizes this dilemma when he acknowledges to Gwendolen that "experience differs for different people. We don't all wince at the same things" (624); and the divide such differences create is made clear when Daniel confesses that he feels himself helpless to "rescue" Gwendolen. The epigraphs thus become symptomatic of the opposition between lived experience and structure that Jameson articulates and that finds its expression in the formal practice of irony. The literal contradiction between the structural frame that the epigraphs erect and the actual narration of experience upsets any notion of either a coherent internal identity or a continuity between structure and experience. As Theodor Adorno phrases it, "the identity of experience in the form of a life that is articulated and possesses internal continuity—and that life was the only thing that made the narrator's stance possible—has disintegrated."[46]

The signs of this disintegration are nowhere better found than in the deep skepticism within the novel about the role of literature itself. Not only does the opening epigraph suggest how tenuous the practice of realism is, and how confined the tenets of the *Bildungsroman* are, in its acknowledgment of the fiction of any "true beginning," but reading, too, is continually questioned for its usefulness. Whereas traditionally the romance is maligned as a form of reading that corrupts its readers, within *Daniel Deronda* realism is equally insufficient as an edifying means of mediation between literature and life. After meeting Lydia Glasher and hearing her tale, the narrator comments that "Gwendolen's uncontrolled reading, though consisting chiefly in what are called pictures of life, had somehow not prepared her for this encounter with reality" (193). The problem, the narrator continues, results from the distance even "pictures of life" afford: "What horrors of damp huts, where human beings languish, may not become picturesque through aerial distance! What hymning of cancerous vices may we not languish over as sublimest art in the safe remoteness of a strange language and artificial phrase! Yet we keep a repugnance to rheumatism and other painful effects when presented in our personal experience" (193). The "aerial distance" the narrator speaks of has its complement in the writer's relation to society. As Jonathan Arac comments in a different context, the "overview" perspective, which "allowed a working distance from society" and which helped produce the social novel of the early 1850s and its interventions, loses its purchase in the later half of the century when that distance becomes alienating rather than enabling: " 'Experience' no longer was something easily shared in a public work through an apprehensible shape of action; instead it became an obscure private domain only to be hinted at with a language itself contaminated by convention."[47]

While the brunt of this new situation will not find its full expression until the advent of modernism proper, *Daniel Deronda* nonetheless narrates the beginnings of a process that will result in "the sense that consciousness is a closed world, so that a representation of the social totality now must take the (impossible) form of a coexistence of those sealed subjective worlds and their peculiar interaction, which is in reality a passage of ships in the night, a centrifugal movement of lines and planes that can never intersect."[48] What can then be read in the Gwendolen narrative is a double relationship to imperialism: at the level of lived experience (or content), imperialism is (metaphorically) critiqued, while at the level of structure, it is reenacted, both in terms of the opposition between public and private, lived experience and structure, that afflicts Gwendolen, Grandcourt et al. and in terms of its antagonistic relation to the Deronda plot.

Finding the Will to Work

In *Beginnings*, Edward Said claims a likeness between *Moby Dick* and *Great Expectations*, seeing in both of them "works of will." As Said explains, he uses "will" to mean both "volition" and "inheritance." He goes on to argue that both Ishmael and Pip substitute volition for inheritance and that this substitution leaves them standing "to one side of life's generative processes" at the same time that "each occupies the narrative center of his novel."[49] In the context of his larger argument about the novel as "beginning intention," Said concludes that "all this illustrates how narrative returns to discover its beginnings in the act whereby the generative faculty was sacrificed to celibate individuality."[50]

The play Said describes between will as volition and will as inheritance is also at the center of *Daniel Deronda*'s narrative. Indeed, the process of Daniel's acculturation involves a redefining of both senses of will. Moreover, this process is integrally related to the conditions of narrative and its role in the world and becomes in the novel a story in its own right, coexisting alongside Daniel's *Bildungsroman* and generated by it. Whereas *Great Expectations* leaves us, in Said's reading, with a vision of "celibate individuality," *Daniel Deronda* actively struggles against the individual's and the novel's sacrifice of the "generative faculty," trying to maintain the individual in a dynamic relation to "life's generative processes." This struggle is responsible finally for the ambivalence about identity and culture in the novel: on the one hand, the narrative needs to create a position from which individuality can be generative, and it locates this possibility in a "justified partiality" which would maintain the particular in the face of the universal; on the other hand, in order to construct such a partiality, the narrative turns to a certain vision of shared history (in Zionism) that threatens to lose sight of the universal altogether, thereby abrogating any special claims to its generative capacities. In the end, the limits of *Daniel Deronda*'s conception of shared history and the geographical space mapped by that history define the contradictory nature of modernity itself: its tendency toward breaking down boundaries at the same time that it constructs new ones.

The ills of pure inheritance as a mode of social production and reproduction are best epitomized in Grandcourt,

> [whose] importance as a subject of this realm was of the grandly passive kind which consists in the inheritance of land. Political and social movements touched him only through the wire of his rental, and his most careful biographer need not have read up on Schleswig-Holstein, the policy of Bismarck, trade-unions, household suffrage, or even the last commercial panic. He glanced over the best newspaper columns on these topics, and his views on them can hardly be said to have wanted breadth, since he embraced all Germans, all commercial men, and all voters liable to use the wrong kind of soap, under the general epithet of "brutes"; but he took no action on these much agitated questions beyond looking from under his eyelids at any man who mentioned them, and retaining a silence which served to shake the opinions of timid thinkers. (644–45)

With no need to work, Grandcourt is untouched by and unconcerned with anything larger than his own maintenance. Isolated and immune to everything except money and power, Grandcourt falls prey to an undiscriminating sensibility, in which differences are all easily assimilated under sweeping epithets in a monolithic, debilitating worldview.[51]

Against the "condition" of imperialism which this worldview embodies, Daniel Deronda's initial lack of an inheritance marks the other extreme. So impartial that he can take no position whatsoever, his sympathy extends to just about everyone; the more needy, the more moved Deronda is to help. Although he has grown up with his aristocratic uncle, Sir Hugo Mallinger, he nonetheless remains an illegitimate heir to his property—as a "nephew" rather than a son—and hence an outsider to the social world of the landed aristocracy. Instead of already possessing a social position and a home, Deronda is actively in search of one. Paradoxically, he is thus looking for something that is rarely acquired, but, importantly, his looking redefines the object of his search. While inheritance generally refers to land, for Deronda it signifies a different kind of worth, measured not in acreage but in the potential for a sense of connectedness to the world. Judaism and Daniel's relationship to Ezra Mordecai are meant to supply the materials for this structure of social "relatedness."[52]

At the center of Daniel's search is the need to find his origins. In this discovery lie his hopes for an inspiriting sense of duty that would provide direction to his desires and, more prosaically, spell a career for him. The knowledge of his parentage, he speculates, would "[save] him from having to make an arbitrary selection where he felt no preponderance of desire" (526). For Daniel, a purposeful, directed "selection" involves more than the realization of individual or personal desires. Offset against Gwendolen's search for passion at the roulette table, Daniel's desires can only be fulfilled collectively: he is looking as much for a meaningful context for his life as for something to give it individual meaning. Unlike Grandcourt's existence, "will" becomes less about the passive receipt or passing on of property and more about a redefined notion of work, of what he can actively *do* in the world. A minor comment by Gascoigne, in response to his son Rex's enthusiastic choice of the law as a profession (after spending most of the novel getting over Gwendolen's jilting of him), is telling for the incidental way it brings together the components of Daniel's vision. Using Brewitt the blacksmith as his example, Gascoigne pontificates, "Well, my boy, the best augury of a man's success in his profession is that he thinks it the finest in the world. But I fancy it is so with most work when a man goes into it with a will. Brewitt, the blacksmith, said to me the other day that his 'prentice had no mind to his trade; 'and yet, sir,' said Brewitt, 'what would a young fellow have if he doesn't like the blacksmithing?' " (773).

Gascoigne's advice is significant on two counts. First, the reference to blacksmithing implies a parallel between this kind of manual labor and the labor that comes to define the middle class, whether it be Rex's work as a lawyer or Daniel's as a statesman of sorts or social reformer. (It is interesting to note how difficult it is even to define what Daniel does as a profession.) The criterion for work that comes out of this definition has at its heart actually liking the work, regardless of its nature. In stark contrast to Pip's forced and tepid enthusiasm toward his job, the vision of work *Daniel Deronda* hopes to realize argues against such a routinized, mechanical approach to labor. Liking one's work gains equal importance to the necessity of it; the notion of necessity itself is transformed by the novel's emphasis on actively choosing a vocation that coincides with one's desire. By linking blacksmithing and other forms of work, Gascoigne's comments also indicate how work in the novel comes to be synonymous with identity, so much so that it is virtually indistinguishable from it. (One measure of the success of the subsumption of work into identity is the absence of almost any mention of work in discussions of *Daniel Deronda*.) But, clearly, Daniel's finding of himself in his Jewish heritage is also the discovery of his life's work. Once he knows he is a Jew and is pressed by his father's friend, Kalonymos, as to his vocation, the two easily collapse into one another. As Deronda declares, " 'I hold that my first duty is to my own people, and if there is anything to be done towards restoring or perfecting their common life, I shall make that my vocation' " (792). Work is no longer something one does, but rather what one *is*. Kalonymos's response makes this connection explicit: " 'Ah, you argue and you look forward—you are Daniel Charisi's grandson' " (792). Even more so than in *Great Expectations*, work has been made so abstract that it is practically invisible *as work*. The labors of nation building have lost their material grounding, refigured primarily as intellectual labors and modeled more after the artist than the artisan or worker.[53]

Yet, even as labor becomes abstract, the desire to see it joined to pleasure motivates Deronda's search. Eliot's model of intellectual labor already assumes that work should be pleasurable, hence Deronda's struggle to find work that is truly meaningful rather than simply adequate or sufficient or worse. He is, after all, looking for a calling. Moreover, the narrative implicitly recognizes that the desire to bring labor and pleasure together necessitates a reorganization of the social structure as a whole. To return to Jameson's language, the novel is clearly struggling to represent the larger structure determining lived experience and, as we will see below, attempting to provide an alternative model for that structure. Right now, it is important to note that the structure Eliot invokes ultimately prevents the expression of an expansive notion of labor precisely because it reproduces the very processes of abstraction and division limiting labor's capacities in the first place. Not only does labor disappear as it gets absorbed into an abstract notion of identity but Eliot's weddedness to the idea of a common inheritance as the basis for identity ends up dividing the social world into separate cultural spheres. Within this paradigm, labor remains alienated; the novel concentrates on Deronda's "identity" to the exclusion of the underlying structure of labor on which any identity becomes possible.

A return to Kalonymos's formulation makes clear that Daniel's identity/vocation is simultaneously given and chosen. It comes from his actions—"you argue," "you look forward"—*and* from his grandfather. It is both inherited and willfully taken up. Like the sentiments that come from a sense of rootedness to place, it flows from the "sweet habit of blood" and provides the ground in which "affection can take root" (50). In this way, obviously, it is an antidote to the "homelessness" defining dominant British culture. But the tension between these two notions of "will" also speaks to how complicated this "grounding" becomes as a means of envisioning a revitalized modern community. Is the community the narrative hopes to construct finally based on racial or ethno-religious ties or on the work and actions of its members? What role do culture and cultural difference play in this construction? The particularity of Daniel's vocation contributes to these complications: he not only discovers that he is a Jew but his Judaism is linked to a proto-Zionist project that seemingly offers the possibility of resolving the contradictions within a modern, increasingly international community by allowing for the differences between peoples and cultures while preserving the community as a whole. Daniel's father's concept of "separateness with communication" captures the double-duty performed by the novel's incipient Zionism.[54]

In concert with the specific nature of Zionism as distinct from Judaism, the novel is equally about envisioning and creating a new kind of state. Mordecai, and eventually Deronda, are defined by their deep spirituality and the social vision that would put this spirituality in the service of a concrete, realized form of social action, the project of nationalism. One brief, early indication of this desired combination of intellect and action is foreshadowed when Daniel as a child opts for the heroic figures of Pericles and Washington, both statesmen, over the purely contemplative faculties of Porson and Leibnitz. It is not just that these men are not philosophers and are thus "men of the world" but that they also both founded national states. Additionally, Daniel is likened to Mazzini and his nationalist campaign in Italy.[55] At some level then, as Christina Crosby has pointed out, Eliot's treatment of Judaism becomes inseparable from Zionism; that is, the thrust in the novel toward a materialization of thought and belief *in statehood* ultimately collapses the one into the other.[56] Yet, as Amanda Anderson has compellingly argued, the novel actually generates two narratives of Jewish nationalism, one by Mordecai, the other by Deronda. Whereas Mordecai advocates "the collectivist-romantic model" coming from the German idealist tradition, replete with a notion of a "unified national will and a projected national destiny," Deronda speaks for a "universalist civic model of nationality often associated with John Stuart Mill and built on the principle of democratic debate."[57] Against Mordecai's model of a kind of "prereflective cultural embeddedness," Deronda vocalizes the need for "self-reflective and dialogical affirmations of cultural heritage."[58] Taking to heart both of these perspectives on Judaism in the novel, the question remains why Eliot turns to statehood or nationalism at all. What is it that keeps Eliot attached to some form of statehood in order to realize a model of cultural difference? What is it about Judaism, and Zionism in particular, that is so compelling for Daniel's *Bildung* and its vision of community?

Within the context of nineteenth-century nationalist movements, Zionism occupies a unique position. The clearly "borrowed nature" of its program, to use Eric Hobsbawm's term, with respect to both language and territory, dramatizes the acquired processes whereby a sense of national identity was created.[59] Owing to the exigencies of mass migration, most notably the lack of any claim to an exclusive territory, among the Jewish Diaspora (as well as in the Habsburg Empire), an alternative definition of nationality was developed: "It was here seen as inherent, not in a particular piece of the map to which a body of inhabitants were attached, but in the members of such bodies of men and women as considered themselves to belong to a nationality, wherever they happened to live. As such members, they would enjoy 'cultural autonomy.' "[60] In contrast to a territorialist view of nationality (which established the identification of nations with an exclusive territory, modeled after the French Revolution), this severing of "home territory" from "nation" more accurately reflected the relation between a geography and a national identity. These nonterritorialists recognized, in a way a territorialist view did not, the metaphorical, imagined nature of the nation, which, as Hobsbawm underscores, was no more akin to home territory than the father in fatherland is to a real parent. Zionism thus represents the "extreme example" that proves the rule: it foregrounds the artificial, *constructed* nature of "nation" operative in any consolidation—nonterritorialist and territorialist alike—of national identity. Within the parameters of *Daniel Deronda* this kind of national "belongingness," or claim to cultural autonomy, carries applicability not only for the Jews themselves but for the English as well.

Like the notion of vocation, then, Zionism as a model of national identity deftly balances choice with "belongingness," holding out the possibility for the kind of dialogism to which Amanda Anderson sees Daniel's practices aspiring. It allows a relationship to one's cultural heritage that is both given and constructed. Moreover, Daniel's version of this project is, above all, about constructing an economy in which no one loses: where differences are not eradicated by the leveling sameness of a moneyed economy and personal gain is inseparable from the gains of the collective. As Mordecai claims, "the world will gain as Israel gains" (595). The duty and vision Zionism encapsulates thus counteracts the disintegration of experience that threatens English society and which, by implication, is associated with imperialism.[61]

The status of Zionism as an anti-imperialist project, however, is fraught with contradiction, intractably caught up in *Daniel Deronda*'s knotty treatment of racial difference. Cultural difference easily slips into racial difference, the expression of separateness into a racial divide. Sander Gilman provocatively notes that Eliot's treatment of racial difference within the novel slips dangerously into what may be termed a polygenetic view, a nineteenth-century pseudoscientific theory which posited an innate genetic difference between the races.[62] Basing his argument on the seemingly offhand comment made by Eliot's narrator that "one man differs from another, as we all differ from the Bosjeman, in a sensibility of checks, that come from variety of needs, spiritual or other" (370), Gilman goes on to argue that Eliot's "we" effectively establishes an absolute racial divide: a view of racial difference buttressed by genetics and the innate difference it implies.[63] Within this kind of racial configuration, Jews, as Gilman concludes, fall just this side of human on the "scale of humanity," yet still unequivocally on the right side of the racial divide. In other words, in some profound sense, they still occupy a position potentially on the "inside."[64] Hence the clear distinction between two kinds of Jews in the text—the Ezra Cohens versus the Ezra Mordecais—which seems to imply that the national state would be a sorry one were a pawnbroker to be its model. As Eliot pithily distinguishes within her own taxonomy, "there are Ezras and there are Ezras" (628).

But even in its most stereotypical form, the figure of the materialistic, pawnbroker Jew ranks above "the peoples of the East," who are never even differentiated in terms of the different nationalities constituting "the East," let alone in terms of actual individuals. In fact, they are absent from the text altogether, mentioned only to be dismissed for their "barbarity." Representations of the East or Easterners are thus relegated to a purely marginal status, referenced only in order to reinforce through repetition an "Oriental despotism" in stark contrast to Western freedom. In this respect, the novel undoubtedly participates in an Orientalist narrative. Addressing Zionism specifically, Edward Said makes two points that need to be reiterated in this context: first, he underscores the view of the despotic "orientalized" East on which the Zionist project is premised and which is supported by the vision of Palestine as an unpopulated piece of land; second, he reminds us that such an attitude toward the East says less about the East than it does about the Occident's construction and representation of itself vis-à-vis the "Orient."[65]

In its most extreme formulation, Mordecai assigns to Judaism the status of a national collective which carries "the culture and the sympathies of every great nation in its bosom" as the transmitter of "the brightness of Western freedom amid the despotisms of the East" (595). Despite Deronda's advocacy of a more democratic view of the collective in his vision of the state, the "despotisms" assigned to the East as an undifferentiated mythic space are never contradicted. Unlike the Jew, then, whose stereotyping by others in the novel works for the most part to critique the narrowness of the English vision—and moreover is continually undercut and overturned by alternative representations which belie the stereotype—the Easterner is never represented as anything other than despotic; in fact, the Easterner is never really represented at all. The sheer invisibility of the East—as nothing more than a land without people, and most easily and summarily summed up in one word—"despotic"—contributes ideologically to a seamless fulfillment of the goals of Zionism. Once the map of the East has been rhetorically depopulated, erased even, there is no longer anything blocking its transformation into the Jewish homeland. Like the spatial history that reveals the relations of work in *Great Expectations*, *Daniel Deronda*'s topography also exposes, by its absences, the exploitative relations underlying its vision of nationalism.

The so-called split or opposition here is no longer between country and city as in Eliot's other fiction, or between social classes as in *Felix Holt*, but rather is international. Eliot finds herself somewhat at a loss when it comes to representing, or more literally mapping, a vision of such an international community, given her attachment, especially in the later novels, to an organic model of class and social relations. Whereas in *Felix Holt*, for instance, Eliot's organicism could be productively employed to quell the incipient violence of what Eliot perceived as an all-too-rapid (read as well: all-too-working-class) movement for social change, literally by slowing it down, in *Daniel Deronda* this kind of organicism no longer seems an adequate blueprint for reconstituting a meaningful community of some sort. While organic language largely defines Mordecai's views of the collective, the community Daniel hopes to build relies on consciously and actively constructing a collectivity that is not assumed but rather in need of creation. Unlike in *Felix Holt* or *Middlemarch*, organicism per se is no longer the organizing principle of *Daniel Deronda*. Instead, the operative model or metaphor replacing that of the body is the nation itself: in place of biological functions, which by homology become social duties, racial/cultural difference is translated into separate nationalities which then coalesce as an international community. Whereas the former model of organicism by its nature denies individual organs/domestic subjects autonomy, the latter national model operates precisely by carving out regions of difference premised on national and cultural autonomy.

As we have seen, the ground for such a model of national identity has been prepared by the implicit construction of a racial chain of being—of white vs. African, Westerner vs. Easterner—within *Daniel Deronda*. Despite this preparation, however, Daniel's own figuration testifies to the hybridity underlying any construction of racial or national purity that the narrative attempts to create. It is even emphasized that Daniel *cannot* lose his English upbringing entirely, that he could in no way abandon his very English education (724). Moreover, when Grandcourt, in the context of a conversation about the Jamaica uprising in 1865, characterizes the "Jamaican negro as a beastly sort of baptist Caliban" (376), Daniel confesses that "he always felt a little with Caliban, who naturally had his own point of view and could sing a song" (376). Later, when the conversation turns to "half-breeds," he reminds his listeners "that the whites had to thank themselves for the half-breeds" (376). At the same time, however, these intimations of hybridity ultimately reflect an ideal more than a reality or practice within the text. In short, the Calibans and "half-breeds" with their "own point of view" are abstractly represented but never concretely realized. Given the numerous ways in which even some slim notion of hybridity is challenged, it is doubtful whether it can be said that any sustained vision of racial, national, or cultural mixing is proffered. Throughout the novel, long before it is revealed to Daniel that he is a Jew, he is repeatedly either (directly) interpellated by other Jews as a Jew or (indirectly) viewed as somehow different, the latter occurrences most often stemming from some differentiation posed in terms of physical appearance.[66]

But these counterclaims themselves work two ways: the insistence on one level of a racial purity is counteracted on another level by the mere fact that Daniel is nonetheless figured as both a Jew *and* an Englishman. In this sense, then, despite the narrative's thrust toward a history of pure nationality, Deronda is symptomatic of a hybrid national reality, of an expression of "Englishness" which undermines that of his uncle, Hugo Mallinger, in that it marks the presence of difference *within* it. As both insider and outsider, Deronda, heading off to Palestine at the end of the novel, thus bears the traces of hybridity underlying any construction of national identity. The historically specific boundaries of late-nineteenth-century British nationalism are here being constructed and renegotiated, with the East now figuring as the negative space on which a properly English, that is, civilized as opposed to uncivilized, identity can be projected; a national identity that can through negation constitute itself as a coherent internal unity.

Shifting registers for a moment, if we return once more to the domestic shores which *Daniel Deronda* ultimately attempts to circumnavigate, this process of negation and its implied assumption of a domestic sameness over and against a foreign otherness itself is unmoored. Significantly, when Daniel transports his national message abroad, he leaves Gwendolen behind. As the narrator understates, "the distance between them was too great" (767). But while the narrative, like Deronda, may be unable to bridge this distance, it does circumvent the obstacle preventing this joining—even as it flees the domestic sphere of the "national" in order to establish a community no longer possible within those national borders. Notably, *Daniel Deronda* is not able to incorporate or absorb Gwendolen seamlessly into its denouement. A figure of the excesses of the new economy, she is subject to and a subject of a "new gambling in which the losing was not simply a *minus*, but a terrible plus" (659). This new gambling is as much about the specific loss of the "organic" community as it is about the qualitative transformation of the community wrought by expansionism and a commodity culture. Consumed by "world-nausea," yet immune to the redemptive cures of nationalism prescribed by Deronda, Gwendolen is left, literally and figuratively, "crushed on the floor," her grief displaced but not entirely eclipsed, as the narrator concludes ironically that "such grief seemed natural in a poor lady whose husband had been drowned in her presence" (767). Thus Gwendolen too is implicitly a critique of British nationalism and of the system of representation that defines the nation-state; a system from which she is not only provisionally excluded but in whose exclusion, given her allegorical positioning as figure of domestic (and domesticated) experience, rests the preconditions for such a nationalism.

These limits are not confined to Gwendolen either. While Mirah appears, in contrast to Gwendolen, to be neatly contained, conveniently willing and even "made to submit" (as in "made to order," not forced) simply because "she has no notion of being anybody but herself" (253), she nonetheless also reveals the fault lines in the narrative's vision of national unity. In an otherwise uneventful scene with Mordecai in which they argue over the meaning of a Midrash story about a woman who willingly sacrifices her life in order to express her love for a Gentile king, the disavowal of Mirah's lived experience becomes clearly necessary to the overall design of the text. As Ezra narrates the story, the woman "entered the prison and changed clothes with the woman who was beloved by the king, that she might deliver that woman from death by dying in her stead, and leave the king to be happy in his love which was not for her." He interprets the woman's actions as exemplary of a selfless love, "the surpassing love, that loses self in the object of love" (803). But Mirah reads this story differently. According to her, the woman "wanted the king when she was dead to know what she had done, and feel that she was better than the other." Far from being a selfless act, it "was her strong self, wanting to conquer, that made her die" (803). When Mirah refuses to bow to Mordecai's interpretation, he accuses her of reading too many plays and judging by them instead of by her own heart. To this comment, Mirah neither capitulates nor continues to argue; she simply doesn't answer. But, given the context of this discussion, Mirah *is* speaking from the heart, for just prior to this conversation, Mirah realizes that the "mortal repugnance" she feels toward Gwendolen stems from the "love that makes jealousy" (800–801). In her love for Deronda, she experiences what she had previously only acted and sung about; she now knows what it is to have desires that are not selfless and that give rise, in Mirah's estimation, to "horrible feelings" (802). Mordecai thus has it all wrong: as Mirah, judging from her own experience, attests, "the Jewish girl must have had jealousy in her heart, and she wanted somehow to have the first place in the king's mind. That is what she would die for" (803). While the possibility of such an expression of love is preempted obviously in Mirah's case, the conflict between these two views of love is never resolved. As a result, the problem of female desire is left productively to plague the narrative.

Finally, were one to ask hypothetically what would happen if Mirah did refuse to submit, the answer would be fittingly close at hand: one would need only turn to Daniel's mother, Alcharisi, suggesting just how tenuous and ambivalent even the articulation of unity between Daniel and Mirah is within the "imagined community" of the novel. Hence, the benign vision of nationalism meant to find its embodiment in the coupling of Mirah and Deronda is itself built on the same structure of domination—of conqueror and conquered—being criticized in Grandcourt's and Gwendolen's relationship. Mirah's subjection and the continuing "homelessness" of Alcharisi and Gwendolen all structurally compromise the democratic desires motivating the text; gender hierarchy is revealed as constitutive of the new as well as the old order. The utopian longings of *Daniel Deronda* thus rest equally on refiguring its international as well as domestic contours, with the intimacy and interconnectedness of the two being revealed in the exclusions necessary to but finally incapable of providing closure.

In terms of the collective, the separateness that defines Eliot's sense of nationality carries with it the possibility for a revitalized community, embodying both a historical continuity with the past as well as a present relationship with the future. Deronda, as the spokesperson for such a nationalism, recovers what, as the novel's ideology underscores, he has always been when he discovers his Jewish paternity. A crucial aspect of that recovery is the apparent uniting of past and present, of lived experience and structure that such a recuperation signifies, underscored by Deronda's rhetorical question: "Unless nationality is a feeling, what force can it have as an idea?" (583). Paradoxically, then, the "threat" of imperialism is resisted by a domestic nationalism. Eliot's narrative thus enacts the contradictory stance of critiquing imperialism from the perspective of British nationalism as if imperialism and nationalism did not, at this particular historical juncture, in fact work in concert with one another.

Indeed, it is precisely these two impulses that can be read as the defining coordinates of modernity. On the one hand, the European nation-state and its concomitant development of national cultures served as the motor of capitalist expansion. On the other hand, this process of expansion—of the increasing globalization of capital, labor, and goods—moved across and thus broke down those selfsame national boundaries. As Stuart Hall has observed, "the so-called 'logic of capital' has operated as much *through* difference—preserving and transforming difference (including sexual difference)—not by undermining it."[67] From this perspective, the tension between the two plots in *Daniel Deronda* can be viewed as symptomatic of the tension between, on the one hand, the tendency of capitalism to develop the nation-state and national cultures and, on the other hand, its transnational imperatives: whereas the historical development of a *national* culture is "invented" through Eliot's representation of the Zionist project (that is, through the so-called Jewish portion of the novel), the detrimental effects of the *transnational* imperatives of capital are delineated through the Gwendolen plot. These two tendencies are inseparable from one another; each is a figure of the other.

A direct homology is drawn between the English and the Zionist project, as Daniel claims of his mission: "The idea that I am possessed with is that of restoring a political existence to my people, making them a nation again, giving them a national center, such as the English have, though they are scattered over the face of the globe" (875). It is in this context that Eliot's own "scattered" comments about Britain's colonial possessions take on a deeper and more sustained relevance within the text of *Daniel Deronda* as a whole. For it is as a result of imperialism—itself a product of capitalist development—that the English are covering the map with their now scattered national population. The fear for Eliot in such a scattering is all too clear, involving, as it does, the loss of an organic center and an encroaching corruption of lived experience. Urban cosmopolitanism figures as that which supplants "organic" community; its aesthetic instrumentalizes all social relationships, reducing them to the reified "sport" of gambling. Given this recognition, the equivalency which Eliot's text draws between British nationalism and Zionism is an odd one. Zionism, taking English nationalism as its model, is to somehow answer to the national and cultural impasse which England itself has reached. But as *Daniel Deronda*'s text so convincingly relates, nationalism is part of the problem, not a solution to it. In other words, Eliot's critique of imperialism, with its resultant vision of an alternative nationalism via Zionism, bears within it the structure of the object of its critique.

A partial explanation for this contradictory stance is the fact that for the most part Eliot's critique of imperialism remains aimed at home: that is, she locates the horrors of empire on the domestic shores of England, not abroad, in the actual sites of British colonial rule, sites which, as noted above, only enter the novel as asides, be it in the reference to Gwendolen's family fortune coming from West Indian plantations, or in the scattered remarks about the Jamaica Uprising in 1865. At once, this is both a traditional novelistic trope inherited from Austen and Charlotte Brontë, among others, and a more significant indication of a radically altered state of affairs.[68] Whereas such references to the colonies never fundamentally affected the cohesiveness of these earlier narratives, in *Daniel Deronda* these "foreign" realities have come to disrupt the representation of the national domestic sphere. Moreover, they delineate the boundaries of the narrative's conception of shared history, insofar as *Daniel Deronda* cannot yet imagine that the shared history it hopes to crystallize through Deronda's project also includes these actual sites of colonial rule and their peoples.

The split which Eliot's narrative embodies registers this changed state of affairs—of the increasing interpenetration of the foreign and the domestic, of the move toward a more global economy that imperialism represents—in which a national narrative is no longer cohesive. Thus while Eliot's neat lining up of paternity, race, and nationality in the final coupling of Mirah and Deronda promises to master the excess that is imperialism, the nationalism she invokes to do so is already only the marker for a loss, the loss of an organic community that is itself a product of the permanent structural imbalance that is capitalism and its means of expansion, imperialism.

In this respect it may be most useful to think of *Daniel Deronda* in a Brechtian sense, reading its antagonistic plots and its only provisionally resolved tensions—Gwendolen, after all, is never absorbed completely within the narrative unlike Dorothea in *Middlemarch* or Esther in *Felix Holt*—as its most radical content. Perhaps, then, it is this structural antagonism itself, the antagonism that Leavis would cut away, that is the novel's strength. For as Slavoj Žižek warns in his discussion of the resurgent nationalism emerging in Eastern Europe in the 1990s and continuing today, the danger at this historical juncture is not one of feeling too alienated but rather of not feeling alienated enough.[69]

PART III

Itineraries of the Utopian

....

As we saw with the late *Bildungsroman*, an increasingly global world order found its way into the Victorian novel via the spatial histories of colonialism, imperial markets, and a cosmopolitanism that came more and more to define the modern British subject. This imperial history was fueled by an international division of labor that carved up the world much as the system of capitalism divided its individual subjects into so many "hands." At its heart lay the idea that labor was by definition abstract.

In contrast, the narratives of utopia forming this last section cull the potential in a living labor freed from the dictates of commodity logic, a notion of labor, that is, that can never be fully reduced to mere abstract labor and as such always maintains traces of resistance to full subsumption by capital. In so doing, these narratives not only return us to the residue of unredeemed experience latent in realism but also give us different tools with which to apprehend that experience. By imagining an as-yet impossible future, they paradoxically unsettle the past, thereby opening up the possibility for recouping the present.

A number of factors specific to the utopian narrative and its history make my discussion here slightly different from that in previous sections. First of all, unlike the industrial novel and the *Bildungsroman*, the utopian narrative is not a distinctly nineteenth-century generic form. As is generally known, Thomas More's *Utopia*, written in 1516, unwittingly named and inaugurated the genre. Additionally, the utopian genre has long outlasted the nineteenth century. As a result, my interest in the utopian narrative rests less in making a case about the historical specificity of the genre to representations of labor in the nineteenth century than in looking at two versions of the genre which directly engage the very problems of representation figured in the realist texts considered so far. Bringing to this representational bind a different form of problem solving altogether, the utopian narrative, I want to suggest, enables different "solutions" to the problems which coalesce around industrial labor, modern pleasure, and narrative representation. In the process, the conventions of realism (but not its cognitive project, an issue to which I will return) are up-ended.

Narratives of utopia begin, in a sense, where realism left off, by assuming the malleability of the social order created by those texts.[1] More accurately, in keeping with the increasing urgency within a global economy to think spatially, utopian narratives construct alternative itineraries that challenge the organization of space within realism. The notion of an itinerary as opposed to a map, drawn from the historian Paul Carter's analysis of Britain's colonization of Australia, is meant to emphasize the way in which these utopian narratives focus on the processes of social organization rather than their end result.[2] In other words, they trace journeys (rather than producing finished maps) which implicitly value the traveling over the getting there. These itinerant histories have at once a critical and a generative component. On the one hand, they produce the conditions that define realism's "reality"; and in the act of producing these conditions, of drawing attention to the act of their "making," their mutability is affirmed. On the other hand, they also contain the means for future, potentially alternative "productions." In other words, they partake not only in ideology critique but also in the formation of a utopian counterproject. This last creative move rewrites the terms of realism vis-à-vis labor and pleasure almost as if retrospectively, not by reinventing them but rather by reinvesting them with a different future. Narratives of utopia thus complete the genealogy of the labor novel, but not in the usual sense of marking its end. Instead, they parse from its roots (to borrow one of Carter's metaphors) alternate routes. Where the industrial novel starts from the premise that labor is by nature abstract and alienated—and hence pleasure something to be found only outside of labor—the narratives of utopia examined here begin by questioning this premise and the divisions it entails. They resolutely insist on the intimate relationship between labor and pleasure and the utopian possibilities therein. As such, they constitute a "counterculture of modernity."[3]

In the following two chapters, I examine two different but nevertheless related articulations of such a counterculture in the utopian thought of William Morris and Oscar Wilde. I argue that both Morris and Wilde locate the deep structure or determinate conditions underlying the industrial novel's and the *Bildungsroman*'s representations of labor and pleasure. In his theories of labor and in his utopian romance *News from Nowhere*, William Morris examines the capitalist division of labor and the consequent social divisions that arise from it and identifies in these divisions the basis for the separation of labor from pleasure. Wilde's fictional and nonfictional writings, including *The Picture of Dorian Gray*, recognize the utter reliance of current social relations on the capitalist system of private property and illustrate that it is only "under socialism," once private property has been abolished, that new forms of sociality, including new forms of pleasure, will be made available. In both cases, capital and its relations of production lie at the heart of their respective critiques as well as forming the basis of their divergent utopias. This may be easier to see in Morris because he focuses so centrally on the issue of work but it is no less operative in Wilde despite appearances. If anything, the fact that Wilde has been read so univocally as speaking only to matters of pleasure says more about the cultural hold the division of labor (and pleasure) has on us than it does about Wilde's work itself.

All utopias, to paraphrase Ernst Bloch, are both of their time and new to their time.[4] As will become clear in the individual readings, I have given far less notice to the limitations of either Morris's or Wilde's utopias, to the ways in which, of necessity, they are bound by their own historical moment, and far more attention to what I see to be the potential "newness" they articulate. It should go without saying, however, that such limitations do exist. In the case of Morris, problems arise particularly around his treatment of gender and sexuality. With Wilde, the question of class is always a troubling one. Nonetheless, my aim in emphasizing the potentially radical aspects of their thought is to show that these limitations do not have to hinder our own use of these texts. In other words, despite their ideological constraints, they are still available for, and indeed promote, wholly "other" future projects. Less blueprints than signs of life, they register the existence of a living labor not fully appropriated by capital and hence open to other possible forms of valuation and other models of pleasure.

The possibilities thus engendered are hardly utopian in the pejorative sense of impossibly ideal or, even worse, hopelessly naive. Instead, they project a future world (or the possibilities of one) that is radically different from the present but not severed completely from it.[5] They are simultaneously of the present and the future, their tense conditional, both in terms of their orientation toward the future and in their laying out of the conditions of possibility for the present. Far from being part of all narratives of utopia, this fully conditional stance (especially with respect to the means whereby one gets to the future) is consonant with the specific nature of Morris's and Wilde's projects. Both of them are writing within the context of a newly emergent socialist movement that was committed to changing the present order through direct social action. While Morris was directly involved in the creation and development of socialism in England as the head of the Socialist League (a splinter group of the Social Democratic Federation, founded by H. M. Hyndman in 1883), Wilde was, as I will argue, a fellow traveler. My hope in resituating Wilde within this context, while simultaneously redefining that context by arguing for a richer understanding of Morris's own utopianism, is to make both of these writers newly useful—in the sense Oscar Wilde gives to this term. Taking to heart what I will show to be Wilde's challenge to establish a radically different, nonutilitarian notion of "use" as pleasure, I have tried to make similar use of these utopias. This is finally as much an exercise in a different kind of reading as it is a different reading of Morris and Wilde, given the present fate of the utopian within fully unfolded commodity production.

CHAPTER 4

WILLIAM MORRIS
AND A PEOPLE'S ART

....

Reimagining the Pleasures

of Labor

The mass of society is made up of morbid thinkers, and miserable workers. Now it is only by labour that thought can be made healthy, and only by thought that labour can be made happy, and the two cannot be separated with impunity. — John Ruskin, *The Stones of Venice*

We need the most powerful telescope, that of polished utopian consciousness, in order to penetrate precisely the nearest nearness. — Ernst Bloch, *The Principle of Hope*

The same year that George Eliot published *Daniel Deronda*, William Morris completed one of his many freely rendered Icelandic sagas, *Sigurd the Volsung*. On the face of it, these two works seem to have nothing in common: the first takes us to the heart of the British Empire in the 1870s with both its literal and figural dislocations and fragmentation, while the second returns us to the heroic age of twelfth-century Iceland—a time, for Morris, epitomized by the fullness and wholeness of an integrated, nonalienated life. In terms of literary historiography, *Daniel Deronda* and 1876 mark the end of the road for Eliot, whereas a good case can be made that it was the Icelandic sagas that helped get Morris on the road—to socialism and to the kind of critical realism which I will argue defines his best work.[1] But Eliot and Morris do have something in common: both are social critics of modernity, seeking some form of cultural regeneration. In their different ways—whether in the more obvious differences of genre, literary sensibility, and plain old politics or in the subtler nuances of tone and temperament—each was responding to what she/he saw as the disruptive effects of industrialism and modernity: the destruction of the traditional fabric of rural communities and the decline of a shared context of communicable experience. If, in the search for a vital community, Eliot finds Zionism and, in it, the seeming possibility for a new cultural nationalism, in Morris the hope of a new type of free collective comes from a variety of sources—Gothic architecture, Icelandic sagas, socialist theory, and social action—and finds its full expression in the principles of revolutionary international socialism.

Perhaps this difference alone—on the one hand, a revitalized notion of cultural nationalism, on the other hand, revolutionary internationalism—goes some distance toward explaining why Eliot has maintained a central place in the literary canon while discussions of Morris, unlike those of, say, Carlyle or Ruskin or Arnold, have been limited by and large to more specialized sub-areas of literary interest, such as utopian or science fiction literature. Doubtless this difference reflects a break along literary-historical lines and the politics of canon formation, with Arnoldian notions of an elevated bourgeois culture separate from and unsullied by politics qua politics marking the divide. At a time, too, when many are wary of older political blueprints for community, yet simultaneously desirous of community, the kind of ethnic or social partiality which Eliot offers seems to speak to these contradictory impulses. Certainly, given the current political climate in which we are witnessing the proliferation of new nationalisms and neoracism, along with the extension of American economic influence through NAFTA and other international trade agreements (brokered by the IMF, the World Bank, the WTO, etc.), all part of the so-called defeat of communism and the end of the cold war, it should come as no great surprise that William Morris, socialist agitator extraordinaire (and a whole lot more besides), is not part of the dialogue.[2]

Even when William Morris is the focus of critical attention, the nature of that attention tends to be fairly limiting. Often his work and his writings are used almost instrumentally for the purposes of one or another debate, the context of which is other than or outside the focus of William Morris himself. The most well-known of such debates is of course that between Perry Anderson and E. P. Thompson, in which William Morris figures as one chapter in the history of arguments within English Marxism—the specifics of which I will return to later. Another perspective would have it that Morris's politics, (mis)construed as essentially quasi-Luddite in orientation, argued anachronistically for the end of machine production and so surely are no longer of interest to twenty-first-century critics squarely situated amid the spectacular hi-tech hard (and soft) ware of the postmodern. Finally, and perhaps most troubling, is a third view which does not even use Morris opportunistically to score forensic points: he has simply been forgotten altogether (save perhaps as a favored designer of wallpapers and fabrics in contemporary yuppie culture).[3] I will argue in the present chapter that what these various positions share is a lack of real engagement with how Morris experienced, thought, and theorized about work.[4] Understanding the significance of his concept of work will explain how labor functions for Morris as the foundation of all social relations and hence the basis of an emancipatory politics, and why much of his theory has lost none of its relevance or its radicalness today. It will go a long way as well toward explaining why Morris has been historically reconfigured or forgotten in the particular ways he has.

Art Is the Expression of Pleasure in Labor

The sheer variety of Morris's work and pleasures testifies to a different kind of intellectual and a different kind of intellectual *space* than that of the compartmentalized, specialized habitus in which, for the most part, contemporary intellectuals think and live. Throughout his life, Morris worked as a printer, painter, decorator, designer, architect, prose romance writer, socialist agitator, translator and writer of Icelandic sagas, and utopian thinker. The most telling difference to which this long list of accomplishments speaks is its combination of mental and manual labors. Its mix of activities and media are reminiscent of Marx's description of the individual in communist society, hunting in the morning, fishing in the afternoon, rearing cattle in the evening, and criticizing after dinner, complete with the important proviso that all these activities can be done "without ever becoming hunter, fisherman, a shepherd, or critic."[5] Edward Carpenter remarked once that "it was very characteristic of Morris that his chief recreation was only another kind of work."[6] Morris himself, working at Merton Abbey workshop dyeing and weaving, was known to challenge, "if a chap can't compose an epic poem while he's weaving a tapestry, he'll never do any good at all."[7]

Perhaps the fullest picture of just how eclectic Morris's unusual mix of talents and energies was comes from Morris's son-in-law, Halliday Sparling, on witnessing Morris at work:

> He would be standing at an easel or sitting with a sketchbook in front of him, charcoal, brush, or pencil in hand, and all the while would be grumbling Homer's Greek under his breath . . . the design coming through in clear unhesitating strokes. Then the note of the grumbling changed, for the turn of the English had come. He was translating the *Odyssey* at this time and he would prowl about the room, filling and lighting his pipe, halting to add a touch or two at one or other easel, still grumbling, go to his writing-table, snatch up his pen, and write furiously for a while—twenty, fifty, and one hundred or more lines, as the case might be . . . the speed of his hand would gradually slacken, his eye would wander to an easel, a sketch-block, or to some one of the manuscripts in progress, and that would have its turn. There was something well-nigh terrifying to a youthful onlooker in the deliberate ease with which he interchanged so many forms of creative work, taking up each one exactly at the point at which he had laid it aside, and never halting to recapture the thread of his thought.[8]

What all these anecdotal remarks point to is a fundamentally different *everyday* relationship to labor, one radically opposed to the organization of labor in the processes of capitalist production. The key to this difference is the division of labor itself.

In large part, many of Morris's attitudes and beliefs about the detrimental effects arising from the capitalist division of labor initially were developed not from within the Marxian tradition but in the context of his English predecessors, Thomas Carlyle and John Ruskin.[9] There are strong and obvious affinities, for instance, between Morris's constant emphasis on the value of work as something more than purely wage labor and Carlyle's argument about labor in *Past and Present*.[10] It is Carlyle, after all, who locates labor as the root of all life.[11] Moreover, his polemic against the demagoguery of the cash nexus provided grist for Morris's attacks on the array of displaced values—from the privileging of mental over manual labor to the false separation of "major" from "minor" arts—accrued under the capitalist system of production. Drawing liberally on Carlyle, and in common cause with Marx, Morris also ultimately saw the division of labor in terms of the compartmentalization of individual men and women. As Marx writes in *Capital*, "not only is the specialized work distributed among the different individuals, but the individual himself is divided up, and transformed into the automatic motor of a detail operation, thus realizing the absurd fate of Menenius Agrippa, which presents man as a mere fragment of his own body."[12] This equation allows for the kind of critical move largely lacking in the industrial novels and *Bildungsromane* discussed in earlier chapters: the drawing of a concrete relationship between the mode of production and the relations of production, a relationship that then becomes consolidated at a social level. Within such a formulation, labor is firmly established as the basis of the social processes of valorization. At the same time, it is precisely the manner in which labor is socialized under capitalism that produces alienation—at both the individual and social level. What has disappeared from the specific processes of socialization under capitalism and what Morris spent his life theorizing and practicing, as the above anecdotes attest, is the enjoyment of labor.

Here, especially, the influence of John Ruskin is clear. Ruskin's dictum "there is no wealth but life," coupled with his emphasis on creative satisfaction in labor, further inspired Morris's belief in the existence of creativity and enjoyment latent in labor yet all but destroyed by the capitalist division of labor given its development toward increasing mechanization and the alienation of workers from their labor and its fruits. In particular, Ruskin's writings on the nature of Gothic in *The Stones of Venice* offered not only an implicit critique of present-day conditions of labor but helped Morris elaborate a vision of another kind of noncapitalist labor, one in sharp contrast to the present in terms both of the *mode* of production and the *social relations* of production.[13]

But Carlyle and Ruskin remain essentially negative critics: soothsayers of the doom of present-day civilization, yet unable to harness their hatred of that civilization to existing social forces of resistance. While it would be far-fetched to draw any hard and fast relationship between this kind of critical hatred of society bereft of any concrete social outlet and the strange personal and political quirks that beset both Carlyle and Ruskin, it is irresistibly tempting to see these thinkers' respective withdrawals into isolated eccentricity—whether the strange political peculiarities of Carlyle's vitriol as he grew older, or the badly seasoned sexual politics of something like Ruskin's "Sesame and Lilies"—as symptomatic of an increasingly distanced retreat from social reality.[14] In any case, part of Morris's originality is his ability to step into the gap created by these social critics' inability to move from the theoretical (and visceral—in terms of their shared revulsion for and hatred of civilization) to the practical, and from the aura of a romantic anti-capitalism to an active struggle against capitalism and *for something*—in Morris's case, socialism. Labor, as I will argue, is the linchpin which holds together the elements of Morris's critical/political complex: his critique of so-called civilization, his artisanry, his love of beauty, his belief in an alternative culture to that of bourgeois culture, and his hope in socialism. Labor, far from just industrial toil, is, for Morris, culturally formative; it constitutes the basis of sociality.[15]

The concept of labor as constructive informs almost all of Morris's work, from his poetry to his prose to his work with the Anti-Scrape (Society for the Protection of Ancient Buildings). Yet the clearest articulation of his views on labor are found in his political writings and speeches, initially written or delivered for the Social Democratic Federation (SDF) and later, in *Commonweal*, under the banner of the Socialist League.[16] Interestingly, both George Bernard Shaw, writing at the end of the nineteenth century just after Morris's death, and Raymond Williams, writing almost a century later, support a change of emphasis with respect to a critical assessment of Morris, away from the prose and verse romances toward these smaller political writings. Although I have chosen to focus on these writings as opposed to his romances, I do so less from a direct endorsement of such a shift and more because this approach is most revelatory of the ways in which Morris attempts to redefine labor, and with it pleasure.[17] My interest in Morris's contribution is twofold: to identify how Morris works to reunite labor with pleasure and to show how this reunion speaks to contemporary divisions both within the Marxist problematic and between Marxism and feminism.

....

In "Useful Work versus Useless Toil" (1884) Morris sets forth his vision of the reasonable conditions of labor. An important aspect of the piece is its disputation of liberal, laissez-faire ideology, what Morris terms "the semi-theological dogma that all labour, under any circumstances, is a blessing to the labourer."[18] Rather, for Morris, such an uncritical valorization of labor, regardless of the conditions of its existence, perverts work. Instead, he counters a blind advocacy of labor at any cost with the notion that "labor is good when due hope of rest and pleasure accompanies it" (*U* 107); a straightforward notion on the face of it, but one which carries a remarkable dialectical complexity within its disarming simplicity.

"Useful Work versus Useless Toil" exemplifies Morris's rhetorical style and powers of storytelling. Always, he moves easily from premise to premise, in simple language and format, yet continually invokes an active participation on the part of his listeners or readers. The essay is framed by the simplest of pleas: "But think, I beseech you, of the product of England, the workshop of the world, and will you not be bewildered, as I am, at the thought of the mass of things which no sane man could desire, but which our useless toil makes—and sells?" (*U* 92). Characteristically, the thought here moves from the product or result of current economic conditions—in this case, a prescient image of the proliferation of commodity aesthetics— toward its cause, with Morris encouraging the reader to see the kinds of connections and relations the logic of capital attempts to mask: the move from appearance to structure, from product and distribution/circulation to the act of labor and the process of production. In other words, his elaboration of these connections works toward making visible the abstract logic of commodity production and of the abstraction of labor-power itself, thereby reestablishing, by linking, the obscured connections between workplace and marketplace.

Morris investigates his framing question through a series of conjectures and observations. To begin with, he sets up what he sees as two interrelated premises to be granted: (1) the race of man must either labor or perish and (2) the compulsion to labor should be compensated in the form of pleasure (just as, the logic goes, nature compensates us for other acts necessary to the continuance of existence). Given that most laborers find little pleasure in their labor, it must follow that there are two kinds of work—one good, the other bad—with the difference between them resting on whether hope resides in the work or whether it is simply useless toil, Morris's coinage for unproductive labor and a crucial element of the Morrisian vocabulary.

Unproductive labor for Morris is work that produces wares that are not worth having and that no one needs. Both of these criteria are as slippery in their operation as they sound in their definition. But rather than seeing this as a weakness, I think it points to one of Morris's greater strengths: his understanding of the complexity of the notion of needs. In terms of his representation of what one needs and how those needs come to be defined, Morris tends to paint in fairly broad brush strokes. At one point, he says of the overcoming of present waste (by making labor fruitful: "to be used for the good of all alike") and the concomitant elevation of the meeting of needs over profit, "We shall no longer be hurried and driven by the fear of starvation, which at present presses no less on the greater part of men in civilized communities than it does on mere savages. The first and most obvious necessities will be so easily provided for in a community in which there is no waste of labor, that we shall have time to look round and consider what we really do want, that can be obtained without over-taxing our energies; for the often expressed fear of mere idleness falling upon us when the force supplied by the present hierarchy of compulsion is withdrawn, is a fear which is but generated by the burden of excessive and repulsive labour, which we most of us have to bear at present" (*U* 99). Later, he reiterates that "as people freed from the daily terror of starvation find out what they really wanted, being no longer compelled by anything but their own needs, they would refuse to produce the mere inanities which are now called luxuries, or the poison and trash now called cheap wares" (*U* 106). Needs are thus inextricably related to reasonable use, in direct opposition to waste. Yet, simultaneously, needs, like the notion of reasonable use, are ambiguous in that they only become meaningful in a communal context and hence are always themselves socially mediated rather than transparent, historically and culturally contingent rather than universal. To be sure, Morris grants some basic needs, namely, those that would eliminate anxiety as to mere subsistence. But aside from food, clothing, and housing he never dictates what people should want or do want, beyond trying to provide a glimpse of the kinds of social and political considerations that at least could begin to be addressed in a society organized on the basis of need. In other words, he maps the broad contours of an alternative culture and the political and economic conditions that could make such a culture possible.[19]

"Wealth" is one of the keywords with which Morris turns present valuations of use and need upside down. If waste is the causeless destruction of raw material and the diverting of labor from useful production, "Wealth is what Nature gives us and what a reasonable man can make out of the gifts of Nature for his reasonable use. The sunlight, the fresh air, the unspoiled face of the earth, food, raiment and housing necessary and decent; the storing up of knowledge of all kinds, and the power of disseminating it; means of free communication between man and man; works of art, the beauty which man creates when he is most a man, most aspiring and thoughtful — all things which serve the pleasure of people, free, manly and uncorrupted. This is wealth. Nor can I think of anything worth having which does not come under one or other of these heads" (*U* 91).[20] Here and elsewhere Morris resists falling into an overly simplified notion of the certainty of needs as opposed to wants or desires.[21] While he will acknowledge that the current system breeds desires that cannot be satisfied by that system, he is careful not to counter this recognition with a blithe slip in the other direction, into an overly reductive, functional account of need and use value. Instead, he provides a "pair of scales" in which to measure the worthiness of work done in the world. These consist of three kinds of hope, which, when present, make work worth doing: hope of rest, hope of product, and hope of pleasure in the work itself. The realization of these apparently innocuous hopes promises more than merely a change in economic relations; it reverses the entire order of the present state of things, from art to culture to the basis of human existence.

Morris starts with the simple observation that by all appearances work done in civilization is portioned out unequally among different classes of society. Indeed, on examination, it is clear that the state is composed of three classes of people: (1) a class of people who do no work and do not even pretend to work (i.e., the aristocracy); (2) a class which works but which produces nothing (the middle class); and (3) a class which works ceaselessly, compelled by the other two classes to do work which is often unproductive (the working class). This third point, especially, begins to formulate a response to the question of how the workshop of the world has developed to the point where, in the name of progress and civilization, it flaunts the useless production of shoddy wares. Morris emphasizes here the way in which a class system necessarily generates inferior goods for the inferior class of workers (a "real inferiority, mind you" Morris stresses, "involving a degradation both of mind and body" [*U* 91]): "For if many men live without producing, nay, must live lives so empty and foolish that they *force* a great part of the workers to produce wares which no one needs, not even the rich, it follows that most men must be poor; and, living as they do on wages from those whom they support, cannot get for their use the *goods* which men naturally desire, but must put up with miserable makeshifts for them, with coarse food that does not nourish, with rotten raiment which does not shelter, with wretched houses" (*U* 92). Much like later critics in the Frankfurt School tradition, particularly Herbert Marcuse, he goes on to suggest that such a result is wildly incommensurate with the victory over the forces of nature and the respective development of productive capabilities more than sufficient for the elimination of all material need and poverty.[22] In short, he asks how this can be "progress."

Although the lack of these necessities betokens the perversion of values in the present social order, the attainment of them is still only the ground on which to cultivate a future society. Far from the mechanical economic determinism of the Second International or the asceticism of a more doctrinaire utilitarian outlook, and unlike even other socialists of Morris's day, the meeting of only the first and second of his criteria—hope of rest and hope of product—would by themselves not be enough: "Some Socialists might say we need not go any further than this; it is enough that the worker should get the full produce of his work, and that his rest should be abundant. But though the compulsion of man's tyranny is thus abolished, I yet demand compensation for the compulsion of Nature's necessity. As long as the work is repulsive it will still be a burden which must be taken up daily, and even so would mar our life, even though the hours of labour were short" (*U* 95). Pleasure is thus never secondary but always of equal importance, if not foremost: the goal is to "add to our wealth without diminishing our pleasure" (*U* 95); to make labor in all its expanded capacities and potentialities attractive and pleasant. Morris's stance is therefore resolutely anti-ascetic. Ornament, sensual pleasures, enjoyment, sex even (!) are all inseparable from a free and full life.[23] Indeed, in "The Society of the Future" he calls directly for the extinction of asceticism: "I demand a free and unfettered animal life for man first of all . . . If we feel the least degradation in being amorous, or merry, or hungry, or sleepy, we are so far bad animals, and therefore miserable men. And you know civilization *does* bid us to be ashamed of all these moods and deeds, and as far as she can, begs us to conceal them, and where possible to get other people to do them for us."[24] Not only does such an attitude reflect the joy and pleasure which infuse Morris's notion of something being useful but it also suggests how his schema of labor is central in reconciling the opposition between individual happiness and social organization rather than domiciling each to their respective spheres of private and public. It is the opposition between these spheres that will form the basis of Morris's understanding of alienation, which I will return to shortly.

The working toward an alternative vision of useful, pleasurable labor involves a number of basic pragmatic changes in the present system, each of which would work toward the fulfillment of the hopes constituting worthy work. First is the demand for shorter work hours and days. The shortening of compulsory work hours would allow for the concomitant building up of the "ornamental part of life": "its pleasures, bodily and mental, scientific and artistic, social and individual—on the basis of work undertaken willingly and cheerfully, with the consciousness of benefiting ourselves and our neighbors by it" (*U* 100). Second is support for a variety of work, both mental and physical, the immediate goal of which would include a restructuring of current forms of education away from commercial education ("At present all education is directed towards the end of fitting people to take their places in the hierarchy of commerce") toward what Morris terms "due" education, which "concerns itself in finding out what different people are fit for, and helping them along the road which they are inclined to take"

(U 101).[25] Third, and perhaps most radical from our present standpoint, is the necessity of pleasant surroundings in which to work. Musing on what even factories could be like in the society of the future, Morris projects that they "might be centres of intellectual activity also, and work in them might well be varied very much: the tending of the necessary machinery might to each individual be but a short part of the day's work" (U 103). To be sure, Morris was well aware of just how impossible a conjecture such as this would appear to his audience given current factory conditions. Nonetheless, for this reason it is signature Morris: the sheer impossibility of any hope of variety or intellectual activity being part of factory work registers the sharp disjuncture between present work conditions and reasonable conditions of labor, which would provide hope of rest, product, and pleasure.

Each of these elements exists in an interdependent relationship, the whole of which comprises Morris's notion of useful work. Taken together, they constitute a structural transformation of the entire environment of daily living. In order to provide hope of rest, the apportionment of work must be altered, since, under current conditions, the working class (used most literally by Morris in contrast to the nonworking classes of the aristocracy and the middle class) not only must support itself but the other two classes who consume in great quantities but produce nothing. Similarly, in order to guarantee hope of product—the production of goods that people want and actually can use—the whole system of production (and with it, class relations) would have to be radically restructured, with productive priorities shifted from profit to use. Finally, in order for hope of pleasure to be possible, not only must hope of product and hope of rest be present but *conscious* effort must be directed toward making labor attractive. This triad of social relations is in essence materially conditioned, historically circumscribed, and above all, radically relational.

A Morris for Our Times

In this light, Morris's turn toward medievalism as an antidote to the empty, profit-driven utilitarian values of his day and a repository of an art that in its form embodied a counterforce to the prevailing commercialism of Victorian England takes on a different hue. Rather than a desired "return" to a simpler "golden age," Morris instead harks back to what he sees as a radically different relationship to work (in Gothic architecture primarily) not as a way of evading present relations of labor and production but rather, as Vincent Geoghegan has stated, with "[full awareness] of the ideological advantage to be gained in showing that free labor had existed historically."[26] Like the pair of scales used to weigh the value of work, the return to the past provides a glimpse of another way of being in a world in which art has not yet been destroyed. The past therefore functions on two fronts: it serves as a hermeneutic aid to those so tainted by the present that they can imagine no outside or no other to it and, at the same time, it jars the memory of the loss of that other—specifically the memory of living labor, of a labor which respects the integrity of the object and its producer.[27] In medieval handicraftsmen and day laborers, that is to say, Morris discovered the foundations of a materialist and utopian approach to technological development and the instruments of production.

Two different types of medievalism are to be distinguished, then. The first, like the architecture of many American campuses, simply mimics the Gothic *style*. The second, Morris's type, is concerned wholly with "the *manner* of work" which could produce the Gothic, with the actual "handling of materials by the medieval builder and craftsman" and the social relations making such work possible.[28] Hence Morris's appropriation of Gothic emphasizes substance and structure rather than merely style, with the goal of showing how aesthetics and ethics, culture and work are intimately connected, indeed dialectically related, to one another. In "Art and Socialism" Morris describes this relationship in terms of a balancing of gains against loss.[29] As he elaborates, the so-called gains of the present society, light and freedom, themselves past images of emancipation, have been bought at too high a price, the price being the loss of pleasure in daily work. "We gave up Art," Morris regrets, "for what we thought was light and freedom, but it was less than light and freedom which we bought . . . to the most of men the light showed them that they need look for hope no more, and the freedom left the most of men free—to take at a wretched wage what slave's work lay nearest to them or starve" (*A* 121). The comforts and prosperity of the middle classes have been paid for with the death of art; past monuments of art decry the baleful sacrifice that has been made.

At the same time, the mere fact that these monuments live on testifies to the persistence of the past in the present. They stand as traces of a utopian impulse in the form of congealed labor power: a labor power that had not yet forgotten pleasure, that had not yet discovered "that fancy, imagination, sentiment, the joy of creation and the hope of fair fame are marketable articles too precious to be allowed to men who have not the money to buy them, to mere handicraftsmen and day laborers" (*A* 120). Toward the reawakening of such an "anticipatory memory" Morris summons his listeners:

"Let us call to mind that there yet remain monuments in the world which show us that all human labor was not always a grief and a burden to men. Let us think of the mighty and lovely architecture, for instance, of medieval Europe . . . Let us remember there was a time when men had pleasure in their daily work, but yet as to other matters hoped for light and freedom as they do now" (*A* 120).

The massive scale and correspondingly broader social context of architecture in particular highlights the interrelationship between aesthetics and ethics. Architecture, as Northrop Frye outlines, "cannot be separated from its own larger social context in, say, town planning, and so, eventually, of social planning as a whole . . . The real context of social planning, then, is a society in which work has been defined as creative act, and thereby becomes the energy by which an intelligent being expresses his intelligence."[30] Again, work as creative act unravels yet another opposition constituting the bourgeois public sphere: the opposition between work and leisure. Under Morris's expanded notion of labor, work "cannot be separated from leisure and can exist only in a society in which there is no longer a leisure class with another class of exploited workers supporting them."[31] For as long as the exploitation of one class by another exists, there can be no labor that is both productive of useful goods and of itself pleasant to do. In short, the present system of production cannot operate without the division of society into classes, a division that in turn leads to the production of inferior goods and sham wealth or luxury, "the supplanter, the changeling of Art" (*A* 113). The reverse of this, a glimpse of which resides in the Gothic cathedral, is the "splendid aspiration for the total union of structure and decoration, of sculpture, painting and the applied arts," what Eric Hobsbawm refers to as the "visual equivalent of Wagner's *Gesamtkunstwerk*."[32]

Just as architecture inscribes the traces of a lost history of aspiration, popular art makes palpable the labor of noncommodified bodies, serving as a "living witness of the existence of deft hands and eager minds," of "an art made intelligently by the whole body of those who live by their labour."[33] Crucial to Morris's project as a socialist is thus to convey how the loss of popular art and with it the sense of beauty is a baneful rather than a trivial thing. It is, consequently, not merely a question of whether the claim for the refunctioning of labor as pleasure is desirable but that it is indeed *necessary*: "unless we try our utmost to satisfy it, we are but part and parcel of a society founded on robbery and injustice, condemned by the laws of the universe to destroy itself by its own efforts to exist for ever" (*A* 129). There is no real escape, then, no real possibility of ensconcing oneself in a protected enclave or subculture safe from the ravages of commercialism; the (desire for the) making of such a subculture of the elite or its artistic equivalent, the "fine arts," shapes and is in turn shaped by the system of commercial war and waste. Popular art, given its bases of production—the offering of pleasure and hope to the workman—simply cannot live under the full development of competitive commerce. In order to allow for the creation of an art common to the whole people, the class system must be abolished and society in its entirety re-formed: "under the present system of labour, our work is wasted and our rest is spoilt; and why? Because it is a system of war, and therefore necessarily of waste; the parts of the system dovetail into one another, so that no one can escape from the conflict: nation competes against nation, class against class, individual against individual; each of these wars sustains the other and each has its own peculiar waste; only as it is with other war so it is with war commercial, that it is the common soldier that pays for all, in the long run."[34]

As this set of dialectical relationships suggests, Morris's aesthetics continually challenges traditional institutions of culture. Institutionalized art, he argues, maintains art (and culture, more generally) in such a way that it appears to be separate from and unrelated to the social processes which constitute it, and in turn are constitutive of it. The divorce between art and daily life is merely symptomatic of a general state of alienation—one in a series of separations and dislocations. Alienation for Morris thus operates on a number of different levels: at one level, it is the forgetting of these fractures, an unconsciousness of what has been lost: "Grievous indeed it was, that we could not keep both our hands full, that we were forced to spill from one while we gathered with the other: yet to my mind it is more grievous still to be unconscious of the loss; or being dimly conscious of it to have to force ourselves to forget it and to cry out that all is well" (*A* 121).[35] But it is also, at a more physical, sensual level, the broken link between art and daily life, between the intellectual and the decorative arts; the separation of labor from its product and of the different parts of the body and even its emotions from one another; the mundane fact that when one walks around an art exhibit "pedagogic" plaques accompany each piece in order to establish meaning between an audience and an art irreparably severed from one another.[36]

Morris's aesthetics, proffering its vision of a unified, integrated past, would seem to run the risk of degenerating into pure nostalgia. Most often, charges of nostalgia made against Morris focus on his treatment of machinery and what place, if any, it would or could have in his future society. A classic misreading of the mechanics of his return to the past assumes that by dint of Morris's pastoral medievalism, he was a staunch, curmudgeonly opponent of all machinery and, therefore, dismissively antimodern. Any number of direct comments by Morris about technology, however, militate against such a reading. In "How We Live and How We Might Live," for instance, Morris clarifies his stance on machinery: "I have spoken of machinery being used freely for releasing people from the more mechanical and repulsive part of necessary labor; and I know that to some cultivated people, people of the artistic turn of mind, machinery is particularly distasteful, and they will be apt to say you will never get your surroundings pleasant so long as you are surrounded by machinery. I don't quite admit that; it is the allowing machines to be our masters and not our servants that so injures the beauty of life nowadays."[37] This is hardly the voice of a machine-busting Luddite. Morris does go on to qualify his position:

> Yet for the consolation of the artists I will say that I believe indeed that a state of social order would probably lead at first to a great development of machinery for really useful purposes, because people will still be anxious about getting through the work necessary to holding society together; but that after a while they will find that there is not so much work to do as they expected, and that then they will have the leisure to reconsider the whole subject; and if it seems to them that a certain industry would be carried on more pleasantly as regards the worker, the more effectually as regards the goods, by using hand-work rather than machinery, they will certainly get rid of their machinery, because it will be possible for them to do so.

However, he makes clear that he does not believe even this kind of choice (as a viable aspect of social planning) is currently available: "It isn't possible now; we are not at liberty to do so; we are slaves to the monsters which we have created."[38] In other words, while Morris may see the limiting of machinery as an eventual (and desired) consequence of the reorganization of society along the basis of use rather than profit, his analysis of machinery belies any simplistic anti-technological stance. Or to look at the issue from its flip side, "when," as Raymond Williams remarks, "we stress, in Morris, the attachment to handicrafts, we are, in part, rationalizing an uneasiness generated by the scale and nature of his social criticism."[39]

Furthermore, it is important to place these statements in the context of a ruling bourgeois ideology that tended to confuse machines, as instruments of progress, with progress itself, mechanically equating progress with proliferating technology.[40] Thus, at issue was really a means/ends debate: were machines and the Mechanical Age teaching and practicing the great art of adapting means to ends, as Carlyle described the rule of utilitarian bourgeois values, or were machines, instead, a means to a particular end, the goal of which ought to be freely and collectively chosen, as Morris would have it?[41]

Yet, this said, the fact still remains: Morris does have an ambivalent relationship to new technologies and modern development, in short, to modernity. On the one hand, he sees the ways in which machinery can perform the more odious tasks of a modern society. On the other hand, he is unable to go much beyond this, to conceive, for instance, of new technologies actually opening up roads toward a new, collective democratic art form. In this light, the issue becomes whether his ambivalence so clouded his aesthetic and political judgment that (1) he consistently misread his own society's existent relations and (2) he is no longer useful today, given how far removed, technologically, modern society is from anything Morris could have imagined. As I want to argue, Morris's ambivalence should be read in much the same way that Walter Benjamin's reflections on the disintegration of aesthetic aura should be read: at times the operative sentiment is one of mourning what has been lost, but the sorrow this entails does not lead to a nostalgic political advocacy of lost social and cultural forms against modernity.[42] While Morris's optimism never reached quite the dialectical heights of Benjamin's (seeing the decline of aura and the subsequent development of film technology as a condition of possibility for a newly politicized art), he was enough of a historical dialectician to grant that no movement of history was an "unmixed evil": "Now to speak plainly it seems to me that the supremacy of Commerce (as we understand the word) is an evil, and a very serious one; and I should call it an unmixed evil—but for the strange continuity of life which runs through all historical events, and by means of which the very evils of such and such a period tend to abolish themselves" (*A* 109–10).

In terms of pinpointing the real problems with Morris's criticisms of his own society and their usefulness (or not) to us now, a number of approaches, other than the antimodernist one so frequently invoked, would seem to yield more productive results. The first problem involves the sense that Morris envisions the overcoming of capitalism as a move toward a re-unified social state; socialism is hence equated with the achievement of a seamless identity—of subject with object, producer with product, and so on. As I have suggested, however, by focusing on Morris's writings about work, we can use his framework to different ends than he does. The trio of hopes—of pleasure, product, and rest—which make work worth doing need not depend on some final unity. Instead, they can help us talk about needs in new ways. (In both these senses, as I develop in the following chapter, I see Oscar Wilde furthering Morris's project, precisely by imagining a coming to terms with separation—as opposed to a desired unity—positively.)[43] A second issue involves the particular Morris we have inherited. When Morris is remembered these days, it is in the context of the Arts and Crafts movement. But this is hardly the place to find the Morris politically useful for our own times. For as Fredric Jameson notes, the time for "deploy[ing] beauty as a political weapon," of beauty having a "subversive role in a society marred by nascent commodification," has long since passed, superseded by the absorption of all art and the image itself into commercial culture. "The image is the commodity today, and that is why it is vain to expect a negation of the logic of commodity production from it, that is why, finally, all beauty today is meretricious and the appeal to it by contemporary pseudo-aestheticism is an ideological manoeuvre and not a creative resource."[44] Instead, the Morris I am arguing we still need is the one who resolutely insists on imagining an intimate relationship between labor and pleasure; less important for the particular form his own aesthetics took than for its conditions of possibility, this Morris can help articulate a politics of collective struggle in which the preconditions of creative labor mark the divide between reform and revolution.

Now, to return to the comparison between Morris and Benjamin—a generative one, it seems to me, in terms of bringing Morris into our present: what Morris could not have foreseen and Benjamin experienced in his own lifetime was the extent and the enormity of alienation possible. Benjamin witnessed the destruction that Morris could hardly imagine: "mankind's self-alienation has reached such a degree that it can experience its own destruction as an aesthetic pleasure of the first order. This is the situation of politics which Fascism is rendering aesthetic."[45] But their respective responses to the degree of destruction and waste they each experienced share a deep affinity, as evidenced by Morris's call to reclaim a people's art and Benjamin's echoing of that with "Communism responds by *politicizing* art."[46]

Conversely, what Morris sustains and what is often lost in the Frankfurt tradition, is the always-present necessity of yoking the politicization of art to a mass politics. Morris's materialist aesthetics—which finds its more properly modern expression in the social theory and cultural reflections of the Frankfurt School—never loses sight of its connection to and realization in a quotidian politics.[47] The lineaments of this politics not only reveal the way in which Morris was able to marshal the concept of creative labor for political mobilization but also suggest how Morris might most fruitfully be situated within the larger map of left politics.

....

Within the field of Morris criticism, much debate has ensued over just how influential Morris's different sources were, with a good deal of the debate focusing on Morris's relationship to Marxism. At one extreme, E. P. Thompson is at pains to prove that Morris came to his ideas about labor, art, social revolution, and utopia via the *English* tradition, primarily that of Ruskin and Carlyle, with a dose of Thomas More and the early influence of the Romantics, especially Keats. At the other extreme, critics like Paul Meier spend a considerable amount of their biographical energies unearthing the means through which Morris ferreted out Marx's writings—sometimes long before they were publicly available in England—in order to show that the bulk of Morris's ideas came directly from Marx.[48] In my view, neither of these approaches is particularly fruitful. Instead, it seems more useful to pose the problem somewhat differently: to ask, instead, what Morris offers in his vision of creative labor and socialism that remains vital to the collective project of transforming capitalist economic and social relations, regardless of its originary or derivative status.

The beginnings of an answer can be found in Morris's own description of how he became a socialist. The history of his conversion, as he details it, involves the translation of an ideal into a belief in its *practical* fulfillment:

> the study of history and the love and practice of art forced me into a hatred of civilization which, if things were to stop as they are, would turn history into inconsequent nonsense, and make art a collection of the curiosities of the past, which would have no serious relation to the life of the present.
>
> But the consciousness of revolution stirring amidst our hateful modern society prevented me, luckier than many others of artistic perceptions, from crystallizing into a mere railer against "progress" on the one hand, and on the other from wasting time and energy in any of the numerous schemes by which the quasi-artistic of the middle classes hope to make art grow when it has no longer any root, and thus I became a practical Socialist.[49]

In all his endeavors, whether those with the Firm, or the SDF, or the Kelmscott Press, he maintains the indispensability of the utopian to the quotidian and vice versa, never seeming to lose what Perry Anderson refers to as the "*popular* texture" of his work.[50]

Before Morris was always the sense that he was involved in the project of "making Socialists," a process which he saw to be dialogic by its nature. He understood his role not so much as providing utopian blueprints for the future but rather as sparking the desire for any kind of utopia at all. On the one hand, this distinction operates in much the same way as Morris's medievalism: it reflects the importance of projecting a picture of something different, of a different state of social relations which by its mere existence — even if only initially in the realm of dream or fantasy — operates as a forceful polemic against those who would argue for the historical ubiquity of capitalist relations. On the other hand, the open-endedness of the desire for something other, the contours of which are outlined but never filled in, can only be realized by the masses. It is thus always a combination of the utopian and the practical that comprises Morris's radical utopianism.

The various elements of Morris's quotidian politics can be read as so many elaborations of his concept of creative labor. The rootedness of Morris's aesthetics in the notion of creative labor forms the link between his aesthetics and his politics: in the society of the future, the two spheres of culture and material contentment would be integrated. Moreover, the preconditions of creative labor establish the basis for distinguishing between the reformist "machinery" of socialism and "true and complete Socialism," what Morris will refer to as communism.[51] Morris exhibits a remarkable prescience as he outlines the potential errors and resultant effects of mistaking the latter for the former. His doubts as to the benefits of partial gains by the socialist movement — in the form of higher wages, public works such as the creation of parks and the establishment of free libraries, improvements in housing, the London County Council, and so on — present an uncannily prophetic vision of Fordism before Ford and of the current embattled state of left politics in general:

> For I want you to know and to ask you to consider, how far the betterment of the working people might go and yet stop at last without having made any progress on the *direct* road to Communism. Whether in short the tremendous organization of civilized commercial society is not playing the cat and mouse game with us socialists. Whether the Society of Inequality might not accept the quasi-socialist machin-

ery above mentioned, and work it for the purpose of upholding that society in a somewhat shorn condition, maybe, but a safe one. That seems to me possible, and means the other side of the view: instead of the useless classes being swept away by the useful, the useless classes gaining some of the usefulness of the workers, and *so* safeguarding their privilege. The workers better treated, better organized, helping to govern themselves, but with no more pretense to equality with the rich, nor any more hope for it than they have now. But if this be possible, it will only be so on the grounds that the working people have ceased to desire real socialism and are contented with some outside show of it joined to an increase in prosperity enough to satisfy the cravings of men who do now know what the pleasures of life might be if they treated their own capacities and the resources of nature reasonably with the intention and expectation of being happy. (*C* 231)

Through Morris's "street education," as it were, it became clear that there were limits even to the degree of *reform* the middle classes were willing to allow. Instrumental in forcing this realization, E. P. Thompson argues, was the demonstration cum massacre in Trafalgar Square on November 13, 1887, which came to be known as "Bloody Sunday." Initiated by spontaneous weekly and then daily meetings in the square of the unemployed (who were joined later by artisans, radicals, members of the Irish National League, and socialists), the demonstration was planned as a protest against the infringement of the unemployed workers' rights to meet freely in the public space of the square. The various groups participating were all to march there for a rally in demand of the rights of free speech. The demonstrators, however, never made it to the square but were brutally assaulted and quashed en route by an impressive show of police force. After the heady days of Morris's initial association and involvement with the SDF, when it seemed sure that revolution was imminent, Bloody Sunday brought home the full power of the state and the irreducible fact that, as revolutionaries, he and his socialist comrades were going to have to be in it for the long haul. The state's willingness to employ naked force against the demonstrators, to literally mow them down in the streets, impressed on Morris the like need on the part of the left for coordinated, militant organization against the state. In its wake, Morris confessed: "Thus at one stroke vanish[ed] the dream of bringing about peaceably and constitutionally the freedom which we long for."[52]

Like 1848 for Lukács, Bloody Sunday for Morris fortified the boundaries between proletariat and bourgeoisie. While obviously on a much smaller scale (one would be hard-pressed, I think, to claim this as an instance in which the British proletariat "entered upon the world-historical stage as an armed mass"), the confrontation at Trafalgar Square contained a similar ideational force. For Lukács the significance of 1848 lay in the fact that "during these days the bourgeoisie for the first time fights for the naked continuance of its economic and political rule."[53] Not only did Trafalgar Square offer a comparable exercise in the enforced violence of bourgeois rule but, as Lukács goes on to enumerate vis-à-vis 1848, it was also a vivid demonstration of the radical turning away of the bourgeoisie from its earlier democratic political aims and ideals.

In another important aspect, as well, Morris shares something with Lukács: his notion of ideology. While Morris nowhere systematically formulates a concept of ideology, his understanding of alienation as the extension of the "division of labor" into all areas of social life and subjectivity, indeed to the psyche and senses themselves, represents a version of Lukács's notion of ideology as the twin processes of rationalization and reification. Morris describes this in terms of a dual slavery, noting of the working class that "in addition to their other mishaps [they] are saddled also with the superstitions and hypocrisies of the upper classes, with scarce a whit of the characteristic traditions of their own class to help them: an intellectual slavery which is a necessary accompaniment of their material slavery" (C 231). Within Morris's schema, it is the concept of creative labor which resolutely resists this ideological system, embodying, as it does, resistance to division (in all its various social manifestations), or, as we saw above, the resistance of the aesthetic itself. Finally, given the totalizing nature of the system against which creative labor is pitted, resistance can only be imagined as total: one cannot sublate wage labor without at the same time sublating capital.

On a number of different fronts, Bloody Sunday thus played a crucial role in Morris's political and theoretical development. In the broadest sense it provided the impetus toward a totalizing view of the complex of capitalist forces: the violence of the demonstration itself was set in the context of numerous other events and factors which included the execution of the Chicago Anarchists, the continuing agitation for Irish Home Rule (1885–87), the severe depression of 1887, and the imperialist "adventures" of the 1880s. More concretely, it called forth the strategies necessary for a political program capable of mobilizing resistance in the interests of an affirmative politics. Centrally, Bloody Sunday made of Morris an uncompromising antiparliamentarian, who saw the Fabians' program of evolutionary reformism as naively misguided, its vision of parliament as the means toward socialism a grave misunderstanding of the nature of the system. Additionally, the demonstration underscored the need for more than political organization, given the pervasive effects of bourgeois ideology on all spheres of life, material and mental. Organization had to be harnessed to the "education into Socialism of the working classes," by which Morris meant the hope that "the inevitable advance of the society of equality will speedily make itself felt by the consciousness of its necessity being impressed upon the working people, and that they will consciously and not blindly strive for its realization" (*C* 230).

As this definition suggests, Morris's notion of education differs significantly from that put forward by Eliot in her "Address to Working Men": in direct opposition to her plea to working people to assume a position of *passive acceptance* with respect to the inequalities of the present, Morris posits a *consciously active* working class in protest against the present state of inequality. Harboring few illusions as to the immediate scope for such protest, Morris nevertheless held fast to his belief in *revolutionary* socialism; this, in stark contrast to many of his socialist colleagues—the most notorious being George Bernard Shaw—who were led by the events of Bloody Sunday more fully into Fabian reformism. For Morris, on the contrary, the massacre served both to renew and deepen his resolve and to solidify his militance: with remarkable directness, it made abundantly clear who he and the movement were up against, the lengths they would go to maintain themselves in power, and the magnitude of resources at their disposal.[54]

Although Shaw and Morris would continue down different political paths, Shaw's reminiscence, "Morris as I Knew Him," nonetheless offers a portrait of Morris that underscores the invaluableness of the utopian dimension of Morris's radicalism. Reflecting on Morris's diverse and extraordinary talents, Shaw suggests that while the world may be none the worse for Morris's renunciation of some of the arts he briefly pursued (such as figure painting or architecture), this is not the case with respect to his socialism: "It is true that there was no lack of practised and even powerful speakers in the movement, spouting Marxism, Fabianism, and all the other brands; but not one of them could propagate his vision of the life to come on a happy earth, and his values that went so much deeper into eternity than the surplus value of Marx. The vision only he himself could propagate; and so he had to go to the street corner even though he was thoroughly miserable there, and to think out and write out for delivery in public halls lectures which were far too pregnant and profound to be extemporized as

Hyndman and I and the rest extemporized."[55] While granting that Shaw's characteristically provocative posturing needs to be taken with a fair degree of skepticism—Shaw's dismissiveness toward the concept of surplus value, for instance, speaks less to Morris's political beliefs than Shaw's (and the Fabians') own moving away from Marx's analysis of economic exploitation—the nature of his paean, its exaggerations as well as its straightforward, unabashed praise, speaks to the remarkable manner in which Morris was able to maintain, uphold, balance, and, most importantly, make real the relationship between utopian and quotidian politics.

Morris's balancing act was upheld, to a large extent, by a sustained belief in the political equivalent of popular art, namely, proletarian culture. Proletarian culture or the proletarian public sphere, to use Oskar Negt and Alexander Kluge's terminology, was the only viable alternative to the bourgeois public sphere. This belief in the actual *creativity* of the proletariat set Morris squarely at odds with the fundamental tenets of Victorian social and political thought and distinguishes him even from most of his fellow middle-class colleagues in the socialist movement.[56] Recall that Gaskell's *Mary Barton*, as we saw in chapter 1, gestures toward a proletarian public sphere in its identification with John Barton but cannot sustain Barton's view against the pressures of a Christian reformism—in large part because the narrative cannot quite fully envision Barton and the other workers as creative, cultural agents in their own right. In essence, Morris's notion of proletarian culture derives its meaning from the concept of an art for the people. In opposition to the social processes of valorization defining the bourgeois public sphere—the elevation of exchange over use, of the abstract universal over the concrete particular—the proletarian public sphere functions as a counterconcept, as a "state of things as nearly as possible the reverse of the present state of things" (*A* 112). Paralleling Negt and Kluge's emphasis on the material basis for this new "state of things," Morris finds the grounds for such a reversal in labor. While he was savvy to the material and ideological pressures of the bourgeois public sphere, and the ways in which it threatened to assimilate all remnants of an alternative system of valorization, he also held that the threat of assimilation could never be fully realized: there would always remain a kernel of resistance in the form of living labor itself. (In *News from Nowhere* Morris locates this kernel in the "instinct for freedom.") As Negt and Kluge characterize the position of workers, "they have two characteristics: in their defensive attitude toward society, their conservatism, and their subcultural character, they are once again mere objects; but they are, at the same time, the block of real life that goes against the valorization interest." As they conclude, "as long as capital is dependent on living labor as a source of wealth, this element of the proletarian context of living cannot be extinguished through repression."[57] In the post-Freudian language of Negt and Kluge an expression of this raw material lives in the extraeconomic, forbidden zones of fantasy; in the semantics of Morris's nineteenth-century imagination, it exists in the realm of dreams—of the artist-workman and a people's art. As Shaw's reminiscence and Morris's political and fictional writings attest, Morris's gift lay in his ability to image the proletarian public sphere as a counterconcept to the bourgeois public sphere, whether in the minds of those he stood before when delivering his open-air speeches, or in those who read his sagas, his political tracts, or his utopian romances.

Utopianism, or Action Is the Sister of the Dream

Morris's best-known literary work, *News from Nowhere*, provides an ideal site in which to understand the relationship between form and content in Morris's view of the proletarian public sphere. Keywords of the utopian mode pick up on concerns enumerated in the previous chapters on the industrial novel and the *Bildungsroman*: community, identity, and stability.[58] In virtually inverse proportion to these novels' representations of work, Morris's utopian romance *News from Nowhere* highlights the centrality of labor to this triad of social relations—an emphasis Morris seems to have felt instinctively could not be made within the generic constraints of the realist novel. "After abandoning his one attempt at a novel with a contemporary setting," Northrop Frye writes, "Morris remarked that he would never try such a thing again 'unless the world turn topsides under some day.'"[59] Indeed, Morris turns the realist novel on *its* head, showing that its order is disorder, its "true society" false. This reversal is most palpably felt as a change in spatial orientation. In the industrial novel and the *Bildungsroman*, work is almost always performed offstage, seemingly beyond the borders of these novels' domains. It is the outside that fortifies the border and marks the limits of the bourgeois public sphere. Within such a configuration, as we saw in earlier chapters, labor is offset against pleasure; the realm of bourgeois pleasures becomes a cordoned-off space, topographically and ideationally separate from work. Work, by its absence, circumscribes the public space of these novels; it, more than the terror of the mob or the ubiquity of the convict, is the real specter haunting these texts, constantly threatening to make its presence public.

Generic tools of the utopian romance in hand, Morris, in *News from No-where*, issues his manifesto against such an ordering of space. Starting from the premise that social spaces (and the individuals that inhabit them) are infinitely open to reconstruction, the mechanics of the utopian narrative provide a vehicle through which to imagine a possible revaluation of labor and the public sphere. Within this reordering, all spaces become sites of creative labor. The distinction between the workplace and the public sphere collapses: work in Morris's expanded form is omnipresent. The placement of work at the center of the processes of social valorization repositions it as *the* problematic of value.[60] Far from being peripherally located, work is the most highly valued thing there is: it is what creates value. Work is value-creating labor but not in the sense of what creates surplus value; instead, value is transformed into a truly intersubjective value, and human labor becomes the activity which mediates among individuals. Labor is thus not only omnipresent but constitutive in a now fully social landscape.[61] The expansion of labor across the social spectrum reunites what come to be represented as separate economies in the industrial novel: labor and pleasure, the political economy and the economies of desire and sexuality.

At the same time, the utopian narrative, historically, has been tied to issues of national identity.[62] Thomas More's *Utopia* founds the genre just as England itself is in the process of becoming a modern nation-state. These two communities, the one literary, the other political, share a similar set of questions and concerns: each fashion models of individual and group identity, of belongingness to a community or place, of the notion of "nationness."[63] Morris's *News from Nowhere* clearly partakes in this tradition. Sections of the romance are devoted to topics "concerning government," "the arrangement of life," and "how matters are managed." Covered are questions of national language, national culture, relations with foreign nations, and so on. Published in serial form in *Commonweal* in 1890, *News from Nowhere* participates in a larger national discussion about the role of England in the world and within her own borders—the beginnings of which we looked at in Dickens's and Eliot's respective *Bildungsromane*, and which really gathers steam in the latter part of the nineteenth century. By the 1880s, England's estimation of herself and her place in the world had certainly begun to suffer.[64] The luster of the 1851 Crystal Palace exhibition had waned, tarnished by problems both at home and abroad. There were only so many ameliorative pageants possible and, as the Jingo Jubilee was to prove, even these began to lose their mesmerizing charms in the midst of widespread unemployment, dockers' strikes, and urban poverty. England was experiencing the end of her monopoly of the world market and with it an ac-companying letdown of imperialist euphoria and national self-confidence. Like Eliot's *Daniel Deronda*, then, *News from Nowhere* interrogates the co-ordinates of national identity and renegotiates the increasingly tenuous na-tional borders of the British Commonwealth.

In this section, I limit the focus of my discussion of *News from Nowhere* to two strands of these concerns: to read the tale as a dramatization of the discursive logic of Morris's ideas on creative labor outlined and analyzed in the previous two sections and to tease from this fictive representation the beginnings of what I see as a provocative critique of the notion of na-tional identity. In this way I hope to provide a reading of *News from Nowhere* which neither forfeits the experimental, open-ended aspects of its construc-tion nor relegates its content to the historical back burner—as merely an idealized fable of feudal England.

....

"I am only going to assert that if individual men are the creatures of their surrounding conditions, as indeed I think they are, it must be the business of man as a social animal, or of Society, if you will, to make the surroundings which make the individual man what he is."[65] This assertion encapsulates in shorthand the social landscape that *News from Nowhere* traverses. At the most general level, the act of making the landscape social defines the chal-lenge of *News from Nowhere*'s utopianism. On the many walks and journey-ings throughout the narrative, there always seems to be a house over the hill; or, people emerge from the fields or woods as if they had materialized from the air: "Romantic as this Kensington wood was, however, it was not lonely. We came on many groups both coming and going, or wandering in the edges of the wood."[66] There is no wilderness to speak of; rather, *News from Nowhere*'s cartography is at once literally social. But social structures (even literal ones, such as architecture) people the landscape in a radically altered context of mutuality: "This whole mass of architecture which we had come upon so suddenly from amidst the pleasant fields was not only ex-quisitely beautiful in itself, but it bore upon it the expression of such gener-osity and abundance of life that I was exhilarated to a pitch that I had never yet reached. I fairly chuckled for pleasure" (*N* 20). At a less directly literal level, the way in which Morris fashions this land of mutual determination through a multilayered narrative structure offers a glimpse of the kind of identity and the theory of history enabled by his concept of creative labor.

A crucial feature of the landscape is that we are never fully sutured in its environment. "*Being some* chapters from a utopian romance" [title page, emphasis added], the narrative is unfinished and fragmentary, an ongoing creation of a continuous present. Like its close sibling, the time-travel narrative, it parades all the tricks of that familial trade: the fracturing of time, space, place, and identity.[67] "Up at the League, says a friend . . ." (*N* 1) the tale begins. But it turns out not to be the friend who will narrate, but a friend of the friend, who will stand in as if he were the friend, part friend, part himself: "I think it would be better if I told them in the first person, as if it were myself" (*N* 3). That guest will be our Guest, William, self-named, and someone whose identity presumably only lasts as long as his relation—as guest—does. Identity thus becomes mutable rather than fixed, historical rather than natural, and something that is therefore constructed. Since people are brought into being, they can also be dismantled and something else put in their place.[68] The possibility for multiple personalities, as it were, emerges once personalities are recognized for their historicity.

Later in Guest's travels this possibility makes itself felt as Guest encounters Dick Hammond's great-grandfather, dressed, teasingly, in Morris's characteristic costume of blue serge, worn threadbare, with matching pants and gray worsted stockings. Seeing him, Guest has the odd sensation of looking in a mirror: "As for me, I was now looking at him harder than good manners allowed of, perhaps; for in truth his face, dried-apple like as it was, seemed strangely familiar to me; as if I had seen it before—in a looking-glass it might be" (*N* 44). Guest fades into the old man, who fades into Morris, who fades into us, as readers, who, then, each become, as Andrew Belsey suggests, the "text's political accomplice."[69] It is a fracturing, the narrative invites us to believe and take part in, which leads to the construction of new forms of subjectivity.

Time and place too acquire a coterminous rather than continuist quality: past, present, and future are intermingled and overlapping; and place becomes an evacuable space that is both "nowhere" and still England. Guest travels along the Thames, finds himself in his own house at one point, visits the Houses of Parliament, and smokes his favorite tobacco. But simultaneously the scene and sensations are radically the "other" of any place. A postindustrial Thames teems with running salmon, Parliament now fittingly houses the Dung Market, and the amount of tobacco Guest "purchases" is based on desire not price—the oddness of which is signified a number of times in the text through Guest's reflexive reaching into his pocket to pay for things only to catch himself and be reminded that money no longer forms the basis of exchange in this future world. Indeed, the situation for Guest is so radically altered that any comparison to an English past necessarily involves a sense of estrangement.

But as with Brecht's notion of *Verfremdungseffekt*, *News from Nowhere*'s estranging effects are never total, never so complete as to sever its two worlds irreparably. Instead, by way of the jarring dissonances and nonsynchronicity of time and place, the narrative foregrounds the *process of becoming* rather than the arrival at any predetermined place or state of being. On the most basic level, this is stressed by the fact that Guest ultimately does not arrive anywhere; at the end, we travel with him back into an ongoing present, with the silent injunction of Ellen's glance—inclusive of *News from Nowhere*'s readers—to "go on living while you may, striving, with whatsoever pain and labour needs must be, to build up little by little the new day of fellowship, and rest, and happiness" (*N* 182). Throughout the text, too, events that in the nineteenth century look like endpoints are reconfigured as part of a process of constant but determinate change. A prime example of this kind of recasting is Morris's description of Bloody Sunday. When Guest hears Hammond describing the massacre, he completes his recounting by what he assumes (from his Victorian perspective) to be its logical conclusion: "'And I suppose that this massacre put an end to the whole revolution for that time?'" to which a shocked Hammond cries, "No, no, it began it!" (*N* 100).

Morris, furthermore, leaves no doubt as to what has effected the transition from the present to this future, from commercial slavery to freedom. All that *News from Nowhere* offers is only possible by rethinking the concept of labor. The precondition for the kind of world the narrative imagines is that labor has ceased to be a commodity; only once it is no longer alienated can integrity and pleasure be restored to the processes of labor: "*All* work is now pleasurable; either because of the hope of gain in honour and wealth with which the work is done, which causes pleasurable excitement, even when the actual work is not pleasant; or else because it has grown into a pleasurable *habit*, as in the case of what you may call mechanical work; and lastly (and most of our work is of this kind) because there is conscious sensuous pleasure in the work itself; it is done, that is, by artists" (*N* 78). This is Morris's artist materialized: a figure who can only come into being once freed from the market forces defining labor-power as a commodity.

The specificity of this change and its import can be seen best perhaps by comparing the nature and role of work in *News from Nowhere* to Edward Bellamy's representations of work in his 1898 utopian romance *Looking Backward*, which, as is well known, served as a strong impetus for Morris's writing of *News from Nowhere*. (In Darko Suvin's terminology, *News from*

Nowhere functions as a "counter-project" to *Looking Backward*.)[70] In stark contrast to Morris's emphasis on work, the most significant aspect of labor in *Looking Backward* is its absence. Bellamy's future, in effect, erases all sites of productive labor from its Bostonian cityscape, containing no workplaces whatsoever. Instead, the future has become one giant marketplace of middle-class consumerism, paralleling the evolution of the nation itself into one giant corporation. (Hardly too taxing an imaginative leap for Bellamy's readers today!) Attention has shifted from production to circulation; in the process, workers themselves have been "disappeared," along with their work. This change essentially does nothing to alter the present (nineteenth-century, or, for that matter, twentieth-century) view of work. Work continues to be neither "the most important, the most interesting, [nor] the most dignified employment of our powers," but simply "a necessary duty to be discharged before we can fully devote ourselves to the higher exercise of our faculties, the intellectual and spiritual enjoyments and pursuits which alone mean life."[71] As duty rather than pleasure, work remains a site of division, marking the divide between necessity and enjoyment, the physical and the intellectual. Morris, in his own review of *Looking Backward*, attributes this difference to the fact that Bellamy cannot think beyond the present "machinery" of society: "the multiplication of machinery will just—multiply machinery; I believe that the ideal of the future does not point to the lessening of men's energy by the reduction of labor to a minimum, but rather to the reduction of *pain in labour* to a minimum, so small that it will cease to be a pain . . . Mr. Bellamy worries himself unnecessarily in seeking (with obvious failure) some incentive to labour to replace the fear of starvation, which is at present our only one, whereas it cannot be too often repeated that the true incentive to useful and happy labour is and must be pleasure in the work itself."[72]

Critics of Morris's utopia have pointed to the ways in which *News from Nowhere*, in contrast to more technologically oriented, machine utopias such as Bellamy's, presents a preindustrial world, not a future world. While they are justified in their claims that machines have all but disappeared from Morris's landscape, they have been less illuminating as to the motivating force behind the marked absence of machines—one which takes us back to Morris's theory of work and the distinction between useful labor and useless toil (or what he refers to at other times as the difference between necessary and unnecessary labor). As we have seen and is reiterated in *News from Nowhere*, Morris viewed nineteenth-century production as the production of measureless quantities of goods that were primarily useless (and shoddy besides).[73] Increased productive capabilities, in the form of new technologies and new media, thus in and of themselves held no great allure for Morris nor any guarantee of ushering in more equal and just social relations. If anything, technological improvements signal ever more ways to produce ever more useless and cheap commodities—at the increasing expense of those producing the goods, the laboring classes.[74] As Hammond recalls, with respect to the dictates of the world-market, "it was a current jest of the time that the wares were made to sell and not to use" (*N* 81)—the final irony being that the only class of goods that was made well were the machines themselves.

At the root of the old society, *News from Nowhere* ultimately upholds, lay the false separation between "nature" and "mankind": "Was not their mistake once more bred of the life of slavery that they had been living?—a life which was always looking upon everything, except mankind, animate, and inanimate—'nature,' as people used to call it—as one thing, and mankind as another. It was natural to people thinking in this way, that they should try to make 'nature' their slave, since they thought 'nature' was something outside them" (*N* 154). Within the new society, the possibility of such a distinction is no longer even thinkable; it has lost all social meaning. The concept of "nature" as such—as something which exists outside of and hence in opposition to mankind—has been rendered obsolete: " 'nature,' *as people used to call it*." The overcoming of this opposition frees the new society from the treadmill of useless production and the world-market. Most importantly, this freedom opens up a social space in which individuals, fully in relation to the collective, can make choices as to what they actually *want*. The exact nature of these wants is left open—to the processes of history and present social struggles.

This open-endedness corresponds to Morris's expanded notion of labor, which in turn shapes *News from Nowhere*'s representation of revolution. Like the concept of creative labor, Morris's utopia affirms new values and new social arrangements: utility and ornament (as complementary rather than contradictory), pleasure in labor, collectivism rather than individualism. Yet, just as Morris's understanding of labor can only be realized as a collective human task, revolution too is understood as a *process* actively and collectively desired and struggled for by individual men and women. Raymond Williams identifies this aspect of the narrative as its definitive contribution: "But what is emergent in Morris's work, and what seems to me increasingly the strongest part of *News from Nowhere*, is the crucial insertion of the *transition* to utopia, which is not discovered, come across, or projected—not even, except at the simplest conventional level, dreamed—but fought for. Between writer or reader and this new condition is chaos, civil war, painful and slow reconstruction."[75]

This distinction and the central role revolutionary struggle occupies in Morris's utopia militate, in my view, against any simple reading of *News from Nowhere* as an escapist retreat into fanciful medievalism. If anything, the medieval characteristics of this future world engender historical consciousness rather than dull it or eradicate it altogether, as the claim of escapism would imply. The chasm between the reader's now and the text's then is never presented as unbreachable; nor is its overcoming merely projected. Rather, the disjuncture between these worlds provides a space in which to momentarily experience or register the mutability of any present social reality. Not only is the present of our Guest in the process of being rewritten but the process of such revision is equally entertained with respect to the utopia *News from Nowhere* creates. At one point, Guest exclaims, "Dear me! how apt history is to reverse contemporary judgments" (*N* 59), thus leaving open a commensurate kind of reversal, or movement of history in the future.

What is ultimately highlighted is the deeply historical nature of the present: the energies of the text are most invested in this understanding of the present rather than in some sort of return to the past or even the accuracy of any specific detail of its imagined future. Elsewhere Morris acknowledges the inescapable place of the present in any utopian project, allowing that "it is impossible to build up a scheme for the society of the future for no man can really think himself out of his own days; his palace of days to come can only be constructed from the aspirations forced upon him by his present surroundings, and from his dreams of the life of the past, which themselves cannot fail to be more or less unsubstantial imaginings."[76] As this statement suggests, the imaginings of any kind of other are necessarily deeply imbricated in one's own historical-cultural present.

Throughout *News from Nowhere* Morris playfully cajoles his reader toward this view of history and social change. In his description of the change in economic relations, for instance, he imagines a reversal of the processes of industrialization whereby the towns invade the country. This reversal, during which the difference between town and country grows less and less, involves a combination of past and present moments rather than a simple reversion to preindustrial times: "it was indeed this world of the country vivified by the thought and briskness of townbred folk which has produced that happy and leisurely but eager life of which you have had a first taste"

(*N* 61). These kinds of reversals extend to feelings and emotions as well. Guest is struck, for instance, by the fact that Ellen has feelings that he cannot even comprehend. His meeting with the Obstinate Refusers underlines this point. In one of *News from Nowhere*'s characteristically estranging effects, Guest finds that the Obstinate Refusers are thus named because they refuse to stop working. They are so interested in the work they are presently doing, the muscle-wearying but imaginatively constructive job of rebuilding a house, that they cannot bear to leave off and join their fellow haymakers in their annual haymaking festival, a kind of work the narrative makes clear is easier in terms of skill and overall expenditure of energy.

Lest Morris's utopia consist of a happiness just too homogenous to be believed, it also houses throwbacks from the "old days," such as Ellen's sulky grandfather, referred to as "a grumbler." The grumbler warrants that people were brisker and more alive in the past as a consequence of unlimited competition. He makes his case based on the quality of the past's cultural artifacts, primarily its books: "I can't help thinking that our moralists and historians exaggerate hugely the unhappiness of the past days, in which such splendid works of imagination and intellect were produced" (*N* 129). The grumbler's barbs prompt an exposition of Morris's notion of the present (i.e., nineteenth-century) relationship between everyday life and culture, a notion presaging Walter Benjamin's statement, "there is no document of civilization which is not at the same time a document of barbarism."[77] In particular, Ellen vehemently argues that not only were the cultural pleasures depicted and read in the novels of the past enjoyed on the backs of those who "dug and sewed and baked and built and carpentered round about these useless—animals" but the whole experience of culture as something separate from daily life is itself only expressive of a deep and generalized alienation, from both the world and sensuous bodily pleasures: "Books, books! always books, grandfather! When will you understand that after all it is the world we live in which interests us; the world of which we are a part, and which we can never love too much?" (*N* 129). Curiously, this is one of the characteristics of Morris's utopia that irks critics the most. On the one hand, this is understandable, given the fact that their livelihood and pleasures are deeply indebted to the continuing production of culture. On the other hand, this clinging to the present reflects a baleful short-sightedness and paucity of imagination, especially on the part of leftists: the attack on the disappearance of culture as we know it revealingly exposes an inability to envision a radically different relationship inhering between individuals and their environment; to imagine a truly "other" social landscape.[78] What all these conjurings ask us to entertain is the possibility of a social order based and organized on something other than commodity logic and the world-market. But, as importantly, these appeals are only engaging precisely insofar as they penetrate *current* relations of production and hence contain within them (retroactively from the perspective of the future) the seeds of their own subsumption.

Perhaps this last criterion accounts in part for the uneven effect of Morris's treatment of women. On the one hand, his discussion of property laws and their relationship to issues of gender continues to resonate with social meaning. Positing a future world in which commercial interests would no longer determine matters of love, Morris unravels a series of Victorian conventions of gender that would consequently disappear with the end of "the sacred rights of property" (*N* 47). Without property as the defining contract of marriage, such a thing as Divorce Court, for instance, becomes meaningless; passion or sentiment replaces contracts of property. Moreover, what Morris terms the "artificial foolishness" of the expectation (and enforcement) of the "until death do us part" vows of marital perpetuity is also overturned: "If there must be a sunder betwixt those who meant never to sunder, so it must be: but there need be no pretext of unity when the reality of it is gone: nor do we drive those who well know that they are incapable of it to profess an undying sentiment which they cannot really feel: thus it is that as that monstrosity of venal lust is no longer possible, so also it is no longer needed" (*N* 49). Given the Victorian context in which Morris was writing, his thoroughgoing critique of what he terms elsewhere "the family tyranny" cannot be underestimated. It unearths to a remarkable degree the complicity between commerce and sexuality under capitalism and likewise their artificially maintained separation within Victorian domestic ideology. Enabled by Morris's non-gender-specific notion of creative labor, these views presage a reunion of labor and pleasure, of the private and the public sphere, which does not simply reduce one side of the division to the other but overcomes the underlying structure making such a division meaningful. Politics as such disappears not because the personal is blithely claimed as the political but because the political is revealed as an artificial category of division which no longer obtains once its underlying structure of alienated consciousness—of which it is merely a symptom— has been superseded.

On the other hand, there remains an unevenness to these suppositions that arises when Morris turns to personifying them in the flesh of his female characters. His two heroines, Ellen and Clara, have long frustrated readers,

especially female ones, with their conventionally assigned roles and predict-
ability. They disappointingly undermine Morris's claims elsewhere about
the mutable nature of identity. Women still serve men, causing Guest himself to query whether this is not a little reactionary. Morris assures us, in
response, that housekeeping is no longer designated as unimportant but is
now considered worthy of respect and, moreover, a source of pleasure for
the women performing it: "don't you know that it is a great pleasure to a
clever woman to manage a house skilfully, and to do it so that all the house-
mates about her look pleased, and are grateful to her? And then, you know,
everybody likes to be ordered about by a pretty woman: why, it is one of the
pleasantest forms of flirtation" (*N* 51). Some assurance. While feminist arguments can be made for valuing forms of labor traditionally devalued under
a commercially dominated economy, there is nonetheless something more
than a little suspect about the way in which Morris's future tends at these
moments to perpetuate and enforce an uncannily Victorian gender division
of labor.

Similarly, Dick and Clara's courtship reads as cloyingly sweet and utterly
banal despite Morris's assurances otherwise. Paradoxically, Morris's argument against bourgeois sentimentality smacks of sentimentality. Describing
a moment in which Clara appraises herself in relation to Dick, Morris qualifies that "she looked down at her own pretty feet with a half sigh, as though
she were contrasting her slight woman's beauty with his man's beauty; as
women will when they are really in love, and are not spoiled with conventional sentiment" (*N* 125). At these moments, any sense of estrangement is
lost; instead of defamiliarizing the present, it comes back with a vengeance,
the intractably "feminine" more intractable than ever. Female subjectivity
appears closed to reconstruction and radical new forms of social expression.
More so than any other aspect of the romance, these passages pinpoint the
limits of Morris's own thinking and simultaneously those of utopian narratives more generally, which can never entirely escape their own historical
moment.

These failings of imagination illustrate, by way of contrast, the relative
success of other parts of the narrative. For what makes these descriptions
inadequate is their lack of newness. Meant to underscore the interest now
garnered in the ordinary occupations of life, to show how the new society
has learned to "look enough to the present pleasure of ordinary daily life"
(*N* 61), their surface mirroring of existing conditions (present gender inequalities) undercuts their hermeneutic value. They are ultimately neither

quite strange enough nor penetratingly near enough to be effectively defamiliarizing.

The same cannot be said of Morris's treatment of national identity. By questioning the concept of the nation as a meaningful form or expression of social identity, *News from Nowhere* posits nothing less than the disappearance of the English nation altogether.[79] The underlying argument for the obsolescence of the nation follows from the distinction between classes and nations. As Morris lectures, through the mouthpiece of Hammond, nationalism as an ideology attempted to mask class differences; but class rather than national identification was what was operative in any so-called national conflict: "it is said that even when two nations were at war, the rich men of each nation gambled with each other pretty much as usual, and even sold each other weapons wherewith to kill their own countrymen" (*N* 66). From here, it is a short step toward seeing the nation as a constructed category, the assignation of a false, reductive sameness to heterogeneous peoples, in the interest, primarily, of commerce. Indeed, Guest's concerns about the loss of the nation as a unit of social identification and Hammond's response to these concerns provide the essentials of Morris's analysis of the state-form in Victorian culture and its potential supersession through socialism. Responding to Guest's concern about the loss of variety that would seemingly accompany the loss of distinct and separate national identities, Hammond asks rhetorically, "how should it add to the variety or dispel the dulness, to coerce certain families or tribes, often heterogeneous and jarring with one another, into certain artificial and mechanical groups, and class them nations, and stimulate their patriotism—i.e. their foolish and envious prejudices?" (*N* 72–73).

The advent of socialism frees them from this folly: "it is obvious to us that by means of this very diversity the different strains of blood in the world can be serviceable and pleasant to each other, without in the least wanting to rob each other: we are all bent on the same enterprise, making the most of our lives" (*N* 73). An artificial system of national conflict subtended by a nationalist ideology holding "political strife" to be "a necessary result of human nature" (*N* 73) is replaced by a diversity finally open to expression. The enforced "oneness" of the nation, its reduction of *internal difference* to a fortified *sameness* against an external Other, is here negated; diversity and difference become the means toward freedom and happiness rather than that which threatens their attainment. In the process, the category "national" itself becomes meaningless, as Dick's misapprehension of the former meaning of the National Gallery playfully illustrates: "It is called the National Gallery; I have sometimes puzzled as to what the name means: anyhow, nowadays wherever there is a place where pictures are kept as curiosities permanently it is called a National Gallery, perhaps after this one. Of course there are a good many of them up and down the country" (*N* 37). Like the pictures contained within them, national galleries have been reduced to mere curiosities, severed, as they are, from any singular *national* referent and thus subject to potentially limitless proliferation.

If, as Fredric Jameson suggests, history is what hurts, *News from Nowhere* presents us with a world in which history has been redeemed—a world which portends the end of strife and suffering, the satisfaction of all desires, and, not least, the end of history. But, as it continually reminds us through the mechanics and incompleteness of its narration, we are far from such redemption. Rather, it returns us finally to the unfinished project of modernity, a project that does not lead inexorably toward the normative progressive teleology of ever-greater "civilization." When Guest marvels, "I could hardly have believed that there could be so many good-looking people in any civilized country," an incredulous Hammond "[crows] a little, like the old bird he was. 'What! are we still civilized?' " (*N* 52). This self-same incredulity extends to *News from Nowhere*'s readers, functioning as a provocation to render that "still" a thing of the past, relevant only to future retrospection.

. . . .

In the 1976 postscript to his biography of Morris, E. P. Thompson wagers that "the case of Morris" extends beyond its significance for Morris studies alone. "So that what may be involved . . . is the whole problem of the subordination of the imaginative utopian faculties within the later Marxist tradition."[80] Under "imaginative utopian faculties" Thompson includes "moral self-consciousness" and "a vocabulary of desire" as well as the more straightforward understanding of utopianism as the ability to project images of the future. The first two characteristics especially are crucial aspects of Thompson's concern to properly establish the relation in which Morris stands to contemporary thought. For it is "as a Utopian and a moralist" that Morris "can never be assimilated to Marxism." Indeed, these virtues serve quite the opposite function: they prompt a (self-) critique of Marxism because they highlight exactly what the Marxist tradition has been unable to accommodate. To Thompson's mind, this inability is ultimately explained "not by any contradiction of purposes but because one may not assimilate desire to knowledge, and because the attempt to do so is to confuse two different operative principles of culture."[81] The solution, exemplified for Thompson in the life of William Morris, is to leave desire to the utopians and moralists and knowledge to the Marxists: "So that what Marxism might do, for a change, is sit on its own head a little in the interests of Socialism's heart. It might close down one counter in its universal pharmacy, and cease dispensing potions of analysis to cure the maladies of desire. This might do good politically as well, since it would allow a little space, not only for literary Utopians, but also for the unprescribed initiatives of everyday men and women who, in some part of themselves, are also alienated and utopian by turns."[82]

In his reading of this passage, Perry Anderson argues that Thompson simply reproduces the antithesis between romanticism and utilitarianism here in the form of an opposition between utopianism and Marxist theory or materialist knowledge. Revealing his own political cards, Anderson characterizes the opposition between desire and knowledge as typical of what he terms the "subjectivist *Schwärmerei*" following the disillusionment with the social revolt of 1968. (Gilles Deleuze and Félix Guattari's *Anti-Oedipus* figures as a prime celebrant of this "dejected post-lapsarian anarchism.")[83] When it comes to Thompson's involvement with this *Schwärmerei*, Anderson grants him the benefit of the doubt: Thompson has inadvertently fallen in with unsavory bedfellows via his interest in the French scholar and libertarian Miguel Abensour and his advocacy (in a reading of *News from Nowhere*) of utopian thought as a vehicle uniquely geared to the "education of desire," an aspiration in stark contrast to the dictates of conceptual knowledge. The gravity of this fall, especially in terms of its political effects, is something of which Thompson is, alas, blamelessly unaware.

I think Perry Anderson is on solid ground in his claim that Thompson misreads the opposition between desire and knowledge as an ontological rather than a historical one. At the same time, the considerable energy behind Anderson's own invective against desire ends up, paradoxically, ceding a certain weight to Thompson's claims against Marxism—even if those claims reflect historical rather than ontological processes. Specifically, Anderson attacks Thompson's uncritical use of Abensour's notion of desire ("the category operates as a license for the exercise of any fantasy freed from the responsibility of cognitive controls"), which, according to Anderson, functions merely as a "cloudy tautology," part and parcel of an invidious Parisian irrationalism. He goes on to challenge, more generally, attention to desire at all, suggesting that it is ultimately politically suspect because of "the metaphysical vacancy of the term [desire] itself." From this he (too) easily concludes that "neither Marxism nor socialism have anything to gain from traffic with it, unless it is given what in this irrationalism it is so expressly constructed to refuse—a clear and observable meaning."[84] Unwittingly, Anderson's response ensnares him in the oppositional dynamic he elsewhere claims the need to move beyond.

To different effect, but in similar fashion, Anderson and Thompson reconstruct the divisions—between desire and knowledge, utopian and Marxist—that William Morris's work belies. Thompson is right to point out the ways in which the Marxist tradition has tended, at times, to write utopianism out of its political program. But it is equally important to remember that Thompson is responding to one historically specific strand of the Marxist tradition, one coming out of the ideology/science split of the Second International and orthodox Marxism. In this context, too, it is not inconsequential that Thompson felt deeply betrayed by this "tradition" and that, during the dark days of 1956, it was the work of William Morris that gave Thompson "the will to go on arguing."[85] In other words, within Thompson's own personal history, William Morris figured as a counter to the excesses and abuses of Stalinism, which, for Thompson, came to irrevocably taint and become synonymous with "the Marxist tradition." Other developments within Marxism are largely ignored, a fact Anderson attributes to Thompson's brand of cultural nationalism: an impulse felt, for example, in the urgency with which Thompson claims Morris as part of an *English* tradition rather than a continental one. As Anderson notes, the names of Lukács, Gramsci, the members of the Frankfurt School, and even Lenin and Trotsky are conspicuously absent from Thompson's work. In the context of Thompson's work as a whole, this leaves him claiming Morris as a major English theorist at the same time he is bemoaning the poverty of theory.

Anderson recognizes correctly the folly of Thompson's sweeping dismissal of international Marxisms, but does so primarily in the interest of establishing the nature of Thompson's thought rather than Morris's—on the face of it, understandable, given Anderson's focus on Thompson's polemic with Louis Althusser, *The Poverty of Theory*. Less tenable, however, is the fact that, in his zeal to shore up Thompson's failings, Anderson tends to conflate Morris with Thompson. As a result, the ways in which Morris's project may be different from Thompson's are largely lost.[86] While Thompson may be heavily invested in showing how Morris and his utopianism are beyond the scope of historical materialism, certainly that was not Morris's theoretical stance; whereas Thompson may want Marxism "to cease dispensing potions of analysis to cure the maladies of desire," Morris wanted nothing more than to improve the potion and up the dosage. In short, Morris, unlike Thompson, did not counterpose Marxism and utopia, nor knowledge and desire. Indeed, Morris's challenge to such a counterposition accounts in large part for the remarkable contribution of *News from Nowhere*.

From this perspective, then, both Thompson and Anderson may be thought of as posing false problems with respect to William Morris. The point is not to leave desire out of the Marxian framework, either in order to honor its autonomy as an "operative principl[e] of culture" or to dismiss it as unmanageably irrational and politically suspect.[87] Of course Morris's notions of productive labor and a people's art prompt a rethinking of certain classical Marxian terms and, concomitantly, suggest a number of alternatives to the political strategies corresponding to that terminology. But they do so precisely insofar as they avoid the pitfalls of the Thompson/Anderson polemic, without throwing out the proverbial baby with the bathwater. Instead, the "case of Morris" urges us to reach beyond these kinds of oppositions: to imagine a social order in which the divisions between the sensual and intellectual, mental and manual labor, desire and knowledge, work and pleasure would be defamiliarized and transformed to such an extent that the current structural necessity of their separation would seem too incredible to be believed.

CHAPTER 5

UTOPIA, USE,
AND THE EVERYDAY

....

Oscar Wilde and

a New Economy

of Pleasure

Dear, dear! How Queer everything is today! And yesterday things went
on just as usual. — Lewis Carroll, *Alice in Wonderland*

In 1966, Herbert Marcuse, returning to *Eros and Civilization* to add a "political preface," asked the crucial question, "Can we speak of a juncture between the erotic and political dimension?"[1] This question was prompted by
what Marcuse saw as his overly optimistic assumption when the book was
originally published in 1955 that "the achievements of advanced industrial
society would enable man to reverse the direction of progress, to break the
fatal union of productivity and destruction, liberty and repression — in other
words, to learn the gay science of how to use the social wealth for shaping
man's world in accordance with his Life Instincts, in the concerted struggle
against the Purveyors of Death."[2] Our alienation from the language alone
which Marcuse uses (and even from his more tempered reflections in the
preface) speaks to the distance that now separates us from the 1960s and
its language of liberation. If in 1966 Marcuse could still turn to the international arena and the revolution in Vietnam, specifically, as a site for at
least "the historical chance of turning the wheel of progress to another di-

rection," what we now face is the opening of Vietnam to the West and market-oriented economic reforms.[3] Clearly, given our changed historical moment, the liberation of both eros and civilization does not lie with an (impossible) return to an equation of the two. But, as I want to argue in the present chapter, nor does it lie with a rejection of the language of eros or pleasure itself. Rather, it is the nature of the "juncture" between the erotic and the political of which Marcuse speaks that needs to be reconsidered.

The seeds for this reconceptualization, I suggest, lie in the work of Oscar Wilde and his attempts to create a new economy of pleasure based on the paradoxical notion of what I will call the labors of hedonism; the notion, that is to say, that pleasure is something to be worked at and worked for. As Bertolt Brecht fashions it, "pleasure takes some achieving, I'd say."[4] A reading of Wilde's work in this light involves two important theoretical shifts: first, to show how the notion of pleasure in his texts dovetails with notions of use versus exchange value, commodification and commodity logic, the utopian and the everyday; and second, to uncouple the concept of pleasure from sexuality per se and to link it instead to a more expansive notion of use. These twin operations—the detachment of pleasure from sexuality and the connection of pleasure to a new kind of use—not only link pleasure to what Marcuse refers to as the "political fight" or the larger political and economic structures which define and delimit pleasure but, in turn, excavate the space for a more complex and varied understanding of pleasure.

A reconsideration of how use and the utopian function in Wilde equally requires a reassessment of his genealogy as a political thinker. Wilde's gestures toward socialism have commonly been disregarded as mere polemic, yet another rhetorical feint in Wilde's repertoire of personae. Renewed attention to his notion of use, however, shows him more firmly placed as a fellow traveler of sorts whose work represents a continuation of the English socialist project of the 1880s, and especially of William Morris. Morris and Wilde, despite their stylistic differences, each focus on ways of overcoming the increasing separation of labor from any notion of pleasure. As surplus value and profit, that is to say, become the primary motive of production, labor is instrumentalized as a commodity that can only realize itself within the terms of capitalist production. As such, it becomes merely a means of existence, alienated from its own self-realization. Pleasure is opposed to abstract labor, but simultaneously defined by it negatively—as that which is not work—as capitalist logic colonizes ever greater domains of experience.

Both William Morris and Oscar Wilde implicitly acknowledge this conceptual and real divide and try to overcome it in their own ways. William

Morris, as we saw in the previous chapter, attempts to redefine labor and with it, pleasure, by envisioning a kind of *creative* labor which places pleasure at the foundation of society. Art is defined by Morris as the expression of pleasure in labor, and his utopia in *News from Nowhere* is one of artisans. Oscar Wilde provides a counternarrative to Victorian conventions by imagining, also through art, an expanded notion of needs and use which privileges pleasure and the imagination over utility. What their utopian visions share is the premise that alienated labor results in an alienation from the objects of human production. As such, any attempt to overcome that fundamental alienation is connected to labor. Where they differ is in their purview: while Morris focuses our attention on the processes of labor and its revaluation as pleasure, Wilde points us to the commodity world, challenging us to taste of the pleasures of a varied and expansive object world liberated from the reductive dictates of commodity exchange and the necessity of possession as private property. Wilde, much more so than Morris, speaks directly to a modern developed world: where Morris harks back to a medieval artisanship, Wilde fully embraces the multitude of offerings of modernity. His attention to consumption and the seductions of commodity fetishism provide a greater sense of the degree to which pleasures have been developed by capitalism and, accordingly, will only be truly liberated by its positive sublation.

The placement of Wilde in the company of Morris significantly expands our reception of both his politics and his pleasures. First, it demands that we reinstate the "under socialism" in his essay "The Soul of Man under Socialism" to its rightful place as the precondition for the pleasures Wilde's collection of texts invites us to celebrate. Second, it challenges a common reading of Wilde as an idealist whose aesthetic ultimately becomes a way of escaping the material world. Finally, it establishes for pleasure a dual function: it is not only to be celebrated in and of itself but also as a figure for a larger social transformation yet to occur.[5] From this viewpoint, then, Wilde's decadence and aestheticism, his self-generation of the personality "Oscar Wilde," his multiple posturings, sexual practices, and epigrammatic style of mimicry and reversal can be seen as interventions into the increasingly limited and limiting public sphere of late-Victorian capitalist culture. These interventions not only provide a useful and, to my mind, inspiring critique of bourgeois definitions of labor and pleasure but usefully put into question the productivist biases that have haunted much socialist thought since Marx, and provocatively suggest how pleasure, much ignored by such thought, can—and must—be articulated within a left-wing project.

Like William Morris, Oscar Wilde dares to ask: What is work? And following hard on its heels: Why work? An early response of Wilde's, "The Decorative Arts," even looks uncannily similar and indeed at times mimics (if not directly repeats) Morris's more sustained replies. "The Decorative Arts" was a mainstay of Wilde's rather scant repertoire of talks for his American speaking tour in 1882. (When he first arrived in New York, in fact, he had under his belt just one lecture, "The English Renaissance," and quickly found himself at a loss, once newspapers began printing his comments before he arrived at his new destination.) In essence, "The Decorative Arts" argues that the worker and the artist are interchangeable. The notion of "decorative art" itself is defined by Wilde as "the value the workman places on his work, it is the pleasure that he must take in making a beautiful thing." In other words, one *works* to make art and to make art is to take pleasure in one's work. Following from this claim, Wilde concludes à la Morris that "a democratic art [will be] made by the hands of the people and for the benefit of the people, for the real basis of all art is to be found in the application of the beautiful in things common to all and in the cultivation and development of this among the artisans of the day."[6]

On the same American tour "The Decorative Arts" was coupled with Wilde's "The House Beautiful." In this piece Wilde moves into a different register altogether in terms of both style and effect, as he takes us on a walking tour of the typical bourgeois household. Here he provides an inventory of nitty-gritty details. Seemingly nothing is left untouched, from the question of flaring gas chandeliers (a definite no-no, destined to discolor and ruin everything else you might do in the way of decorating the room) down to Queen Anne furniture (which gets a thumbs up, much favored over its Gothic predecessor which was "very well for those who lived in castles and who needed occasionally to use it as a means of defence or as a weapon of war," but rather out of place in nineteenth-century America).[7] The whole essay proceeds apace in this manner: "But to return to our room," "About the ceiling," "As regards windows," "As regards dress," down to such fine points as trousers get dirty, and knee-breeches are more comfortable; high boots should be worn in the streets to ward off mud, while low shoes and silk stockings are for the drawing room; and, cloaks, unquestionably, are to be much preferred to coats.[8] Given these criteria, Wilde, the master of upsetting audience expectation, finds the Rocky Mountain miner to be the best-dressed man in America.

There is more than humor (although plenty of that, too) in each of these essays, and between them, in their juxtaposition. If the first essay on the decorative arts represents Wilde's philosophy, and the second, his tour, as Richard Ellmann suggests, this raises the question of why in Wilde the one always threatens to collapse into the other. As Wilde continually and substantially changed "The English Renaissance," it came to look more and more like "The Decorative Arts," which, in turn, evolved into "The House Beautiful." (Sometimes whole passages even are lifted from one text to the next.) The point, though, is not to read the blurring of philosophy and tour as a failure on Wilde's part but rather to see the tour itself as the form of Wilde's philosophy: composed as it is of a series or collection of objects, it embodies the form and method of Wilde's thought and of his appropriation of the object-world. Just as he will collect other people's words— Morris's, Ruskin's, Whistler's, to name but a few—he will, throughout his work, collect and continually reassemble the objects of Victorian society, its furniture, its dress, its conventions, not to mention his own words and his own actions. The most significant aspect of this listing, this collecting, this serial assemblage of objects and so on, is that Wilde does not attempt to imbue them with an overarching sameness; he does not attempt to equate them in any way but instead enjoys their multiplicity and variety and unlocks them from the homogeneity to which their existence as mere objects of exchange consigns them.

Another important point, and something that is very Wildean and perhaps one of his more utopian moments, is that need becomes indistinguishable from taste ("You've just *got* to have that Queen Anne furniture"); similarly luxury is reinvented as use. This development is interesting to consider as a figure in Wilde for what the early Marx referred to as the "richness of historical human needs"—that is, these are needs that only develop after the base needs of survival (food, clothing, shelter) are historically met and the diversity of human wants expands. Taste, pleasure, and luxury are thus inseparable from the concept of use yet ideally separate from necessity.

In this sense, the space mapped by Wilde's "tour" functions less in terms of Ellmann's contrast between philosophy and tour and more in terms of the distinction between place (*lieu*) and space (*espace*) Michel de Certeau draws in his discussion of modern narrations that describe apartments and streets. A place involves relationships of coexistence: "The law of the 'proper' rules in the place: the elements taken into consideration are *beside* one another, each situated in its own 'proper' and distinct location, a location it defines." A space, on the other hand, has none of this stability or univocity; it "exists when one takes into consideration vectors of direction, velocities, and time variables. Thus space is composed of intersections of mobile elements."[9] The tour, as an oscillation between seeing and going, as an organization of movements, makes space a "*practiced place.*" The tour becomes a unique site for what Certeau terms "enunciative focalizations," or "the practice of the body in discourse."[10]

This practice—of the body *in* discourse, rather than *as* discourse—is suggestive for describing the effect of Wilde's prose more generally, moving somewhere between essay and dialogue, prose and drama, philosophy and tour, life and art, written and spoken word. For Certeau space operates in a manner homologous to the spoken word: "On this view, in relation to place, space is like the word when it is spoken, that is, when it is caught in the ambiguity of actualization, transformed into a term dependent upon many different conventions, situated as the act of a present (or of a time), and modified by the transformations caused by successive contexts."[11] It is this ambiguity of actualization, the nonequivalence of place and space, the linguistic and the material, and a whole series of other nonequivalencies that delineates the social topography of Wilde's work—one that defies the statically topographical in its emphasis on what can be done to and made out of a pre-established geography or an imposed order.[12]

Thus while Wilde's later, more properly "literary" works will supplant the figure of the artisan with that of the artist, the philosophy underlying their role in his aesthetics remains the same: "the application of the beautiful in things common to all."[13] Similarly, the method of the tour will manifest itself in new styles, from the diversionary style of *The Picture of Dorian Gray* to the aphorisms prefacing it.[14] But what will draw all these disparate elements together and yet maintain them as qualitatively different is a new notion of use which emerges in the *form* through which Wildean social space is defined, namely, the form of the collection.

Lists, Catalogues, and Collecting

Oscar Wilde was an inveterate collector—a collector of nineteenth-century platitudes, imperial jewels, beautiful young boys, scandalous tales, rich tapestries, fin de siècle flowers, and yellow press. The now-famous chapter 11 of *Dorian Gray* inventories the resultant objects of Dorian's evolving passions for collecting, which lead from the spoils of empire to the substance abuse of opium dens. In its intimate relation to imperialism, Dorian's collection apparently lends itself, as Eve Sedgwick has noted, to an Orientalist reading. But as Sedgwick also observes, this display of imperial booty denies the logic of Orientalism it might seem to invoke in its simultaneous occlusion of any singular Occidental sexual and national body against which the exotic Other is to be offset: "With orientalism so ready-to-hand a rubric for the relation to the Other, it is difficult (Wilde seems to want to make it difficult) to resist seeing the desired English body as simply the domestic Same. Yet the sameness of this Same—or put another way, the *homo*-nature of this sexuality—is no less open to question than the self-identicalness of the national borders of the domestic."[15] This questionable self-identicalness, I want to argue, contains within it a radical notion of the nonidentical; an epistemological relation, that is to say, in which there is a necessary gap between subject and object which the subject does not in turn necessarily try to overcome.

Theodor Adorno describes the relationship of nonidentity between subject and object in terms of a nonidealist dialectics. He sees the separation of subject and object as both real (because it expresses a real, operative separation) and illusory (because it hypostasizes the separation): "Though they cannot be thought away, as separated, the *pseudos* of the separation is manifested in their being mutually mediated—the object by the subject, and even more, in different ways, the subject by the object. The separation is no sooner established directly, without mediation, than it becomes ideology, which is indeed its normal form . . . the mind will then usurp the place of something absolutely independent—which it is not; its claim of independence heralds the claim of dominance. Once radically separated from the object, the subject reduces it to its own measure; the subject swallows the object, forgetting how much it is an object itself."[16]

The whole dynamic of chapter 11 resists just such a collapse of subject and object in its movement from object to body (or subject) to object. Dorian's list proceeds from perfume to music to jewels to embroideries and ecclesiastical vestments. Each description brings Dorian back to himself, to his body. His exploration of music ends with his return to Wagner's *Tannhauser*, "seeing in that great work of art a presentation of the tragedy of his own soul" (*DG* 166). In the chasubles he collects and "in the mystic offices to which such things were put, there was something that quickened his imagination" (*DG* 172). Looking at the ancestral portraits in his picture-gallery, "they seemed to follow him wherever he went" (*DG* 176). But, always, the movement back to the self refuses a resting place. These returns are equally an expansion outward to new objects and new sensations; a continual recreation of what Wilde refers to as a "strangeness" like that essential to romance. It is never a question of holding out the possibility of a return to some Edenic identity between subject and object nor its opposite, the liquidation of the subject. Subject and object are neither undifferentiated from nor independent of one another. Dorian's picture underscores this differentiated state: as an object, it has constituted Dorian; at the same time, Dorian as subject is separate from yet united with it: "He hated to be separated from the picture that was such a part of his life" (*DG* 172).

What Wilde imagines is a nonutilitarian form of use which circumvents the transformation of use value into exchange value in the commodity form and thus recreates a different relationship to the objects of the commodity world. That is, the *form* of collecting serves both as a recognition of the temptations of commodity fetishism and yet also as a resistance to it. Collecting refuses any easy recourse to an overvaluation or simplification (through transparency) of use value in opposition to exchange value. "A collected object possesses only an amateur value and no use value whatsoever"; thus, as Walter Benjamin formulated it, "things are liberated from the drudgery of usefulness."[17] The rejection of use value is not, however, a wholesale rejection of use itself but of an instrumental use value that can only relate to objects in terms of mere utility. What is thus liberated from the drudgery of use value is a different valorization of use, which, in its refusal of mere utility, maintains the integrity of objects and, crucially, makes possible an intimate relationship to them.

Relations of nonidentity function in *The Picture of Dorian Gray* on a number of different levels. In terms of defining the national body, as Eve Sedgwick argues, Wilde's own life and its specularization embodies national *difference* within national *definition*. Moreover, the literal body of Oscar Wilde—from his bulky physical make to his gay homosexual gestures and persona—calls into question the self-identicalness of the male English body: "it dramatized the uncouth nonequivalence of an English national body with a British with an Irish, as domestic grounds from which to launch a stable understanding of national/imperial relations."[18] These relations of nonidentity imply an economy of excess: a queer economy that seeks to make of character not an essence but a mobile set of reactions.[19]

The kind of doubleness (at the very least) that this nonequivalence implies is equally applicable to the male sexual body. Dorian's collection is a collection of histories, which is also a coded collection of gay history, an intervention in the history of men desiring men. In this register, chapter 11 functions as a gay manual, a repertoire for an identity—but, crucially, one that is always already not identical to itself.[20] To return to the metaphor of space, this repertoire opens or makes space in female spaces—interior decorating, the collecting of bibelots, dress fashion, flower arrangement—for men. Men in *this* London move languidly: they lounge and loll on sofas, sip chocolate, and lose themselves in Wagnerian opera. At the most basic level, divisions of gender are thus undermined as domestic space is made available for and luxurious to men. Domestic space is thus both redecorated and undomesticated. Once its doors are flung open and the Wildean tour begun, all sorts of products flow into its previously fortified, sanctified space. Instead of the architecture of an earlier "industrial" domestic space—structured on divisions of labor, gender, nationality, and sexuality—the domestic as escape hatch or hermetic counterspace to the economic does not exist in this Wildean world. These are the kinds of compartmentalization that Wilde's texts ceaselessly complicate and prove insupportable. The same men recreating the domestic in Wilde are also English gentlemen who patronize proper English male clubs and freely circulate in the wider public sphere. They are men made of and by many social and sexual relations and situations that are recognized as public rather than artificially relegated to the putatively "private" sphere. So that, even as the novel closes down so many things, in its coupling, for instance, of substance abuse with addiction or its construction (at times) of a natural/unnatural divide, it simultaneously offers a new model of the subject predicated, significantly, on a new understanding of the object.

At the same time that Wilde recreates a different relationship to the objects of the commodity world, his materialist aesthetic grapples with the lure of those self-same objects as commodities. In short, Wilde is fully aware of what he is up against. Most vividly, Wilde's description of the opium den in *The Picture of Dorian Gray* conjures the strange transmogrifying powers of commodity fetishism: "Dorian winced, and looked round at the grotesque things that lay in such fantastic postures on the ragged mattresses. The twisted limbs, the gaping mouths, the staring lustreless eyes, fascinated him. He knew in what strange heavens they were suffering, and what dull hells were teaching them the secret of some new joy" (*DG* 224).[21]

Wilde's understanding of the commodity is not unlike that of Marx, who finds the commodity to be "a very strange thing":

A commodity appears at first sight an extremely obvious, trivial thing. But its analysis brings out that it is a very strange thing, abounding in metaphysical subtleties and theological niceties. So far as it is a use-value, there is nothing mysterious about it, whether we consider it from the point of view that by its properties it satisfies human needs, or that it first takes on these properties as the product of human labour. It is absolutely clear that, by his activity, man changes the forms of the materials of nature in such a way as to make them useful to him. The form of wood, for instance, is altered if a table is made out of it. Nevertheless the table continues to be wood, an ordinary, sensuous thing. But as soon as it emerges as a commodity, it changes into a thing which transcends sensuousness. It not only stands with its feet on the ground, but, in relation to all other commodities, it stands on its head, and evolves out of its wooden brain grotesque ideas, far more wonderful than if it were to begin dancing of its own free will.[22]

That which constitutes its acrobatic enigmatical character is the *form* of the product of labor—as commodity. Wilde's amateur value frustrates the equation of all value with exchange value and thus at times permits one to see behind the veil of the commodity to the labor which produced it. A sociality is thus produced that goes beyond the reductive sociality of commodity fetishism, which Marx so pointedly summed up as the transformation of the relations between people into the mere relations between things.[23] This amateur value, identified in Wilde with the collector and the act of collecting, thwarts the abstract quantification of qualitative difference (the conversion of use value into exchange value).

Writing specifically on book collecting, Walter Benjamin links the collector's passion to the aleatory and to memory: "Every passion borders on the chaotic, but the collector's passion borders on the chaos of memories. More than that: the chance, the fate, that suffuse the past before my eyes are conspicuously present in the accustomed confusion of these books."[24] The books function as Benjaminian ruins, containing within them a whole host of memories: memories of the cities in which they were found, of the past, and of the selves congealed in them as objects.

Benjamin's essay ends on a note of collector's *jouissance*: "O bliss of the collector, bliss of the man of leisure! . . . inside him there are spirits, or at least little genii, which have seen to it that for a collector—and I mean a real collector, a collector as he ought to be—ownership is the most intimate relationship one can have to objects. Not that they come alive in him; it is he who lives in them."[25] *The Picture of Dorian Gray* offers glimpses of a similar jouissance, but with a crucial difference: the collector's bliss of which Benjamin speaks is not sustainable within the evolving relations of Dorian's story or its eventual culmination. His progression toward an ever-greater narcissistic identification with his portrait ultimately denies the kind of distinctness between subject and object making possible an intimate relationship to objects. To recover that relation of intimacy without the domination of the object by the subject: that is the utopian promise of Wilde's collection. Still caught between the utopian and the present, The Age of Dorian stages a dialectic of contradictions, a dialectic which does not so much offer solutions as pose problems.[26] One form the dialectic as problematic takes is that between art and utility or, more generally, between freedom and necessity.

The Counterconcept or the Green Flower

In order to carve out the realm of freedom from the realm of necessity, Wilde needs to attack the bourgeois forms that reduce needs to mere utility and reduce the objects that meet those needs to mere commodities; he needs to denaturalize and defamiliarize them, in order that they may be reappropriated in all their richness and variety. (This is a two-step process: first, to defamiliarize, disassociate, disassemble; second, to reassemble, reconfigure, reappropriate.) Reminiscent of the goals of Brechtian *Verfremdungseffekt*, Wilde sees the need to put accepted truths on the high wire before they can be evaluated. As he puts it, "To test reality we must see it on the tightrope. When the verities become acrobats we can judge them" (*DG* 64).

One of Wilde's weapons of estrangement is the epigram. Like Walter Benjamin's description of the modern function of quotations, the epigram is "born out of despair": "the despair of the present and the desire to destroy it."[27] As Basil counters Lord Henry Wotton, "You cut life to pieces with your epigrams" (*DG* 126). The epigram functions to tear things out of context while simultaneously maintaining the concept wrenched out of place in an altered state. In *The Picture of Dorian Gray*, strewn with countless examples of such epigrammatic wit, Dorian proclaims, "I don't think I am likely to marry, Henry. I am too much in love" (*DG* 71). Here the concept of love is sustained (Wilde and Dorian indeed like it) but is critiqued in its social expression in the institution of marriage. The aphorism works and is humorous precisely because it enacts a dissociation of the senses; a severing of the feeling—of love, in this case—from its common-sense second-nature expression. In fact, its expression—marriage—is revealed to be incompatible with the feeling—love. The turn of thought involved is ingenious insofar as it marks the borders of what is considered thinkable and, in so doing, makes alterable those borders. These turns insinuate a slippage between meanings and institutions commonly thought of as existing in a relation of expressive identity. Once unmoored from its anchoring in marriage, love is potentially free to circulate in myriad forms and realize itself more fully.

Meanings and institutions are equally estranged by a kind of recycling in Wilde which at times seems like an almost endless reproduction or re-use of the same objects, phrases, quotes, even character names. Perhaps the most extreme example of this is to be found in Wilde's response during his trial in 1895 to the question from the prosecution: What is "the love that dare not speak its name?"[28] In the midst of acting finally to expose the nature of his relationship with Lord Alfred Douglas, Wilde borrows from his own past notes and combines two separate speeches from *The Picture of Dorian Gray*, one by Lord Wotton and one by Dorian. As the critic Neil Bartlett asks: "If this, the truest of all his speeches, is a quotation, or worse, a quotation from his own work, then what answer can we hope to have to our question, the only question we ever want to ask of history, the first question we must ask of ourselves, *is this true*?"[29] In a sense, Bartlett, via Wilde, answers this question himself. Describing the manner in which nineteenth-century gay men operated in relation to bourgeois norms, narratives, and histories, Bartlett claims that "they read between the lines of history, stole its best lines for their own use. They were magpies, thieves, *bricoleurs* for whom the past could be reassembled, given new and wicked meanings."[30] Within this mode, notions of truth, or Bartlett's first question, "Is this true?," should be the *last* question to be asked. Indeed, this is the most un-Wildean of questions. Instead of an epistemology grounded in authenticity or identity, and thus, in competing truth claims, Wilde's play with history asks us to concern ourselves with alterable subjects and processes of social reproduction open to reassembly by magpies, thieves, and *bricoleurs* alike.

In a manner similar to his unsettling of institutionalized meanings, Wilde assaults the notion of uselessness, a value with a more obvious relationship to labor. The fanciful abandon with which Wilde trumpets uselessness is proportionate to the purposefulness with which bourgeois norms instrumentalize use. To the bourgeois valuation of productivity, use, the nobility of labor, heterosexual sexuality and reproduction, Oscar Wilde throws down, as gauntlet, the green flower: "It is superbly sterile, and the note of its pleasure is sterility. A work of art is useless as a flower is useless. A flower blossoms for its own joy."[31] With the green flower Wilde elevates style, beauty, and uselessness over truth, authenticity, or utility. Each of the former negates bourgeois, capitalist valorization; each of the latter involves an arresting of production—of knowledge, self, objects—and consequent reification.

In fact, for Wilde reification is the real crime—a prime example of which is to be found, fittingly, in the story "Lord Arthur Savile's Crime." While attending a party at Lady Windemere's in which the chiromanist, Mr. Podgers, is present reading all the guests' futures, Lord Arthur learns that his particular fate is to commit murder. Plagued by this prediction, and the conviction that surely he cannot go on with his marriage plans until this murder has been duly committed, Lord Arthur decides to take matters into his own hands. Rather than waiting expectantly with no control over when the deed might be sprung on him, he determines to get the murder over and done with, posthaste. Driven by duty, the sheer arbitrariness of a suitable victim for his crime is of no concern. (Throughout the story, we follow Lord Arthur's numerous attempts at murder, ranging from poison to bombs, all of which are miserably bungled until at last, and purely accidentally, Lord Arthur bumps into Podgers while walking by the Thames and neatly does away with him into the river.)

On the face of it, we are easily led, like lambs to the slaughter, to presume that the eponymous crime is murder. But a closer look—and this movement is the truly Wildean one—suggests that the crime in question is really Lord Arthur's false reading of his predicted future. The chiromanist, that is, reads Lord Arthur in the specific context of his practice of chiromancy: as a fortune teller, naturally he must prophesy Arthur's future. In response, Lord Arthur makes of the claim a duty and is unable to see that its meaning is merely provisional, occasioned by the expectations of fortune telling. This misreading is off-handedly enough made clear at the end of the story by Lady Windemere, who, twisting the proverbial knife, objects not to the chiromantist's lack of authenticity but rather to his heartfelt expressions of romantic sincerity: "Do you remember that horrid Mr Podgers? He was a dreadful impostor. Of course, I don't mind that at all, and even when he wanted to borrow money I forgave him, but I could not stand his making love to me. He has really made me hate cheiromancy."[32] For her, his fraud is transparent.

Lord Arthur's false sense of duty has its twisted familial correlates as well. The last scene of the story, one of married bliss (Lord Arthur enters his garden, a beautiful daughter at each elbow, while his wife looks on adoringly), is built on poison, explosive clocks, and in the end, murder. A brief look at just one of these capers, the exploding clock, reveals the kinds of connections Wilde is drawing between the acts of duty performed by Lord

Arthur and their desired end, marriage. In Lord Arthur's second try at murder, he attempts, with the help of Count Rouvaloff, "a young Russian of very revolutionary tendencies" (L 33) and a suspected Nihilist agent, to blow up his uncle by placing explosives in a liberty clock. The explosion, however, misfires and merely knocks the liberty figure off her pedestal, resulting in nothing more explosive than the breaking of liberty's nose. The fiasco is reported to Lord Arthur in a letter from his niece, who relates her father's reaction to the incident: "Papa says [the Nihilists] should do a great deal of good, as they show liberty can't last, but must fall down. Papa says Liberty was invented at the time of the French Revolution. How awful it seems!" (L 37–38).

Like the figure of liberty sitting atop the failed exploding clock, the final family scene is presented as an *invented* one, as a self-consciously dramatic tableau—and equally one which should elicit the response "How awful it seems!" These Wildean twists peel away second nature—in this case, of the family—revealing that which appears to be natural as a product of social invention, and hence subject to reinvention.

This peeling away brings us, as well, to one formulation of Wilde's concept of Individualism with a capital I, which has little to do with bourgeois individualism. Once Mr. Podgers's prophecy is written on his hand, so to speak, Lord Arthur sees himself faced with the choice of living for himself (that is, not murdering anyone and, as a result, not being able to marry) or living for others (murdering someone and thus being free to marry). Hard as the choice may be, he "knew he must not suffer selfishness to triumph over love" (L 24). Just as Wilde will argue in "The Soul of Man under Socialism," he underscores the fallacy of living for others, a choice which, in this case, leads to the ethically fatuous actions taken by Lord Arthur in the name of a putative selfless love. The specious self-denial illustrated by Lord Arthur, in essence, defines for Wilde the limits of bourgeois individualism.

Collective Individualism

Against the limitations of selfless duty, Wilde's view of individualism consists of an "unselfish selfishness" which in turn forms the basis of pleasure.[33] To see what this kind of "selfishness" looks like, I want to turn now to what may at first seem an odd place to find a theory of pleasure: Wilde's *De Profundis*. *De Profundis*, the last piece of prose Wilde ever wrote, is a letter to Lord Alfred Douglas, written in the last months of Wilde's imprisonment.

Wilde, as is well known, was put on trial in 1895, charged with "posing as a Sodomite" by none other than Lord Douglas's father. And it was in fact an earlier love letter to Douglas that became prime evidence against Wilde in the case. He was eventually found guilty and sentenced to two years of hard labor. As Wilde wryly sums up the trial in *De Profundis*, "I go to prison at last. This is the result of writing you a charming letter."[34] Filled with bitterness toward Douglas as Wilde recollects their life together and its ending for him in Reading Gaol, *De Profundis* is generally read as a moratorium on the utopian individualism Wilde puts forward in "The Soul of Man under Socialism." But as I want to suggest, it is precisely in *De Profundis* that Wilde clarifies just what his notion of pleasure entails and what its larger social ramifications are.

Written from Reading Gaol, Wilde's long, soul-baring letter to Lord Alfred Douglas has been enshrouded since its writing in intrigue, personal adversity, and melodrama. In an introduction to the text, Vyvyan Holland lays out all the mysterious details of the letter in fine detective-thriller form: the fact that Wilde was only allowed one sheet of paper at a time in the initial writing of it; the refusal by the prison authorities to deliver the document to Robert Ross as requested by Wilde; the handing of the complete manuscript to Wilde himself as he left the prison on May 19, 1897; the attempt by Alfred Douglas to destroy the manuscript (under the false belief that the copy he was sent by Ross was the one and only original); the presenting of the manuscript in 1909 to the British Museum with the proviso that it remain sealed for sixty years (with the interesting coincidence that it would then be unveiled during the height of the 1960s); and, finally, its early unveiling in 1913 and the subsequent and rapid publication in America of the original carbon copy by Robert Ross, as a means of circumventing Douglas's plans to publish it there himself accompanied by his own comments.[35]

The path of *De Profundis* is at least as ambient as the events and emotions it narrates. In *De Profundis*, Wilde composes a new catalogue, this time one, as Neil Bartlett notes, detailing the costs of his pleasures:

> The pleasures we repeat, and repeatedly enjoy, are necessary to our lives. But the image of the bankrupt Wilde listing the trivial circumstances of his pleasure is a reminder that at any moment this repetition may cease to be effective. The appalled realization that the pleasure has come to an end is not simply the weeping of a rich man who has lost his possessions. Now that the reveller (the lover) is stone-cold sober, the vine leaves, the champagnes and the moonstones must be

catalogued as all-too-accurate signs of the life he has led in this, his chosen city. *De Profundis* is a letter from a man who realizes that the method of his pleasure concealed the fact that pleasure has both origins and consequences, that it takes place within a specific economy and that it can, at any moment, be taken away. Perhaps we require of our pleasures that they conceal these facts. How could we enjoy ourselves if we worried too much that our whole culture is based on the consumption of pleasures, on the pleasures of consumption?[36]

Wilde's own letter offers a provisional response to Bartlett's concerns, for, in reality, *De Profundis* catalogues two kinds of pleasure and two kinds of consumption. On the one hand, as Bartlett identifies, there are the pleasures of which Wilde and Douglas partook, pleasures described variously by Wilde as "appetitive" (*DP* 98); "unintellectual" (*DP* 99); "simply for amusements, for ordinary or less ordinary pleasures" (*DP* 101); characterized by "long spells of senseless and sensual ease" (*DP* 151); and "a weakness that paralyses the imagination" (*DP* 101). All these descriptions share, in Wilde's view, a slavery to things, which, in turn, entails a waste of freedom. Wilde, you see, was not perfect even in his own eyes.

Juxtaposed to these "hard hedonist" (*DP* 169) pleasures is another kind of pleasure, which does not "traffic in the market place, nor use a huckster's scales. Its joy, like the joy of the intellect, is to feel alive" (*DP* 134). This pleasure is the pleasure of love and the imagination; a pleasure, the exercise of which is an end in itself. "The aim of love is to love: no more, and no less" (*DP* 134). Through this latter notion of pleasure lies the possibility for the recreation of the critical faculty—a faculty which would truly understand the uses of things and in this understanding revive the creative and imaginative faculties lying dormant within individuals but with no means of expression within a public sphere dominated by market relations. As Wilde says, "we call ours a utilitarian age, and we do not know the uses of any single thing. We have forgotten that water can cleanse, and fire purify, and that the Earth is mother to us all. As a consequence our art is of the moon and plays with shadows, while Greek art is of the sun and deals directly with things" (*DP* 208).

In place of the "dull lifeless mechanical systems that treat people as if they were things" (*DP* 176), Wilde—via Christ—discovers in objects a multitude of ways of experiencing the material world: "The faith that others give to what is unseen, I give to what one can touch, and look at. My gods dwell in temples made with hands" (*DP* 164).[37] It is thus in the expansion of our possible relations to objects that pleasure is to be found. A new qualitative difference is ascribed to the object, a difference that liberates it from the merely instrumental and leveling relations of exchange value. Like Wilde's collecting, and his disruption more generally of simple equivalences, this kind of expansive, pleasurable use involves a labor that goes beyond base need, a relationship we have seen elsewhere figured as taste, and here as imagination. Taste and imagination are reflective of *human* needs rather than utilitarian, base needs and as such reflect the richness of those needs.

In *De Profundis* Wilde, however, assigns to sorrow the greatest imaginative capabilities. Sorrow is the "ultimate type both in life and art" (*DP* 161) because it wears no mask: "there is no truth comparable to sorrow . . . Other things may be illusions of the eye or the appetite, made to blind the one and cloy the other, but out of sorrow have the worlds been built" (*DP* 161). But this assessment, I think, must be placed within the context of Wilde's prison experience. Wilde himself, in "The Soul of Man under Socialism," interprets the elevation of sorrow or pain (as in the teachings of Christianity to date) as only one step toward the fuller realization of joy and a truly free expression of living labor. "The evolution of man is slow. The injustice of men is great. It was necessary that pain should be put forward as a mode of self-realization."[38] But, as he goes on to argue, "pain is not the ultimate mode of perfection. It is merely provisional and a protest. It has reference to wrong, unhealthy, unjust surroundings. When the wrong, and the disease, and the injustice are removed, it will have no further place. It was a great work but it is almost over. Its sphere lessens every day" (*S* 53). If anything, then, Wilde's move back to pain and suffering as the supreme emotions is most reflective of the intractably materialist basis of his thought. Despite his denials to the contrary, prison, to quote Johnny Cash, changes a man, a fact to which every page of *De Profundis* attests.

Finally, even within the air of doom that pervades *De Profundis* Wilde is able to conjure a social practice firmly rooted in the experiential possibilities of the present. Wilde's imaginings of a new body and new pleasures look within the present for utopian ways of relating to objects and the world which are not reducible to commodification. His assault on the present reclaims the utopian from within and in so doing proffers glimpses of a new modernity in which individual pleasures would no longer come at the expense of the collective. Paradoxically, Wilde sees in socialism the full realization of individualism.

Neither a bourgeois individualist (or liberal democratic) nor an anarchist, Wilde is best situated within a particular strand of Marxism, a utopianism whose basis lies not in valorizing labor (as in much socialist thought) but in a *liberation from labor*. It is at heart a socialism of pleasure: "socialism was beautiful"; "socialism is enjoyment."[39]

In opposition to dominant Victorian culture, Wilde, much like William Morris, does not unthinkingly celebrate manual labor. As he writes in "The Soul of Man under Socialism," "there is nothing necessarily dignified about manual labor at all, and most of it is absolutely degrading. It is mentally and morally injurious to man to do anything in which he does not find pleasure, and many forms of labor are quite pleasureless activities, and should be regarded as such" (*S* 32). Whereas at present machines control humans, in a society of freed individualism, humans will be served by machinery. The past reliance on human slavery—a fact preventing the attainment of true individualism—will be superseded by technology: "On mechanical slavery, on the slavery of the machine, the future of the world depends" (*S* 33). This is so because it is principally through cultivated leisure that individuals are able to achieve perfection.

Before turning to what exactly Wilde means by perfection, it is important to note that the liberation from labor which he espouses is not a turn away from labor per se, that is to say, from all forms of productive activity, or even a Lafarguean claim to the right to be lazy. Instead, the liberation involved is a liberation from the absolute necessity to work under the force of what Wilde calls the "Tyranny of want" (*S* 21). What is fundamentally at issue is a liberated state of labor in which all individuals—not just those few, in the current system, who, as holders of private property, are free from want—would be free to choose the sphere of activity they enjoy and thus which gives them pleasure: "Every man must be left quite free to choose his own work. No form of compulsion must be exercised over him. If there is, his work will not be good for him, will not be good in itself, and will not be good for others. And by work I simply mean activity of any kind" (*S* 24).

The relationship between freely chosen and pleasurable work and perfection is then causal: once individuals are able to choose their own activity, they can fully realize themselves and thus become what Wilde refers to as the "perfect personality" (*S* 26). Perfection is embodied, historically, in such figures as Darwin, Keats, Renan, and Flaubert. Their exceptional talents are able to be realized, according to Wilde, because they have been able to isolate themselves, "to keep [themselves] out of reach of the clamorous claims of others" (*S* 19). (These clamorous claims, however, are not, as they might first appear, the claims of a collectivity against which Wilde will oppose his notion of individualism. Rather, their clamor issues from a misdirected altruism.)

In the future, in order that all individuals may realize perfection or the "perfect personality," current property relations must be abolished. Wilde's reading of the degraded lives and distorted values produced under the present system of private property shares much with Marx's analysis of private property in the early Paris manuscripts—in both detail and tone. Both highlight the elevation of having over being under the system of private property; the measure of value by material things; the lack of free and joyful development of the individual; and the consequent crushing on all fronts of truly *human* needs and values. With the abolition of private property, many Victorian social institutions also must disappear, including marriage and the entire current structure of family life. Even emotions themselves must be transformed and some simply made obsolete. Jealousy, for instance, so closely bound up with conceptions of property, would surely die out under socialism and individualism.[40]

These connections between Wilde and Marx also suggest another affinity between the two: a conception of laboring practices as the motor of historical change. Although Wilde nowhere explicitly focuses on labor to the extent that Marx does (or Morris, for that matter), his analysis of the manner in which private property warps individuals' personalities and, consequently, the larger public sphere is inseparable from an understanding of labor under capitalism as estranged and alienated *and* from an unalienated vision of labor under socialism. As Marx states, "the *subjective essence* of private property—*private property* as activity for itself, as *subject*, as *person*—is *labor*."[41] Moreover, it is only when private property has been grasped as a contradiction, understood, that is, as the base antagonism of society, that resolutions to its logic can be anything but piecemeal: "The antithesis between *lack of property* and *property*, so long as it is not comprehended as the antithesis of *labor and capital*, still remains an indifferent antithesis, not grasped in its *active connection*, with its *internal* relation—an antithesis not yet grasped as a *contradiction* . . . But labor, the subjective essence of private property as exclusion of property, and capital, objective labor as exclusion of labor, constitute *private property* as its developed state of contradiction—hence a dynamic relationship moving to its resolution."[42] Wilde encodes this dynamic in what he refers to somewhat vaguely as the law of life, or the evolution toward individualism. This evolution only makes sense with an understanding of some notion of untapped labor capacities inherent in individuals but unable fully to be expressed within capital logic. At one point, Wilde describes, for instance, "the great actual Individualism latent and potential in mankind generally" (*S* 24–25). Later in the essay, he argues that "to ask whether Individualism is practical is like asking whether Evolution is practical. Evolution is the law of life, and there is no evolution except towards individualism. Where this tendency is not expressed, it is a case of artificially arrested growth, or of disease, or of death" (*S* 49).

Unalienated labor is to be found, then, in the realization of the perfect personality: it is "Humanity [amusing] itself, or enjoying cultivated leisure—which, and not labour, is the aim of man—or making beautiful things, or reading beautiful things, or simply contemplating the world with admiration and delight" (*S* 33). (When Wilde refers to labor, he does so in reference to alienated capitalist labor, or what he calls "necessary and unpleasant work" [*S* 33].) Unalienated labor, in other words, is the joy of living labor, of a form of human activity driven neither by compulsion nor necessity.

In order to free individuals from the necessity of unpleasant work and thus allow for cultivated leisure, the state is to deal with the necessity of unpleasant work. The state is to be an association that organizes labor and manufactures and distributes commodities. It is to be the province of use, its sole purpose to make what is useful. The individual, on the other hand, is to make what is beautiful. Given this vision of the state, coupled with Wilde's stance against authoritarian socialism, many have characterized Wilde's views as more properly anarchist than socialist. Yet the labeling of Wilde as an anarchist is really not accurate. To position him in the anarchist camp is to lose the important ways in which his ideas are thoroughly part of a socialist tradition, not only in terms of his analysis of private property but also in terms of his acknowledgment of the continued need for the state under socialism. Instead of doing away with the state altogether, he simply envisions it transformed from an oppressive, authoritarian body into a voluntary association. His brand of individualism is better thought of as a reaction against a particular form of state government within one strand of socialist thought, a view of the state tainted with ideas of authority and compulsion. As Fredric Jameson conjectures about our own historical moment in which images of centralized planning carry with them the stigma of Stalinism and, with it, the loss of individual freedoms, "a beginning might be made with those contemporary endorsements of socialism that attempt to formulate the great collective project in individualistic terms, as a vast social experiment calculated to elicit the development of individual energies and the excitement of a truly modern individualism—as a liberation of individuals by the collective and an exercise in new political possibilities, rather than some ominous social regression to the pre-individualistic and the repressively archaic."[43] It is just such energies that Wilde draws on and works to develop when, time and time again throughout his prose and essays, he embraces change and the new.

Given this, I think a good deal of the confusion surrounding Wilde's notion of individualism arises from his exemplary use of art as the most intense mode of individualism the world has known. Often the production of art and the ability of artists in the past to attain at least an "imaginatively realized Individualism" (S 34) is presented by Wilde as almost entirely a solipsistic activity. He speaks of the need for artists to be left alone, unhindered by concerns for their neighbors or the public, and unfettered by the constraints or dictates of authority. "An individual who has to make things for the use of others, and with reference to their wants and their wishes, does not work with interest, and consequently cannot put into his work what is best in him" (S 34). It is this line of reasoning that leads Terry Eagleton, for instance, to argue that "though Wilde wishes, like Marx, to universalize individual self-development, this will not for him be achieved through mutuality. On the contrary, it will be achieved by each individual leaving the other alone."[44] But this perspective leaves out a crucial aspect of Wilde's argument in "The Soul of Man under Socialism": it ignores the changed nature of society necessary for an *actual*, rather than a merely imaginative (and hence limited), individualism to be realized.[45] As Wilde argues early on in the essay, "Socialism, Communism, or whatever one chooses to call it, by converting private property into public wealth, and substituting cooperation for competition, will restore society to its proper condition of a thoroughly healthy organism, and ensure the material well-being of each member of the community. It will, in fact, give Life its proper basis and its proper environment" (S 20). It is only after this condition of life, of public wealth and cooperation, has been attained that individualism can truly develop: "But, for the full development of Life to its highest mode of perfection, something more is needed. What is needed is Individualism" (S 20–21).

In this light, Wilde's protestations against authority, the people, public opinion, and so on look less like retreats into a new variation of bourgeois individualism than a spirited revolt against current conditions which make of these collectivities so many forces of social control. For Wilde, as for Morris, the production of the beautiful structurally cannot coexist with the institution of private property. As Wilde cautions throughout "The Soul of Man under Socialism," ownership always comes with its costs: private property has set up an individualism that is false, one which misses the true pleasure and joy of living. In a rare moment in which Wilde positions anything in terms of morality, he goes so far as to declare definitively that "it is immoral to use private property in order to alleviate the horrible evils that result from the institution of private property" (S 20). Thus the nature of false individualism, and, conversely, the possibility for the flowering of a true individualism, is directly dependent on the mode of production. At the end of "The Soul of Man under Socialism," describing the necessary conditions of the new individualism, he claims that "it will be what the Greeks sought for, but could not, except in Thought, realize completely because they had slaves, and fed them; it will be what the Renaissance sought for, but could not realize completely except in Art, because they had slaves and starved them" (S 53).

Taken as a whole, there is nothing reformist about Wilde's socialism. While it may not be able to realize the heights of its own bravado, it holds no truck with gradualist approaches to change or with claims to the contingencies of "practicality": "For what is a practical scheme? A practical scheme is either a scheme that is already in existence, or a scheme that could be carried out under existing conditions. But it is exactly the existing conditions that one objects to; and any scheme that could accept existing conditions is wrong and foolish" (S 48). Instead the socialism Wilde espouses is inconceivable without structural change. Arguing against philanthropy or altruism as remedies which are part of the disease they hope to cure, Wilde calls for a reorganization of the material conditions of society on a revolutionary scale: "The proper aim is to try and reconstruct society on such a basis that poverty will be impossible. And the altruistic virtues have really prevented the carrying out of this aim" (S 20).

Perhaps then the most mystifying aspect of Wilde's socialism still remains the idealist strokes with which he paints his final picture of a world in which the new individualism has been achieved—an achievement that seems at times almost self-propelled: "the new Individualism, for whose service Socialism, whether it wills it or not, is working, will be perfect harmony" (S 53). But lest this last rallying call be taken too much out of context, it is equally important to remember that in the same essay Wilde also describes the drive toward utopia as endlessly generative and never-ending:

"when Humanity lands there, it looks out, and, seeing a better country, sets sail. Progress is the realization of Utopias" (*S* 34).

Wilde's "new Individualism" is thus, finally, best understood as a "new hedonism" or a qualified utopianism.[46] On the one hand, it is a recognition that neither ascetic rejections of consumption nor productivist conceptions about work, technology, and efficiency are the answer. Positioning the utopian as the useful because useless, it counters prevailing Victorian valorizations of use and utility and attempts to establish a radically different relationship to the object-world than that offered by the commodity form. On the other hand, it is not simply pleasure for pleasure's sake. Its erotics of consumption are fully premised on a relationship among producers liberated from the mediating moment of exchange value. Its pleasures are simultaneously contingent, conditional, thoroughly historical, local, complex, and everyday.

It is a hedonism which not only contains the preconditions for the pleasures it provides a brief taste of but simultaneously serves as a baleful marker of how far there is yet to go to make such social transformations possible. To the question of whether there is a link between pleasure and politics (the question with which we began), Wilde's collective individualism provides a qualified "yes, but" whose realization hinges on philosophizing utopia at home, in the everyday use of the very objects that currently hold us in thrall.[47]

CONCLUSION

....

"How little happiness there is for people!"—Lizzie Eustace, *The Eustace Diamonds*

Lizzie Eustace: her name is practically synonymous with lying. When she utters the above exclamation, she has just about come to the finale of a bravura performance, her dramatic powers exhausted, the combined force of all her machinations—from the "stealing" of her late husband's diamonds, to her extraordinary efforts to keep them, to her search for a new husband—put to an end by the much less dazzling investigations of Bunfit and Gager, who finally unravel the mystery of the stolen Eustace diamonds and, with it, the lies of our heroine. So, it is interesting that at this particular moment Lizzie should so emphatically tell the truth.

But, indeed, truth be told, the nineteenth-century novel, along with Lizzie, can easily be heard to wonder at the meager dose of happiness meted out to most people. From the pile of corpses cluttering the industrial novel, to Pip's muted response to the question of his well-being, to Dorian's eventual decline into self-loathing, the texts considered in this study leave us with a rather grim picture of the pleasures of modern industrial life. The wealth of such displeasure alone suggests that the issue of happiness is hardly a minor affair. But what, then, to make of all this unhappiness?

The answer, these same texts suggest, is twofold. On the one hand, the paucity of happiness reflects the harshness of these texts' disciplinary regimes, the fact that they subject their characters to a fairly relentless and thoroughgoing series of impositions and restrictions. On the other hand, this same unhappiness registers a tenacious resistance to these regimes, a refusal to settle for what these texts offer in the way of happiness. In either case, the source of such unhappiness, as I have argued, rests with the processes of labor and pleasure and their particular organization within industrial capitalism. Beginning with the industrial novel, these texts trace what I have called a genealogy of the labor novel whose legacy resides in the lived division between labor and pleasure which currently structures our experience. This genealogy places labor at the center of the nineteenth-century novel: obviously thematized in the industrial novel though not represented directly, labor then goes underground, as it were, as the *Bildungsroman* narrates a new regime of accumulation in which labor becomes increasingly invisible because increasingly dispersed across the globe. No less central than in the industrial novel, labor simply becomes even harder to see, stratified as it is along different geographical lines. The utopian narrative reminds us of the spatial divisions—between private and public, country and city, production and consumption, home and abroad—underlying this disappearing act in its insistence on labor as constitutive: by expanding the notion of labor to include nothing short of the processes of social valorization, these texts imagine a world in which the divisions which the industrial novel constructs and is constructed by would be overcome and labor and pleasure would no longer exist in mutual opposition to one another. A conditional hope, no doubt, the unfettered visions of pleasure these texts hold out are predicated on the overthrow of the present system of labor relations. To liberate pleasure is to liberate labor and vice versa.

In its disciplinary function, the labor novel carves out separate spheres of experience, as the workplace and the public sphere become disengaged from one another. Production is banished from the public sphere, relegated to the sidelines of social experience; pleasure finds itself at the opposite end of the spectrum from production—it is everything that is not work, that attempts to escape the formal rationality of capitalist market relations. This division structures a whole series of divisions that continue to organize our lives today: divisions between mental and manual labor; productive and unproductive activities and sexualities; and different modes and domains of knowledge (objective/subjective, rational/emotional, economic, political, social, etc.). The novel's function in all this is to teach us, much like Gilles Deleuze's and Félix Guattari's Oedipus, to desire our own repression. In the less psychoanalytic language of "regulation school" economics, the novel habituates individual behaviors to the requirements of the prevailing regime of accumulation in order to keep its schema of reproduction functioning smoothly. This process, like the practice of reading novels themselves, becomes increasingly privatized, as individual subjects/readers constitute themselves via the very mechanisms that discipline them.[1]

This is one version of the story, at least, and a not unimportant one either. To be sure, the critical practice of identifying the processes by which the hegemonic categories that largely define our own present came into existence is indispensable. Ideology critique can only lose its urgency once the structures of capitalism that necessitate its practice are no longer operative. But, by itself, it is only half the answer to our initial question about unhappiness and the nineteenth-century novel. For as the novels themselves attest, even the most ideological of texts—ideological in the sense that they provide symbolic resolutions to real conflicts—contain what Raymond Williams, in a different context, referred to as "resources of hope": by which I mean utopian impulses or projects that are not fully delimited by the disciplinary regimes which they inhabit. No less than Morris's William Guest, Gaskell's and Eliot's and Dickens's heroes and heroines struggle with the exigencies of modern life: industrial capitalism and its relations of production; an emergent, urban culture and the new forms of community it produces; the presence of want and exploitation in the midst of "progress" and immense wealth; the gulf between haves and have-nots; the institutional constraints of an increasingly bureaucratic culture. From within the existent structures they bring into being, these novels resist, to varying degrees, the instrumental logic that threatens to colonize all realms of social experience. Whether in the conflict between the narrative and the prophetic registers of *Felix Holt*, or in the search in *Great Expectations* for a space free from production and hence unencumbered by the " 'disenchanted' object world of the commodity system,"[2] they offer glimpses of the utopian, of what it might mean to organize, anew, our pleasures and our labors. Their difference from the more properly generic utopian narratives of Morris and Wilde thus rests less on their respective hopes being radically at odds than on their approaches to the conditions on which those hopes are predicated. If realist texts produce the life world of market capitalism, their utopian counterparts challenge the deep structures of that world: in place of the displacements, reroutings, and aporias which mark realism's attempts to represent labor, they recognize alienated labor as the source of the conflict and imagine a resolution to it. In a paradoxical turning of the tables, these utopian narratives show realism to be "utopian" in the commonplace and often negative sense of impossibly ideal: like Eliot's criticism of Esther Lyons's utopian dreams, their hopes embody "delightful results, independent of processes."[3]

But if one thinks of the utopian in a fuller, more productive Blochian sense, as a "surplus" that speaks to the process of becoming or the always "not yet fulfilled," the fact that realism registers these hopes at all is significant: these inchoate hopes not only belie the seemingly ubiquitous reach of capitalism's "order of things" but deeply question its desirability and inevitability as well.

In looking back to the nineteenth century and Britain's age of empire, I have hoped, as Northrop Frye once said in describing William Morris's project, to get a better look at the future as well as the present. The double vision captured in this kind of looking is instructive, I think, both for the ways in which it asks us to read nineteenth-century texts and for the pedagogical lessons it offers today. In and of itself, looking backward can be a rather self-congratulatory gesture. In the case of texts, in particular, a certain preemptiveness attends such a viewing: a kind of "knowingness" that assumes these novels know nothing that modern readers don't already. But looking backward in the way Morris does, while perhaps a less predictable and confirming experience, is nonetheless a more generative one.

In this view, we may not know all that these texts do; or, they may know things in ways we cannot any longer. As this book has argued, nineteenth-century novels as diverse as *Mary Barton*, *Daniel Deronda*, and *The Picture of Dorian Gray* imaginatively narrate an intimacy between labor and pleasure that exceeds the bounds of our current conceptions of either of these categories. In the realist novel, that intimacy is felt most in the effort needed to pry these two terms apart, and in the unhappiness that attends their separation. Alternately, it is felt in the fragments of experience, the multitude of yearnings, and the diverse dreamworlds that speak of a radically different kind of collectivity or context of living that is neither fulfilled nor fully co-opted by the bourgeois public sphere. Morris and Wilde, then, name the conditions of these dreamworlds: the bringing together of labor and pleasure, which can only occur once both terms have overcome their alienated existence under capitalism.

As imaginings of a future socialism, Morris's and Wilde's projects can be thought of, then, as yet two more "incomplete projects," to borrow a phrase from Habermas, which anticipate a host of other alternative figurations of socialism that would follow in the twentieth century, none of which were able to contend with the sheer might and power of the institutionalized Marxism of the Communist Party in the Soviet Union. In a sense they anticipate a critique recently made by the intellectual historian Susan Buck-Morss, who has argued that socialism failed not because it was so different from capitalism but rather because it shared too much with capitalism's worldview.[4] From this perspective, one can also assert that socialism's vision of labor bore a resemblance to the rigors of abstract labor that dominated capitalism. The sort of pleasurable labor that Morris and Wilde espouse had no place within the productivist account of labor characteristic of Soviet socialism, and neither did their concomitant method of critical realism. Instead, socialist realism—an aesthetic corollary of a productivist vision of labor—asserted itself. A reduced and simplified version of realism, socialist realism forsook the crucial interplay between the cognitive and the aesthetic, which, following Fredric Jameson, I have argued defines the real force of realism, and opted for only half the equation—the cognitive—forfeiting pleasure. In the process, the division between labor and pleasure and labor and the aesthetic became profound. Yet, as the present study's work on the industrial novel suggests, the cleavage between labor and pleasure is itself instructive, as are claims for the transparent representation of labor. As we saw in Gaskell's and Eliot's novels, a genre assumed to contain the visible presence of labor actually turned out to be far more equivocal with respect to that representation. Likewise, socialist realism's narrative of "boy meets tractor" might prove more pliant when viewed through the lens of labor's relationship to pleasure.[5] In any case, a crucial impetus behind the present study has been to reveal a different strand of socialism within the development of realism and vice versa, one that historically did not prevail and that largely disappeared from the cultural landscape until the 1970s, when feminists and others began questioning what happened to pleasure within Marxist discourse.

From the perspective of the problematic of labor, not only could socialist realism be investigated for the particular divisions between labor and pleasure that it enforces but the various modernisms that flourished in the Soviet Union before the triumph and entrenchment of socialist realism could be interrogated for their imaginings of a pleasurable labor. In Alexander Rodchenko's mandate that "our things in our hands must be equals, comrades" one can see a radically different relationship between subject and object that bears resemblance to that I have seen figured in Wilde.[6] Similarly, Dziga Vertov's spectacular portrayal of the aesthetic as a form of pleasurable industrial labor in his film *The Man with a Movie Camera* gives a sense of the countertradition of conceptualizations of labor that animated early Soviet art. In the European context, surrealism and Dada could be interrogated as well for their portrayals of alternative articulations of labor and pleasure. And above all, one can then see Bertolt Brecht as a fellow traveler, if one may put it that way, of Wilde and Morris, for he, as perhaps no other writer in the first half of the twentieth century, attended simultaneously to the issues of labor and pleasure that I have seen animating the literature of the nineteenth century. His poem "Pleasures," for instance, uncannily extends the spirit of Wilde's aesthetic experiments, articulating new forms of pleasure that are as much about form as they are about content.[7] Composed of a list, the poem catalogues a series of activities, events, objects, and feelings:

> The first look out of the window in the morning
> The old book found again
> Enthusiastic faces
> Snow, the change of the seasons
> The newspaper
> The dog
> Dialectics
> Taking showers, swimming
> Old music
> Comfortable shoes
> Taking things in
> New music
> Writing, planting
> Travelling
> Singing
> Being friendly.

In its very form, Brecht's poem works to break down the labor-pleasure division. By virtue of its inclusion here, writing, for instance, takes on new meaning: something normally considered a form of intellectual labor becomes what is commonly understood as its obverse, namely, pleasure. Similarly, the whole medley of activities and objects—from taking things in and being friendly to comfortable shoes and dialectics, which, after all, proceeds from the labor of the negative—plays with our conceptions of what qualifies as pleasure and what as labor. Like Wilde's catalogue, the poem refuses any neat compartmentalization of its constituent parts and encourages us to inhabit a new order of things, which, in turn, figures a new social world equally resistant to the logic of reducibility. Celebrating the pleasures of the nonidentical, Brecht's aesthetic opens up the possibility for a critical realism that abjures the purely "reflective" protocol of classic or socialist realism in its bringing together of the cognitive and the aesthetic.

This view of international modernisms also provides a different context,

I think, for understanding the history of the British novel. The aesthetics of these avant-garde movements suggest, if nothing else, that the problematic of labor does not disappear but rather must be negotiated somehow by the various modernisms. In terms of what this might look like in the British context, it seems important, first of all, to challenge readings of the novel that too easily reproduce a split between social and psychological realism, thereby reinscribing another version of the division between labor and pleasure.[8] Within such a model, psychological realism is equated with an inward-looking emphasis on the aesthetic to the exclusion of the social. Yet, as we saw with Wilde, the problematic of labor should make us wary of these kinds of critical judgments. After all, without this attentiveness to labor, Wilde has often been identified with a form of aestheticism devoid of social vision, his heterodox socialism unseen by reading protocols that essentially and ironically mimic those of "reflective" realism. With respect to the group of British authors writing on the cusp of the twentieth century and actively negotiating the transition to modernism, the perspective of the problematic of labor could similarly inspire new readings of writers on both sides of the social/psychological divide. Thomas Hardy and D. H. Lawrence, for instance, could be investigated for the ways in which mediated representations of labor—especially those involving gender—are rendered invisible as a result of the more overt forms of (male) labor monopolizing our critical attention. With James perhaps the reverse could prove illuminating: interrogating his preoccupation with the aesthetic for the vision of labor it both encompasses and renders opaque.

The category of the "Condition of England" novel—with its explicit goal of trying to come to terms with the new socioeconomic relations of industrial capitalism—can also continue to provide critical traction, as Robert P. Winston and Timothy Marshall have recently shown. In their reading of the intertextual references abounding in David Lodge's *Nice Work*, E. M. Forster's *Howard's End* is seen as an updated, modernist version of Gaskell's *North and South*, which, in turn, takes yet another form in *Nice Work* itself. Together these texts trace a progression of representations of labor indicative of their respective historical moments, with *Nice Work* suggesting how difficult that task can become as the divisions marking the industrial novel are increasingly consolidated: a solitary black gardener mowing the lawn on the novel's college campus and invisible to the students gathered there figures the difficulties of seeing modern labor even when it has not been relocated abroad. Finally, within modernism proper, expanded notions of labor in relation to pleasure might prove instructive to our understanding of modernist women's labors as writers, mothers, fashion editors, home-makers, amanuenses, and journal editors.[9]

Certainly any articulation of modernism today must also include the rich body of twentieth-century literature in which "the empire writes back" and crucially reworks the relations between labor and pleasure. The nineteenth-century novel, as we saw especially with Dickens, cordons off labor from pleasure both conceptually and spatially by "exporting" production to the colonies in order to claim an untainted space for pleasure. This division of production and consumption brought with it other divisions within the realm of colonial production—a social space erased, for the most part, in the nineteenth-century British novel. As the anthropologist Jean Comaroff has shown in her research on the Tswana, for example, cloth made in the colonies was exported to Britain where it became the material for the latest British fashions while South African blacks, conversely, were sold "the em-pire's old clothes," the out-of-date fashions donated to British missionaries to clothe the "heathens." The introduction of clothing brought with it a dis-tinction between different kinds of work within Tswana society, as women's clothing was tailored specifically to the production of a distinct domestic economy. Furthermore, as the concept of self-fashioning took hold, the new customers it created were essentially "putting on the dress of industrial capi-talism, with its distinctions between labor and leisure, and manual and non-manual toil."[10] As this process suggests, colonial relations thus instituted a whole series of changes both in the division of labor and in the concepts of production and consumption and their relation to one another.

The history of decolonization entailed and continues to entail a radi-cal questioning of these relations of production. While this is obviously the subject of another book, a brief look at one postcolonial novel and film, *My Beautiful Laundrette*, suggests the potential usefulness of the labor-pleasure nexus for understanding postcolonial cultural production. Stephen Frears's film (from Hanif Kureishi's novel and screenplay) depicts a postindustrial Britain characterized by the reversal of colonial relations and the collapse of the boundaries on which those relations were, at least nominally, predi-cated—with special attention given to the slippage between industrial and erotic spaces. The title alone reunites the realms of labor and pleasure in its invocation of the aesthetic with the industrial. History "reverses" itself as the Pakistani family at the center of the film and its "future," the central character, Omar, hire the white working-class, unemployed Brit, Johnny, to work in the laundrette. Johnny's white friend, Genghis, articulates what is wrong with this scenario when he bemoans, "I don't like to see one of our blokes grovelling to Pakis. Look, they came over here to work for us. That's why we brought them over, ok?" While this repositioning and the *ressentiment* it engenders might seem to have as its message the need for just such a Fanonian reversal, the use of the erotic in the film complicates such a reading. Rather than simply reversing the colonial narrative, *My Beautiful Laundrette* unsettles its very categories in its blending of work and pleasure. Genghis's plea to Johnny, for example, ends with him saying, "Look, don't cut yourself off from your own people. There's no one else who really wants ya. Everyone has to belong." Given Johnny's and Omar's sexual relationship, this plea, however, carries a double meaning. In fact, Omar does "want" Johnny, both for his work and for sex. And clearly the playfulness of the film's closing shot, following on the brutal violence between Johnny's gang and Omar's family, suggests that there is an alternative to the Manichaeism of both the colonial and Fanonian narratives. After initially rebuffing Omar's attempts to touch him, Johnny and Omar stand at either end of a laundry tub splashing water down the front of each other's pants and laughing, once again intimating a complex and indivisible relationship between work and play. In the end, they exemplify the "in-betweens" whom Omar's Anglo aunt (who nonetheless fully identifies as Indian) rejects at the beginning of the film—"God. I'm sick of these in-betweens. People should make up their minds where they are"—and, as gay lovers who represent the "future," they simultaneously recast sexuality and the family in non-reproductive terms. Further work on the wide range of postcolonial writing, from the early works of African women writers such as Flora Nwapa, Buchi Emecheta, and Mariama Ba to the more contemporary novels and films of those such as Sembene Ousmane, Kidlat Tahimik, and Arandhati Roy could enrich a picture of a global modernism in which the relations between labor and pleasure figure centrally.[11]

Regardless of the different directions one might pursue, there can be no question that all of them must account for and take stock of the processes of modernization. If the afterlife of Morris's and Wilde's utopian visions of labor and pleasure might already have appeared fanciful and blighted within the rapidly unfolding commodification of daily life and modernization that formed the grounds of twentieth-century modernism, one can take heart in the fact that that modernism was nonetheless animated by a similar utopian spirit. Despite the amplification of the divisions identified by Morris and Wilde, that is to say, a dynamic, countervailing vision of labor and pleasure emerged, attesting to the resilience of these utopian energies even in dark times.

Surely, too, the grounding of these energies in everyday practices and experiences accounts for much of their resilience. As Brecht's poem illustrates, the utopian pleasures these different aesthetics gesture toward are located in the mundane and the quotidian (the newspaper, comfortable shoes, being friendly), while nonetheless having the capacity to rediscover the world (the old book found again, new music, the change of seasons) and to embrace movement, change, and creation (writing, planting, traveling, dialectics). Integral to and inseparable from everyday life, labor and pleasure are therefore readily available for use, either in their current capacity or in some future one yet to be determined. As we have seen, labor can never be fully reduced to mere abstract labor; it always maintains traces of resistance to full subsumption by capital.[12] In other words, even within commodity production as we know it today, labor has still not been fully reduced to abstract labor; a certain trace of pleasure remains unconsumed within the transformation of labor as use value into exchange value. It is precisely this trace of pleasure that counterbalances the commodification of labor. The value of pleasurable labor (or of a nonutilitarian notion of use, in Wilde's terms), then, as a concept and a conditional practice, rests both in its critical and in its utopian capacities. It has the ability to discern the underlying structure of the everyday and to proffer a vision of utopia characterized not by a productivist asceticism but rather by a collective plenitude. In short, it can see the separation between labor and pleasure and, in its attempt to put these two bifurcated pieces back together, imagine a radically "other" social world no longer rent by such debilitating divisions and the structures of inequality on which they are based. Much like the movement of my overall argument, the concept of pleasurable labor leads us from the processes of labor to those of pleasure and back again.

As this book and these final speculations about the afterlife of the problematic of labor suggest, criticism today must equally take up this task. After all, who better than cultural critics to address a situation so intimately bound up with the interrelations between the aesthetic and the cognitive? Historically, the genealogy of the labor novel, as I have outlined it here, presages what Brecht called, simply, the New. These Victorian texts and their culture formed the prelude to the collective dream of mass utopia, the construction of which would define the twentieth century and whose moment is now passing, as the vision of mass happiness it embodies seems hopelessly outdated.[13] In its wake it is more important than ever to think the possibility of a still unfinished past open to another future.

NOTES

....

Introduction

1. A sampling of these works includes Miller, *The Novel and the Police*; Cottom, *Social Figures*; Gagnier, *Idylls of the Marketplace*; McClintock, *Imperial Leather*; Nunokawa, *The Afterlife of Property*; Miller, *Novels behind Glass*; Cvetkovich, *Mixed Feelings*; Amanda Anderson, *The Powers of Distance*.

2. I draw the phrase "extraordinary and transforming" from Raymond Williams. As he claims in reference to the division and specialization of labor (which, in turn, created numerous other divisions), "though it did not begin with capitalism, [it] was developed under it to an extraordinary and transforming degree." Williams, *The Country and the City*, 304.

3. Gallagher, *The Industrial Reformation of English Fiction*, xiii. As Gallagher notes, her purpose in identifying this shift is not to "revise the canon" but rather to "[describe] the prehistory of canon formation." Like Gallagher, I am not interested in revising the canon, but unlike her, I do want to suggest that it contains a far richer story about work. This is why I deal exclusively with canonical texts, for it is in these particular works that the story of aestheticism's triumph over labor has been established and made part of dominant ideology.

4. Terry Eagleton provides a reading of this process as well, in which he emphasizes the ameliorative effects of an Arnoldian view of literature, especially with respect to working-class disaffection. As he phrases the threat neutralized by literature, "If the masses are not thrown a few novels, they may react by throwing up a few barricades." See Eagleton, *Literary Theory*, 21.

5. My argument is clearly indebted to this research, as well as to other critics who have dealt with different aspects of the problems labor raises for the Victorian novel, most notably Nancy Armstrong, Bruce Robbins, Mary Poovey, and Jonathan Arac. But while these accounts for the most part emphasize the ways in which the Victorian novel moves away from issues of industrial labor, I will argue that this early problematic of labor remains integral to nineteenth-century British culture and is inextricably bound up with representations of pleasure—an aspect of social experience as fundamentally changed as labor during this period. See Armstrong, *Desire and Domestic Fiction*, esp. 161–202; Robbins, *The Servant's Hand*; Poovey, *Uneven Developments* and *Making a Social Body*; Arac, *Commissioned Spirits*.

6. Gallagher, *The Industrial Reformation of English Fiction*, 87.

7. Armstrong, *Desire and Domestic Fiction*, 23.

8. For a reading of this agency as "aggrandizing" and symptomatic of a certain strain of Victorian feminist scholarship, see Amanda Anderson, *The Powers of Distance*, 36–46.

9. Armstrong, *Desire and Domestic Fiction*, 24.

10. Slavoj Žižek defines the difference between pleasure and enjoyment in the following way: "What should be pointed out here is that enjoyment (*jouissance, Genuss*) is not to be equated with pleasure (Lust): enjoyment is precisely 'Lust im Unlust'; it designates the paradoxical satisfaction procured by a painful encounter with a Thing that perturbs the equilibrium of the 'pleasure principle.' In other words, enjoyment is located 'beyond the pleasure principle.'" See Žižek, *Tarrying with the Negative*, 280, n. 1.

11. Clark, *The Struggle for the Breeches*, 7. Clark is here encapsulating the conclusions of Leonore Davidoff and Catherine Hall in *Family Fortunes*.

12. The term "anti-novel" comes from Patrick Brantlinger, who uses it directly in reference to William Morris, defining *News from Nowhere* as a "conscious anti-novel, hostile to virtually every aspect of 'the great tradition' of Victorian fiction" (35). See Brantlinger, " 'News from Nowhere.' "

13. My use of Raymond Williams here is meant to establish a kinship between labor and pleasure and the interpretive force Williams claims for the opposition between the country and the city. As Williams elaborates on the latter relationship, "most obviously since the Industrial Revolution, but in my view also since the beginning of the capitalist agrarian mode of production, our powerful images of country and city have been ways of responding to a whole social development. This is why, in the end, we must not limit ourselves to their contrast but go on to see their interrelations and through these the real shape of the underlying crisis." See Williams, *The Country and the City*, 297.

14. Dickens, *David Copperfield*, 560. All further page references will be made parenthetically in the text.

15. On the notion of the vanishing mediator, see Jameson, "The Vanishing Mediator; or, Max Weber as Storyteller," *The Ideologies of Theory*, vol. 2, 3–34.

16. Williams, *The Country and the City*, 197–98.

17. Ibid., 210.

18. Ibid., 211.

19. For another reading of the problems with Williams's emphasis on immediacy, see Simpson, "Raymond Williams: Feeling for Structures, Voicing 'History,'" 45.

20. One notable exception is Elaine Scarry's analysis of the ways in which labor resists representation yet nonetheless plays a central role in the novel. In a compelling reading of Thomas Hardy's novels, she outlines the "larger representational context" within which his depictions of work need to be situated: "first, work is a subject extensively represented in the eighteenth- and nineteenth-century British novel, and a subject that has in fact a natural affinity with the novel; second, though it is a natural subject for the novel and though it occurs there far more than has been acknowledged in twentieth-century readings, it is a subject that in some fundamental ways is very difficult to represent . . . it is not the mere fact of his [Hardy's] inclusion of the subject of work that so distinguishes Hardy but, rather, his particular response to certain deep problems in its representation—problems which he solves by making the structure of all narrative action entail (and often even depend on) the physical continuity of man and his materials" (60). She goes on to read this "physical continuity" in such images as the paint of a gate rubbing off on a girl's shoulders in *The Woodlanders* or a footprint left in the dirt.

Scarry also provides a different reading of twentieth-century critics' inattention to work. In her view, it is the result of a passive " 'act' of erasure . . . the natural counterpart to our intense (and in itself benign) preoccupation with courtship and desire" (61). But as she concedes, "What is somewhat startling about this, however, is that the very basis of our critical absorption with courtship is much more self-evidently and elaborately true of work" (61). As she elaborates, our fascination with the marriage contract is a fascination with "the products of man's fiction-making powers" (61), with a kind of making of the world which would seem to resonate even more strongly with the world of work than with that of marriage. What Scarry's analysis does not account for in these kinships, however, are the representational strategies that might evolve when these kinds of "making"—through marriage and work—are placed in relation to one another. See Scarry, *Resisting Representation*, 49–90.

21. Jameson, "Reflections on the Brecht-Lukács Debate," *The Ideologies of Theory*, vol. 2, 135.

22. This is, for me, the weakness of Bruce Robbins's study of servants. In his analysis of George Orwell's search for representations of labor in the novel, Robbins argues that Orwell's politics put him in the position of looking for something that did not exist and then bemoaning its nonexistence. Robbins counters the futility of such an interpretive approach by arguing that the novel "cast its lot with rhetoric rather than realism" (6) and once we own up to that, we can stop looking for the impossible (a realistic portrait of the working class) and deal with what novels do occupy themselves with (servants) rather than what they do not (proletarians). While Robbins provides a compelling argument about how servants function in English fiction, he cedes too much ground by siding so fully with the rhetorical/aesthetic function of the novel. Not only does this tipping of the balance overlook the Victorian novel's attempts to represent industrial labor and the industrial working class but, on a deeper level, it disallows realism's claim to cognitive status; realism becomes simply another aesthetic form. In the process, the ways in which the nineteenth-century realist novel has attempted to understand and represent the changes brought about by a radically new social organization of labor are foreclosed. Even if, in the final analysis, those attempts have been largely unsuccessful or highly mediated, the reasons for their lack of success yield what I hope to show are instructive results. See Robbins, *The Servant's Hand*, 1–23.

23. Wilde, *The Picture of Dorian Gray*, 260.

24. Hardt and Negri, *Labor of Dionysus*; and Negt and Kluge, *Geschichte und Eigensinn*. In Hardt and Negri, labor incorporates a multitude of productive activities, including "the sphere of desiring production, intellectual creativity, caring labor, kin work and so forth." See Hardt, "The Withering of Civil Society," 41.

25. Soper, *Troubled Pleasures*, 8. By the late 1980s, pleasure had gained a central place in a number of theoretical projects, from AIDS activism and queer theory to cultural studies and theories of popular culture. See, for example, Crimp, *AIDS*; Sedgwick, *Between Men* and *Epistemology of the Closet*; Butler, *Gender Trouble*; Fuss, ed., *Inside/Out*; Grossberg, Nelson, and Treichler, eds. *Cultural Studies*; Sinfield, *Cultural Politics-Queer Reading*. In some of its formulations, especially within activist circles, gay and lesbian and queer theory is often linked to forms of identity politics that tend to lose the connection between the individual and the collective and between labor and pleasure. Part of my work here is to build on these models by extending them to the area of labor.

26. Eliot, *Daniel Deronda*, 190.

27. Warner, ed., *Fear of a Queer Planet*, x. For two other articulations of this lacuna, see Sedgwick, *Tendencies*, 1–20; and Edelman, "The Future Is Kid Stuff," 18–30. As Edelman provocatively asks, in response to the head of the conservative American Family Association Donald Wildmon's claim that the homosexual movement will destroy society, "Before the standard discourse of liberal pluralism spills from our lips, before we supply once more the assurance that ours is another kind of love but a love like his nonetheless, before we piously invoke the litany of our glorious contributions to civilizations of East and West alike, dare we take a moment and concede that Mr. Wildmon might be right, that the queerness of queer theory should tend precisely toward such a redefinition of civil order itself through a rupturing of our foundational faith in the reproduction of futurity?" (23).

28. The eccentric Paul Lafargue, Marx's son-in-law and author of *The Right to Be Lazy*, polemically characterizes the nineteenth-century dogma of work as "Work, work, proletarians, to increase social wealth and your individual property; work, work, in order that becoming poorer, you may have more reason to work and become miserable. Such is the inexorable law of capitalist production." See Lafargue, *The Right to Be Lazy*, 36.

29. Negt and Kluge, *Geschichte und Eigensinn*, 38 (my translation).

30. Moretti argues that the *Bildungsroman* loses its historical foundations as a symbolic form with the ushering in of the "age of the masses." *Daniel Deronda* serves as one of his examples of the end of the *Bildungsroman*. I refer to Eliot's and Dickens's novels as late *Bildungsromane* less to mark this distinction (Moretti, after all, considers *Great Expectations* as a classic example of the genre) than to identify how the decades of their writing coincide with the development of a world economy, a development with which I see both of these novels wrestling, albeit in quite different ways. In my reading, then, empire is an inseparable characteristic of the "age of the masses," and one left underdeveloped in Moretti's account of the *Bildungsroman*. See Moretti, *The Way of the World*, 181–228.

31. As Miss Havisham says to Pip, feeling, at last, the enormity of her actions, "until

I saw in you a looking-glass that showed me what I once felt myself, I did not know what I had done." Dickens, *Great Expectations*, 399.

32. Quoted in Frye, "The Meeting of Past and Future in William Morris," 305-6.

PART I   *Realism Meets the Masses*

1. Auerbach, *Mimesis*, 497. All further references will be made parenthetically in the text.

2. Williams, *Culture and Society*, 99-119. All further references will be made parenthetically in the text.

3. Fredric Jameson, in the context of discussing Lukács's conception of totality, refers to the notion of ideology it posits in terms of strategies of containment. As Jameson argues, "Lukács's achievement was to have understood that such strategies of containment—which Marx described principally in his critiques of classical political economy and the ingenious frames the latter constructed in order to avoid the ultimate consequences of such insights as the relationship between labor and value—can be unmasked only by confrontation with the ideal of totality which they at once imply and repress." See Jameson, *The Political Unconscious*, 53.

4. Williams, *Culture and Society*, 101.

5. Cora Kaplan addresses this problem specifically with respect to Williams and feminist responses to his body of work on the 1840s. She offers a compelling way out of the impasse between class and gender relations such a model constructs when she both recognizes the power of Williams's arguments (she allows his treatment of *Mary Barton* to be "the single most illuminating critical analysis of the novel" [216]) and abjures feminists to make use of Williams's broader theorization of culture to complicate his own gender politics. With such an approach, she concludes, "We might then see more clearly how the two narratives with their male and female protagonists and their generic alterity coexist in the same novel" (216). While we come to different conclusions, my readings of the industrial novel take up Kaplan's challenge to read their narratives of class and gender as coexistent rather than mutually exclusive. See Kaplan, " 'What We Have Again to Say,' " in *Cultural Materialism*, ed. Prendergast, 211-36.

6. Recent feminist poststructuralist critics have attempted to address this problem, specifically in relation to the construction of the nineteenth-century novel. Nancy Armstrong, for example, tries to bring the public and private sphere, politics and sexuality, back into relation by historicizing the split between them. She argues that it was precisely during the nineteenth century that the project of gendering subjectivity outside of and separate from "politics" acquired its political significance. She goes on then to claim primacy for the domestic front as the privileged site of ideological battle (and eventual victory) for middle-class dominance. See Armstrong, *Desire and Domestic Fiction*, esp. 28-58 and 161-202.

7. For a discussion tracing our critical heritage back to Arnold and the autonomy he assigns culture, see Gallagher, *The Industrial Reformation of English Fiction*, 219-67.

8. This is by no means a novel criticism of Williams. For readings on the body of his work, see Prendergast, ed., *Cultural Materialism*. For an analysis of his "silence" about imperialism, see especially Gauri Viswanathan, "Raymond Williams and British Colonialism," 188–210.

9. There are any number of examples later in the century of the thematic of the colonial invading England's island, ranging from the Sherlock Holmes detective stories (see especially Arthur Conan Doyle, *The Sign of Four*, 107–205) to narratives of the Englander "gone native." Like representations of the working class in the industrial novel, they reflect a palpable sense of cultural anxiety over the breaking down of clearly demarcated internal/external social and spatial boundaries.

10. Anderson, *Imagined Communities*, 7.

11. This series of displacements from the sphere of production to the domestic and national spheres typifies the structure of the industrial novel generally. Industrial novels exemplifying such a dynamic include Charlotte Brontë's *Shirley*, Benjamin Disraeli's *Sybil*, and Charles Dickens's *Hard Times*.

CHAPTER 1   *"How Deep Might Be the Romance"*

1. Hobsbawm, *The Age of Capital*, 17.

2. Lukács, *The Historical Novel*, 171.

3. Gaskell, *Mary Barton*, 4. All further page references will be made parenthetically in the text.

4. Elizabeth Gaskell to Mary Ewart, 1848, *The Letters of Elizabeth Gaskell*, ed. Chapple and Pollard, 67. In the numerous letters around the publication of the novel, Gaskell repeatedly refers to her concerns about readers' responses. In letter 35, she notes that "some say the masters are very sore, but I'm sure I *believe* I wrote truth"; in letter 37, she acknowledges, "Half the masters are bitterly angry with me—half (and the best half) are buying it to give to their work-people's libraries . . . I had no idea it would have proved such a fire brand"; and in letter 38, she explains to Edward Chapman that "I have not troubled myself about the reviews, except the one or two which I respect because I know something of the *character* of the writers; what I felt was the angry feeling induced towards me personally among some of those I live amongst; and the expressions of belief from some of those whom in many ways I respect that the book wd do harm. I am sure in the long run it will not; I have faith that what I wrote so earnestly & from the fulness of my hear<t> must be right, but meanwhile & when I am not quite well this \angry talking/ troubles me in spite of myself."

5. Like Gaskell's own use of the term, "romance" here signifies less a distinct generic mode—the romance—than a general umbrella term for matters domestic as opposed to political, under which sexual politics would fall. In Gaskell's usage it is perhaps even more broadly inflected. When she wonders "how deep might be the romance" in workers' lives, it seems to include anything about their existences or experiences that is inaccessible in the context of a crowd, i.e., where her initial contact with the working class occurs. Throughout the chapter, my use of "romance" coincides with its commonplace usage (a love story) rather than with its generic variant. For a fuller reading of Williams's analysis of the industrial novel, see part I.

6. See Armstrong, *Desire and Domestic Fiction*, 28–58; Gallagher, *The Industrial Reformation of English Fiction*, 62–87; and Anderson, *Tainted Souls and Painted Faces*, 108–40.

7. A number of critics have read this disclaimer on Gaskell's part as a strong statement of the value of the sexual or emotional realm over and against the political realm. Nancy Armstrong argues that "it is wrong for us to imagine that [Gaskell's] claim to know only the ways of the heart is a humble statement, for if nothing else, her novels prove that love can resolve even the most violent political conflicts." In a different reading, Mary Poovey argues that "for Gaskell, the novel is a mode of representation superior to classical political economy because only the former can transport middle-class readers into the homes and minds of the poor." See Armstrong, *Desire and Domestic Fiction*, 45, and Poovey, *Making a Social Body*, 147.

8. Lovell, *Consuming Fiction*, 87.

9. Ibid., 87–88.

10. Poovey, *Making a Social Body*, 133.

11. Quoted in *Mary Barton*, xxxi.

12. As Gaskell articulates this relationship, "a little manifestation of this sympathy [for the "care-worn men, who looked as if doomed to struggle through their lives in strange alternations between work and want"], and a little attention to the expression of feelings on the part of some of the work-people with whom I was acquainted, had laid open to me the hearts of one or two the more thoughtful among them" (3).

13. This is the tack that Bruce Robbins essentially takes and which prompts his shift, in *The Servant's Hand*, from looking at laborers to analyzing the role of servants in the Victorian novel. As he argues, servants are actually represented in a way that laborers are not. A fuller explanation of Robbins's approach is detailed in the introduction.

14. Later, the question gets phrased as "John Barton's overpowering thought, which was to work out his fate on earth, was rich and poor; why are they so separate, so distinct, when God has made them all? It is not His will that their interests are so far apart. Whose doing is it?" (169–70).

15. Considering the conditions under which women in factories labored, the claim here to too much independence, money, and free time is quite remarkable. Factory labor averaged twelve to fifteen hours a day and eight to ten hours on Sunday. The Factory Act of 1847 shortened the legal workday to ten hours, to which manufacturers responded by cutting wages by 10 percent. Wages for women and children were even lower than they were for men. See Marx, "The Working Day," in *Capital*, vol. 1, 340–416.

16. As Stephen Gill notes, drawing on Leon Faucher's *Manchester in 1844: Its Present Condition and Future Prospects*, the overwhelming catalyst for the increase in prostitution was "commercial distress," leading to the closing of factories and mills and the decline of jobs. Not surprisingly, during the economically troubled 1840s, the extent of prostitution was considerable. Official reports put the number of brothels at 330 and the number of prostitutes at 701, while Faucher argues that these numbers need to be doubled at least. See Gill, "Notes to *Mary Barton*," 474. For a comprehensive discussion of Victorian prostitution, see Walkowitz, *Prostitution and Victorian Society*.

17. In her study of Victorian prostitution, Judith Walkowitz locates the figure of the prostitute as part of a larger structure of class guilt and fear, "a powerful symbol of sexual and economic exploitation under industrial capitalism" (4). Moreover, as she highlights, the stereotyped narrative of the seduced girl represented only a small minority of women working as prostitutes. More often prostitution was a transitional occupation that young working-class women moved in and out of based on their financial circumstances. See Walkowitz, *Prostitution and Victorian Society*, esp. 13–47.

18. A similar structure organizes George Eliot's *Felix Holt*, as will be discussed in chapter 2.

19. In this context, Esther's mistaken view of Jem's relationship to Mary becomes one more way in which their relationship is defined as a nonsexual and hence safe one. When Esther chooses to divulge Mary's dangerous relationship with Carson to Jem, she essentially transforms him from a lover into a brother, articulating directly the work the text as a whole does more obliquely. He is chosen, for both tasks, "because Mary had no other friend capable of the duty required of him; the duty of a brother, as Esther imagined him to be in feeling, from his long friendship. He would be unto her as a brother" (168).

20. Ruth Yeazell provides a version of this reading, in her focus on the absolute and instantaneous nature of Mary's self-discovery with regard to her feelings for Jem. She argues that Mary's declaration, coming so early in the novel, never leaves any doubt in readers' minds about her faithfulness and thus serves to stabilize the text by securing it against the intense passions of John Barton and Gaskell's identification with him. See Yeazell, "Why Political Novels Have Heroines."

21. Anderson, *Tainted Souls and Painted Faces*, 122.

22. The narrative does allow for the possibility of a cross-class marriage, in the earlier marriage of the elder Harry Carson and his wife. In one of Mrs. Wilson's reminiscences, she remembers how her husband, George Wilson, was such a desirable match that before they were married Bessy Witter (now Mrs. Carson) "would ha' given her eyes for him" (120). Immediately, however, the text distinguishes the difference between the working-class Bessy and Carson as less great than the current divide between the Carsons and the Wilsons et al.: "Carson warn't so much above her, as they're both above us all now" (120). This qualification differentiates the class dynamic, then, from its current expression and, in the process, marks the historical specificity of class difference in 1848. In short, it was quite a different matter to bridge the class gap in the 1820s than in the late 1840s, after the passage of the First Reform Bill and its contribution to the development of a coherent middle-class identity. For a discussion of this development in the context of the "making" of the working class, see Clark, *The Struggle for the Breeches*, 1–9. Although much contested by recent feminist historians (such as Anna Clark) for its lack of attention to gender, E. P. Thompson's account of the making of the working class also argues that by around 1830 (and amid the agitation around the Reform Bill) the working class had "discovered" itself as a class. See Thompson, *The Making of the English Working Class*, 781–915. For a critique of the ways in which Thompson writes women out of this history, see Clark as well as Scott, "Women in *The Making of the English Working Class*," *Gender and the Politics of History*, 68–90. Finally, it is important to note that cross-class attachments have the kind of piquancy they do in the novel because the working class forms the focus of the narrative; obviously, it is not the same kind of problem, if a problem at all, when the libertine is the subject.

23. Yeazell, "Why Political Novels Have Heroines," 144.

24. Marx, *Capital*, vol. 1, 272.

25. Ibid., 272–73.

26. Marx, *Early Writings*, 322.

27. Chapters 4 and 5 examine two utopian models of the relationship between labor and pleasure that *do* have the capitalist system of production as their object of scrutiny.

28. Keating, *The Working Classes in Victorian Fiction*, 34.

29. In the passage preceding this one, the possibility that the workers are responsible for the employers' wealth is also raised again, suggesting the extent to which this alternative perspective troubles the narrator's disavowal: "At all times it is a bewildering thing to the poor weaver to see his employer removing from house to house, each one grander than the last, till he ends in building one more magnificent than all, or withdraws his money from the concern, or sells his mill, to buy an estate in the country, while all the time the weaver, *who thinks he and his fellows are the real makers of this wealth*, is struggling on for bread for his children, through the vicissitudes of lowered wages, short hours, fewer hands employed, &c . . . he is, I say, bewildered and (to use his own word) 'aggravated' to see that all goes on just as usual with the mill-owners" (23–24, emphasis added).

30. The distinction between a "charity of consumption" and a "charity of production" comes originally from Rosa Luxemburg, on whom Raymond Williams then draws in his analysis of seventeenth-century pastoral. As he argues, a charity of consumption relies on an image of the communal feast in which all workers and landowners could seemingly partake as equals, while "a charity of production—of loving relations between men actually working and producing what is ultimately, in whatever proportions, to be shared—was neglected, not seen, and at times suppressed, by this habitual reference to a charity of consumption, an eating and drinking communion, which then applied to ordinary working societies was inevitably a mystification." While I think this distinction helps to explain the relationship between production and consumption in Gaskell's text, I do not hold to Williams's general devaluation of the role of consumption. Obviously, the role of consumption operates differently in different texts. For instance, as I will argue in chapter 6, the emphasis on consumption in Oscar Wilde's work does not function as an escape from or masking of relations of production but rather a manifestation of those relations in the commodity form itself. Thus any blanket statement about the value of the sphere of consumption as a site of ideological work is finally both politically and theoretically shortsighted. See Williams, *The Country and the City*, 31.

31. Derek Beales describes the years 1837–42 as a "watershed," both economically and socially, with the British masses facing some of their worst conditions ever. "What seemed so appalling was that such enormous economic advance should improve conditions so little, if at all; more especially that earlier gains should be retrenched; and that it was possible for principals in that advance, the industrial workers, living in its creations, the great new towns, to suffer such squalor and misery." See Beales, *From Castlereagh to Gladstone*, 112.

32. See Hobsbawm, *The Age of Revolution*, 143. For more on Chartism, see also Dorothy Thompson, *The Chartists*; and Epstein and Thompson, eds., *The Chartist Experience*.

33. Hobsbawm, *The Age of Revolution*, 148. Dorothy Thompson charts the development of the Chartist movement from the First Reform Bill on and identifies in particular the Poor Law of 1834 as "the litmus test for distinguishing the radicalism of the middle class from that of the working class." See Thompson, *The Chartists*, 29.

34. Macdonald Daly, editor of the 1986 Penguin edition of *Mary Barton*, also notes the significance of Gaskell's use of the term "combination" when referring to cooperation among the workers but not when referring to cooperation among the employers. In doing so, she mobilizes the term in the same way the anti-union Combination Acts of 1824 did. See *Mary Barton*, 173 and 408, n. 6.

35. By treating labor only in abstract terms, the narrative conceals the reciprocal nature of this relationship. The direct relationship between labor and production, that is to say, is ignored, which, in turn, obscures the worker's creation of the capitalist. Marx states it thus: "through *estranged*, alienated labour the worker creates the relationship of another man, who is alien to labour and stands outside it, to that labour. The relation of the worker to labour creates the relation of the capitalist—or whatever other word one chooses for the master of labour—to that labour. *Private property* is therefore the product, result and necessary consequence of *alienated labour*, of the external relation of the worker to nature and to himself." See Marx, *Economic and Philosophic Manuscripts*, 333.

36. Franco Moretti, from a Marxian perspective, reads the original *Frankenstein* monster as a metaphor for the industrial proletariat; Mary Poovey, within a psychoanalytic framework, identifies the monster as Mary Shelley's literary progeny. See Moretti, *Signs Taken for Wonders*, 85–90; and Poovey, *The Proper Lady and the Woman Writer*, 114–42.

37. It is important to remember, too, that this kind of giddiness defines Esther's "unregulated nature," suggesting that the text reenacts the excess it works so hard to locate and contain in Esther.

38. This same conflation occurs near the end of the novel when the narrator informs us that eventually Mary tells Jem's mother, Mrs. Wilson, the truth about her father. As the narrator explains, "[Mrs. Wilson] gave way to no curiosity as to the untold details; she was as secret and trustworthy as her son himself; and if in years to come her anger was occasionally excited against Mary, and she, on rare occasions, yielded to ill-temper against her daughter-in-law, she would upbraid her for extravagance, or stinginess, or over-dressing, or under-dressing, or too much mirth, or too much gloom, but never, never in her most uncontrolled moments, did she allude to any one of the circumstances relating to Mary's flirtation with Harry Carson, or his murderer; and always when she spoke of John Barton, named him with the respect due to his conduct before the last, miserable, guilty month of his life" (378–79). It is doubly significant that this takes place in the context of Mary's relationship with Mrs. Wilson since, earlier, Jem justifies the need to keep this secret from Mrs. Wilson in order to preserve his and Mary's "domestic happiness." As I will discuss later in the chapter, such political secrets suggest what is at stake in the preservation at all costs of the domestic sphere.

39. Mary Poovey argues that the novel, along with other nineteenth-century novels, "helped delineate the psychological in a way that facilitated its disaggregation as an autonomous realm, whose operations are governed by a rationality specific to it, not to social relations more generally understood." She will go on to argue that in *Mary Barton*, Gaskell's depiction of psychological interiority is still unmistakably social because caused by external forces and thus, at this point, "(proto) psychological." See Poovey, *Making a Social Body*, 143–54. The point I want to make in this context is that, while the external forces may be social in nature, the "cure" for those forces is already purely individually conceived.

40. Catharine Gallagher identifies a different structure of causality in the novel when she places *Mary Barton* in the context of Unitarian debates regarding a "Religion of Causality" (social determinism) versus a "Religion of Conscience" (free will). She links this conflict to the problem of finding an appropriate narrative form for John Barton's story. This leads to her emphasis on the "formal significance" of Gaskell's novel, something I discuss in detail in the introduction. See Gallagher, *The Industrial Reformation of English Fiction*, 62–87.

41. Brooks, *The Melodramatic Imagination*, 15. All further page references will be made parenthetically in the text.

42. Hadley positions her work in opposition to Brooks, arguing that his analysis presents an ahistorical view of melodrama and is more concerned with a "melodrama of consciousness" than with melodrama's place within a specific social and historical context. Her use of the "melodramatic mode" or the titular melodramatic "tactics" rather than Brooks's "melodramatic imagination" is meant to register this difference in approach. While her point is well taken, historians like Judith Walkowitz and Patrick Joyce present readings of the social and political in Victorian England that both draw on Brooks and yet firmly argue from a fully historicist position. See Hadley, *Melodramatic Tactics*; Walkowitz, *City of Dreadful Delight*; and Joyce, "The Constitution and the Narrative Structure of Victorian Politics."

43. Joyce, "The Constitution and the Narrative Structure of Victorian Politics," 182.

44. Walkowitz, *City of Dreadful Delight*, 93.

45. Hadley, *Melodramatic Tactics*, 11–12.

46. The incompleteness of the answer to this question is marked in a number of graphic ways. As Catherine Gallagher points out, the text claims to have already told us about all of John's motivations and the circumstances surrounding his life—"I've said all this afore; may be" (371)—but actually has not. Also, in the penultimate chapter, the novel goes back in time in order to recover Barton's motivations, detailing a scene in which Mr. Carson meets with Jem and Job Legh to ask them questions about the murder that have been left unanswered. Finally, the editor, Macdonald Daly, notes that Gaskell was most probably forced by her publisher to add this penultimate chapter because the novel was too short. See Gallagher, *The Industrial Reformation of English Fiction*, 83–87; *Mary Barton*, chap. 37; and "A Note on the Text," xxxi–xxxii.

47. Amanda Anderson makes this point in the context of examining the limits of sympathizing with a literary representation. The two other instances she focuses on are Jem Wilson's and John Barton's respective encounters with Esther in which both of them fail to help Esther in any way despite their belated feelings of sympathy for her. See Anderson, *Tainted Souls and Painted Faces*, 116–26.

48. Joyce, "The Constitution and the Narrative Structure of Victorian Politics," 186.

49. It also literally does so, since the ballad is written on the flip side of a valentine sent by Jem to Mary, which is then used as the paper wadding for the gun Barton uses to kill Carson. It is this piece of paper that Esther returns to Mary (thinking it implicates Jem in the crime) and which becomes the means whereby Mary learns that her father is the murderer. For a reading of the valentine/social ballad as a "double text" within the novel's discourse of representation, see Anderson, *Tainted Souls and Painted Faces*, 123.

50. Schor, *Scheherezade in the Marketplace*, 32–33.

51. Schor cautions, too, that mothers or matriarchal power more generally requires children. So that, for instance, in order for Mr. Carson to be moved to compassion toward John Barton, Barton must become like a child (that Carson sees in the street) and be forgiven for not knowing what he is doing. Once again, agency is truncated or denied. See Schor, *Scheherezade in the Marketplace*, 32–37.

52. For a study of domestic melodrama, see Vicinus, " 'Helpless and Unfriended.' " As Vicinus notes, "domestic melodrama by its very nature is conservative, however subversive its underlying message. It argues for the preservation of the family and its traditional values—a binding in of the errant son or unforgiving father or wayward daughter" (141).

53. The whole passage naming Barton as a visionary makes clear the opposition here between an individualist approach and a collective one: "John Barton became a Chartist, a Communist, all that is commonly called wild and visionary. Ay! but being visionary is something. It shows a soul, a being not altogether sensual; a creature who looks forward for others, if not for himself . . . And what perhaps more than all made him relied upon and valued, was the consciousness which every one who came in contact with him felt, that he was actuated by no selfish motives; that his class, his order, was what he stood by, not the rights of his own paltry self. For even in great and noble men, as soon as self comes into prominent existence, it becomes a mean and paltry thing" (170).

54. Quoted in Hansen, foreword to Negt and Kluge, *Public Sphere and Experience*, xxxiv; Negt and Kluge, *Public Sphere and Experience*, 297.

55. The full explanation of the Union's and Barton's folly is as follows: "To intimidate a class of men, known only to those below them as desirous to obtain the greatest quantity of work for the lowest wages,—at most to remove an overbearing partner from an obnoxious firm, who stood in the way of those who struggled as well as they were able to obtain their rights,—this was the light in which John Barton had viewed his deed . . . But now he knew he had killed a man, and a brother,—now he knew that no good thing could come out of this evil, even to the sufferers whose cause he had so blindly espoused" (366). As Negt and Kluge describe this process of disqualification, "the proletarian context of living does not as such lose its experiential value; however, the experience bound up in it is rendered 'incomprehensible' in terms of social communication: ultimately, it becomes a private experience." See Negt and Kluge, *Public Sphere and Experience*, 18.

56. Elizabeth Gaskell to Mrs. Greg, early 1849, *The Letters of Elizabeth Gaskell*, ed. Chapple and Pollard, 74.

57. Auerbach, *Mimesis*, 497.

CHAPTER 2   *A Modern Odyssey*

1. Eliot, *Felix Holt*, 75. All further page references will be made parenthetically in the text.

2. In 1841 a rapid coach from London to Exeter took eighteen hours. In 1845 the same journey by rail express took six and a half hours.

3. This distinction between the process and experience of change is crucial to how Eliot will attempt to represent history in the novel, something I develop later in the chapter. In its simplest form, this distinction involves the difference between reading the process or history of change as a diachronic, continuous narrative of development and progress and seeing history as a series of fragments and ruptures, as a narrative of discontinuity in which the past is not passively read to confirm the present. I am here drawing on the work of Walter Benjamin, who distinguishes these two readings of the relationship between past and present as the difference between historicism and historical materialism. Whereas historicism, for Benjamin, "gives the 'eternal' image of the past," historical materialism "supplies a unique experience with the past." See Benjamin, "Theses on the Philosophy of History," *Illuminations*, 253–64.

4. This co-extensivity of the individual with his/her landscape also figures strongly in Eliot's earlier novels, such as *Scenes from Clerical Life* and *Adam Bede*, where identity is structured around a rootedness to place, even while the rural community is disintegrating.

5. The relation of nonidentity between subject and object does not have to be seen necessarily as a loss, as Eliot imagines it. In chapter 5, I show how this same notion of nonidentity fuels Oscar Wilde's generative non-idealist dialectic.

6. Given this, it is with Harold Transome, not Rufus Lyon (as we will see below), that the greater error lies, for he tries to sever himself from the past, "trusting in his own skill to shape the success of his morrows, ignorant of what many yesterdays had determined for him beforehand" (277). In so doing, he moves from the proper position of stewardship to that of contrivance.

7. In chapter 3 I will discuss in particular how such quandaries are approached in *Daniel Deronda*, where the presence of industrial labor and its social effects gets figured in an altogether different way. The connection, too, has been made between *Felix Holt* and *Middlemarch* in terms of the latter's prefatory question regarding how one represents the individual in the flux of history.

8. The epigraph to this chapter opens with the following poem about truth: "Truth is the precious harvest of the earth. / But once, when harvest waved upon a land, / The noisome cankerworm and caterpillar, / Locusts, and all the swarming foul-born broods, / Fastened upon it with swift, greedy jaws, / And turned the harvest into pestilence, / Until men said, What profits it to sow?" (215).

9. When John Blackwood sent proofs of "Address to Working Men" to Eliot he added a note clarifying that in the House the charge that the new franchise made working men masters was issued sarcastically by those who opposed the Reform Bill of 1867. Eliot responded in a letter on December 7, 1867: "I agree with you about the phrase, 'masters of the country.' I wrote that part twice, and originally I distinctly said that the epithet was false. Afterwards I left that out, preferring to make a stronger *argumentum ad hominem* in case any workman believed himself a future master." *The George Eliot Letters*, ed. Haight, 4: 403–04.

10. It was at the behest of her publisher, John Blackwood, that Eliot wrote the "Address to Working Men" in November 1867. Blackwood got the idea after hearing Disraeli's Edinburgh address to the working men in defense of the Second Reform Bill. In terms of the larger argument I am making as to the ambivalent narration of past and present in *Felix Holt*, the significance of the address lies in its historical continuity with the novel. Whereas the novel purportedly portrays the changes of 1832, its formal concerns are those of the 1860s.

11. See Williams, *Problems in Materialism and Culture*, 213–29; and Brantlinger, *The Spirit of Reform*, esp. 1–9 and 205–35. Although there is a slight discrepancy in the time frames of Williams and Brantlinger, the distinction they draw is essentially the same: the first period of reform is identified with middle-class rights and the ensuing crisis of Chartism in the 1840s, and the second with the crisis of suffrage surrounding the Second Reform Bill. In the following discussion of the rising importance of culture in debates about reform, I am paraphrasing Brantlinger's argument. Eric Hobsbawm also notes the shift in class alliances but in the broader context of Europe as a whole. In terms of continental politics he marks 1848 as a turning point for the bourgeoisie: tying their fortunes to reform they cease to be a revolutionary class. See *The Age of Revolution*, 349–62. On the significance of 1848, see also Lukács, *The Historical Novel*, 171–250.

12. Franco Moretti interestingly traces this emphasis on cultural continuity back to the singular nature of the English Revolution, suggesting that 1642 and 1688 figured as "revolutionary" in the etymological sense of the word: rather than a revolutionary break between an aristocratic past and a newly emerging bourgeois present (as in France in 1789), the English Revolution *reestablished* or restored rights deemed temporarily lost, circling back toward English origins, not forward to a revolutionary new future. In the context of the development and analysis of the *Bildungsroman*, Moretti argues that this had profound effects on the English form of this genre. Moretti's specific analysis of *Felix Holt* is developed later in the chapter, while chapter 3 investigates more fully the representation of labor and pleasure in the *Bildungsroman*. See Moretti, *The Way of the World*, 181–228.

13. Brantlinger, *The Spirit of Reform*, 239.

14. The vocabulary Eliot uses when describing the mob and its riot indicates the force of its threat to ordered society. The mob is variously described as "a mad crowd," a "mass of wild chaotic desires and impulses," and "unreasoning men," filled with "destructive spirit," "blind [outrage]," and raising the specter of "horror" should they not be "diverted from any further attack on places where they would get in the midst of intoxicating and inflammable materials" (424–27). Against this chaos of desire and impulse, the "civil force" of Treby Magna "prepared themselves to struggle for order," whose essence lay primarily in protecting the private property most likely to be destroyed by this mass.

15. Catherine Hall convincingly argues that the reconstitution of the English nation as a result of the Reform Act of 1867 cannot be understood outside the context of empire, "for it was impossible to think about the 'mother country' and its specificities without reference to the colonies." As she demonstrates through the chain of connections she draws between Birmingham (England), Britain, and Jamaica, "there was a deep-rooted and widely shared set of assumptions which cut across Radical and Tory that England was without a doubt the greatest, the most advanced and the most civilized nation of all time. The colonies demonstrated this for they were possessed and civilized by the English." See Hall, "Rethinking Imperial Histories," 10.

16. See Marx, *Collected Works, 1857–1861*, vol. 28, 399–421.

17. Interestingly enough, this choice is also distinguished through a literary metaphor as the choice between two different genres, reflected in Esther's comment to Harold that "[he is] quite in another *genre*" (540).

18. Chapter 43, in which Esther explores her primary feeling of just subjection before Felix, begins with an epigraph of two stanzas of Tennyson's *In Memoriam*, the second of which harkens "Dear friend, far off, my lost desire, / So far, so near, in woe and weal; / O, loved the most when most I feel / There is a lower and a higher!" (522). Once again, this illustrates the kind of naturalized hierarchy that is continually being reestablished on different levels of the narrative, be it the economic, the social, the cultural, or the moral.

19. Esther's connection with the real Empress of India, Queen Victoria, offers insight into the issues of power that circulate around Esther. In 1867 Queen Victoria was named Empress of India, thereby linking the queen's domestic rule with the British Empire. But, as a woman, she occupied a unique position with respect to her own power. Analyzing the relationship between Queen Victoria and Victorian women novelists, Margaret Homans identifies Queen Victoria as a queen who kept her power by giving it away; ruling in this manner, she reinforced the separate sphere's argument that women do not rule, and, moreover, are not fit to rule. Instead, she called on her identification as a feminine woman, engendering an authority that came not from the public sphere but from the privatized emotional depths of the domestic sphere. Benedict Anderson points out that the linking of national and imperial rule is a late development—post-1857— which is then consolidated in 1867. See Homans, *Royal Representations*; Homans and Munich, eds., *Remaking Queen Victoria*; and Anderson, *Imagined Communities*, 88–94.

20. A representative historical moment making visible the concealed nature of this exchange was the 1857 Matrimonial Causes Act, which, according to Mary Poovey, was "the first major piece of British legislation to focus attention on the anomalous position of married women under the law" (51). This act challenged the fact that women, once they were married, were legally represented or "covered" by their husbands, thereby equating the interests of the husband with those of his wife. As Poovey argues, this act was important not only on its own terms but also because it "exposed the limitations of the domestic ideal" (52). See Poovey, *Uneven Developments*, 51–88.

21. Deleuze and Guattari, *Anti-Oedipus*, 170.

22. The end of *Felix Holt* closes with the classic image of Oedipal triangulation: the producing of a "young Felix" in the last sentence of the novel completes the "daddy-mommy-me" triangle and, moreover, ensures the reproduction of Oedipal power, which here takes the particular form of scientific rationality: "There is a young Felix, who has a great deal more science than his father but not much more money" (606).

23. When Mrs. Transome speaks to Jermyn about Harold's intention of pursuing his case against him, she recognizes the limited extent of her power, even with respect to her son, as the singularly disempowering "power to feel miserable" (517).

24. See, for example, Barrett, *Vocation and Desire*; Uglow, *George Eliot*; and Beer, *George Eliot*. In his foreword to Daniel Cottom's book on Eliot, Terry Eagleton as well suggests that Eliot's representations of sex and gender "[surpass] a simple project of class-hegemony" (xvii). See Cottom, *Social Figures*, viii–xvii.

25. Moretti, *The Way of the World*, 227.

PART II   *Coming of Age in a World Economy*

1. Hobsbawm, *The Age of Capital*, 47.
2. Quoted in Wiener, *English Culture and the Decline of the Industrial Spirit*, 28. .
3. Arnold, *Culture and Anarchy*, 49.
4. Ibid., 46.
5. Williams, *Culture and Society*, 134.
6. Ibid., 136.
7. Arnold, *Culture and Anarchy*, 82.
8. Ibid., 64–65.
9. Jameson, *Brecht and Method*, 13.
10. For a reading of the female *Bildungsroman* and the alternative kinds of "growing up" it entails, see Fraiman, *Unbecoming Women*.

CHAPTER 3   *Seeing the Invisible*

1. Wiener, *English Culture and the Decline of the Industrial Spirit*, 27. The notion of the "visibility of human progress," quoted by Wiener, comes from Asa Briggs. As he goes on to note, although the economy was strong, there were, nonetheless, significant tensions within the political parties at this time, as Lord John Russell's Whig government struggled to maintain itself in power. As Briggs comments, "The same provoking contrast between economic prosperity and political fragmentation was to persist for a large portion of the middle years of the century, and the Queen and Prince Albert came to see quite clearly that the state of the country and the state of the parties were two quite distinct questions" (17). See Briggs, *Victorian People*, 15–51.

2. Quoted in Wiener, *English Culture and the Decline of the Industrial Spirit*, 34.

3. Hobsbawm, *The Age of Capital*, 34. As Hobsbawm elaborates, "though no dramatic new discoveries were made and (with relatively minor exceptions) few formal conquests by new military conquistadors, for practical purposes an entirely new economic world was added to the old and integrated into it" (34).

4. Hobsbawm, *The Age of Capital*, 47. The full quote for this phrase from Eric Hobsbawm is discussed in Part II.

5. Said, *Culture and Imperialism*, xvi.

6. See, for example, Meyer, *Imperialism at Home*; David, *Rule Britannia*; Lewis, *Gendering Orientalism*; and McClintock, *Imperial Leather*. For an assessment of Said's theory and influence, see Pearson et al., *Cultural Readings of Imperialism*.

7. Harvey, *The Condition of Postmodernity*, 123.

8. Ibid., 121–22.

9. Jameson, *Brecht and Method*, 152.

10. Dickens, *Great Expectations*, 319. All further page references will be made parenthetically in the text.

11. Moretti, *The Way of the World*, 213.

12. Ibid., 213.

13. Ibid., 227.

14. Daniel Cottom observes that the opposite of mastery in the text is not servility but rather plagiarism. See *Text and Culture*, 103–53.

15. In a Darwinian reading of the novel, Goldie Morgentaler argues that *Great Expectations* marks the first time Dickens emphasizes social environment over heredity as the determining factor in the formation of the self. Morgentaler sees this shift as evidence of the effect Darwin's *The Origin of Species* had on Dickens. See Morgentaler, "Meditating on the Low."

16. Hughes, *The Fatal Shore*, 40.

17. Hughes divides transportation to Australia into four phases: (1) 1787–1810, when relatively few convicts were sent; (2) 1811–30, when 50,200 convicts were transported (some 31 percent of the total number); (3) 1831–40, the period when the system peaked and began to decline, with all transportation to New South Wales ending in 1840; (4) 1841–68, when the last group of convicts, all Irish Fenians, was sent to Van Dieman's Island. Given Jerome Meckier's analysis of the dating of events in *Great Expectations*, Magwitch would have been sent to Australia during the second phase of transport and stayed there roughly from 1812–13 to 1827–28. Significantly, this is the period with the greatest amount of social turmoil at home and a corresponding pressure from abroad, as the growth of the pastoral industry after 1815 created a huge demand for convict labor. See Hughes, *The Fatal Shore*, 158–202; and Meckier, "Dating the Action in *Great Expectations*," 157–94.

18. Hughes, *The Fatal Shore*, 168.

19. Fanon, *The Wretched of the Earth*, 102.

20. For a reading of how the "avenging" servant signals Pip's failure to maintain his former family with Joe and Biddy, see Robbins, *The Servant's Hand*, 156–57.

21. To translate this relationship into a slightly different language, it is the horror of lived experience and structure coming together—a relationship Fredric Jameson outlines in "Cognitive Mapping," and that I develop in more detail later in the chapter in reference to *Daniel Deronda*.

22. Geras, "Fetishism," 165.

23. Interestingly, "Handel" means "trade" in German.

24. Kincaid, *Annoying the Victorians*, 85.

25. The romantic realm is no less susceptible to such invasions. Not only does Magwitch turn out to be Estella's father, thereby intertwining his plight with Estella's and, in a sense, fathering the romance between his two "orphans," but Pip's feelings toward Estella are fully inseparable from his desire for money and Great Expectations, whose source once again leads back to Magwitch. As Pip declares when he sees Estella again after being in London: "Truly it was impossible to dissociate her presence from all those wretched hankerings after money and gentility that had disturbed my boyhood . . . In a word, it was impossible for me to separate her, in the past or in the present, from the innermost life of my life" (235–36). For a reading of how romance mitigates the social constraints it also reveals, and ultimately aligns men with the power structure in a hierarchized relationship with women, see Langbauer, *Women and Romance*, 127–87.

26. For a reading of the omniscient narrator in *Bleak House* as a "commissioned spirit," "[lifting] . . . the roofs of the city, street by street" (2), in order to provide the kind of unifying viewpoint such a synoptic overview allows, and which is not present in the first-person narration of *Great Expectation*, see Arac, *Commissioned Spirits*, 1–12; 114–38.

27. While some might argue that Joe and Biddy inhabit such a place, they so clearly represent a historically obsolete position that they can hardly be seen to provide the critical leverage for such a commentary.

28. Benedict Anderson uses the term "imagined community" to designate the invented nature of nationalisms. He carefully differentiates his use of the term from Ernest Gellner's, in which "invention" is counterposed to authenticity, "as if true communities exist that can be advantageously juxtaposed to nations." Following Anderson, I am using the term not as an indicator of falsity as opposed to genuineness but with a focus on the style in which *Daniel Deronda*'s community is being imagined. See Anderson, *Imagined Communities*, 6.

29. *The George Eliot Letters*, ed. Haight, 6:290.

30. Leavis inducts Eliot into his eponymous tradition with the following flourish: "In no other of her works is the association of the strength with the weakness so remarkable or so unfortunate as in *Daniel Deronda*. It is so peculiarly unfortunate, not because the weakness spoils the strength—the two stand apart, on a large scale, in fairly neatly separable masses—but because the mass of fervid and wordy unreality seems to have absorbed most of the attention the book has ever had, and to be all that is remembered of it" (79). Leavis felt so strongly about how unfortunate (but fortunately separable) the Jewish portion of the novel was that he took it upon himself to rename the novel *Gwendolen Harleth*. My point in dwelling on Leavis's dismissal is to underline that what he and others have identified as the failed form of *Daniel Deronda* can be more productively approached as the problematic of the novel itself. In other words, as Lukács reminds us, it is dangerous to equate *having* a problematic with *being* problematic. See Leavis, *The Great Tradition*, 79–125.

31. One version of this kind of reading is Irving Howe's. In contradistinction to the extended "play" of systematic debasement in the Gwendolen/Grandcourt plot, he sees the Deronda plot as the search for a locus for moral standards and obligations, for the "ideals" which Eliot "finds increasingly difficult to authenticate in her own world." See Howe, "George Eliot and the Jews," 374.

32. Hardy, Introduction, *Daniel Deronda*, 10.

33. Quoted in Hardy, Introduction, 10; James, "Daniel Deronda: A Conversation," *Partial Portraits*, 65–93.

34. The best account is Katherine Bailey Linehan's. She delineates the connections drawn between racism, sexism, and imperialism and argues that Eliot's vision of imperialism via the Gwendolen plot forms a central focus of the novel rather than serving merely as a secondary, symbolic background to the character of Gwendolen herself. Ann Cvetkovich, in the context of arguing that Eliot's portrayal of Gwendolen's interiority is indebted to the sensation novel, reads the relationship of domination between Grandcourt and Gwendolen not only as the analogue of imperialism but its extension. See Linehan, "Mixed Politics," 323–46; and Cvetkovich, *Mixed Feelings*, 128–64.

35. Eliot, *Daniel Deronda*, 71. All further page references will be made parenthetically in the text.

36. For a reading that connects Grandcourt's mastery to the logic of property ownership, and specifically the notion of absolute possession, see Nunokawa, *The Afterlife of Property*, 77–99. As Nunokawa argues, the notion of absolute possession evolved from the need to distinguish between slaves and citizens in Roman law and thus suggests a deep "intimacy between the sphere of the formal economy and the shapes of the psychic" (95). In the case of Gwendolen and Grandcourt, psychological domination displaces ownership; unlike property, which must paradoxically be given away in order to be realized, Gwendolen's subjection can be ongoing, stimulated by fancy, in a mastery that never exhausts itself.

37. Eliot's famous passage on the importance a rootedness to place has to a rich affective life opens chapter 3: "A human life, I think, should be well rooted in some spot of a native land, where it may get the love of tender kinship for the face of earth, for the labours men go forth to, for the sounds and accents that haunt it, for whatever will give that early home a familiar unmistakable difference amidst the future widening of knowledge: a spot where the definiteness of early memories may be inwrought with affection, and kindly acquaintance with all neighbours, even to the dogs and monkeys, may spread not by sentimental effort and reflection, but as a sweet habit of the blood." Needless to say, "this blessed persistence in which affection can take root had been wanting in Gwendolen's life" (50).

38. Walter Benjamin draws an analogy between the worker under capitalism and the gambler in terms of the way in which each has been cheated out of experience, their lives mechanistically reduced to those of automatons. See Benjamin, "On Some Motifs in Baudelaire," *Illuminations*, 155–200. For a more Foucauldian reading of the relations of power in the gambling scene, and of the workings of what he terms the "body-machine complex" in the culture of realism, see Seltzer, "Statistical Persons," 82–98.

39. Jameson, "Cognitive Mapping," 349. The relationship between lived experience and structure is another way of conceiving the relationship between appearance and essence, as discussed above vis-à-vis *Great Expectations*.

40. Eliot, *Essays*, 386.

41. In contrast, Eliot defines the "full meaning" of morals "as the conduct which, in every human relation, would follow from the fullest knowledge and the fullest sympathy,—a meaning perpetually corrected and enriched by the more thorough appreciation of the dependence in things, and a finer sensibility to both physical and spiritual fact" (*Essays*, 392). In the negative examples she cites of men falsely lauded for their morality, their situations are, interestingly, the reverse of Grandcourt's: they are praised for exhibiting virtue at home while disregarding the public welfare at large.

42. Lukács, *The Theory of the Novel*.

43. Acts of concealment are not limited to women. Mirah's father actively severs Mirah from her mother and brother by kidnapping her and then lying about her mother's death. Sir Hugo Mallinger also participates in Alcharisi's concealment by not telling Deronda about his parents. Nevertheless, women are punished much more severely than men for these acts.

44. Gwendolen enters into marriage with Grandcourt in large part to avoid having (metaphorically) to sell her body by becoming a governess, a choice whose fetters she feels to be too confining, and which she poses expressly in terms of the bitterness she would feel at being at the mercy of someone else: "I am not at all sure what the Momperts will like me to be. It is enough that I am expected to be what they like" (319). Similarly, Alcharisi rebels against the restrictions limiting her ambition as a female artist and seeks to determine her own life by freeing herself from her father's authority. In a discussion of Eliot's *Adam Bede* and Thackeray's *Henry Esmond*, Eve Kosofsky Sedgwick addresses the relationship between women's sexuality and power in terms of the historicity of the female. As she notes, with regard to the Hetty and Beatrix plots in these respective novels, "for each woman, the sexual narrative occurs with the overtaking of an active search for power of which she is the *subject*, by an already-constituted symbolic power exchange between men of which her very misconstruction, her sense of purposefulness, proves her to have been the designated *object*" (159). Almost the same can be said of Gwendolen, who, like these women, is offset by the female figure of the pitiable woman, in this case, Mirah. As Sedgwick argues, "the sexually pitiable or contemptible female figure is a solvent that not only facilitates the relative democratization that grows up with capitalism and cash exchange, but goes a long way—for the men whom she leaves bonded together—toward palliating its gaps and failures" (160). It is in a similar sense as well that nationalism plays a palliative role, something that I will develop later. See Sedgwick, *Between Men*, 134–60.

45. Benjamin, "The Storyteller," *Illuminations*, 86. Eliot, as well, in her own essay "Story-telling," bases her whole argument about the best way to tell a story on the assumption that communication between a storyteller and her public is of singular importance: "Since the standard must be the interest of the audience, there must be several or many good ways [to tell a story] rather than one best." See Eliot, *Essays*, 240. See also Adorno, "The Position of the Narrator in the Contemporary Novel," *Notes to Literature*, 1:30–36, for a reading of the increasingly paradoxical role of the narrator in a world where individual experience has been replaced by the administered world. In terms of the British novel, specifically, Raymond Williams also identifies the changing compass of community and hence storytelling in the context of a quite newly experienced world. For his discussion of "knowable communities," see *The Country and the City*, 165–81.

46. Adorno, "The Position of the Narrator in the Contemporary Novel," 31.

47. Arac, *Commissioned Spirits*, 11.

48. Jameson, "Cognitive Mapping," 350.

49. Said, *Beginnings*, 145.

50. Ibid.

51. Jennifer Uglow notes that Grandcourt's lack of openness to complexity leads to his downfall. Because he is unable to appreciate the mixed emotions of either Lydia or Gwendolen, he misreads their motivations and actions. See Uglow, *George Eliot*, 226.

52. For critics desirous of drawing a straight and uninterrupted line from the beginning of Eliot's fiction to the end, her choice of Judaism in this context becomes just one more application of her doctrine of sympathy—this time for yet another group in another time and place. Carol A. Martin, for example, concludes, "From *Scenes of Clerical Life* to *Daniel Deronda*, the purpose of fiction for Eliot is to create imaginatively the lives of others so that readers will have that 'fiber of sympathy' that connects them with the lives around them, as the narrator says in the famous chapter 17 of *Adam Bede*." See Martin, "Contemporary Critics and Judaism in *Daniel Deronda*." This is the approach that George Lewes also takes when he writes that just as Eliot "formerly contrived to make one love Methodists, there was no reason why she should not conquer the prejudice against the Jews." See *The George Eliot Letters*, ed. Haight, 6:196.

53. This is not to suggest that the figure of the artist cannot be situated within a materialist framework—I will argue that it is in Oscar Wilde's work—but only that it is not here. For a reading of the relationship between intellectual labor and mid-nineteenth-century representations of professional identity, see Ruth, *Novel Professions*.

54. Interestingly, when contemporary reviews of *Daniel Deronda* dealt with the so-called Jewish portion of the novel at all, or specifically with its Zionist project, they did so, for the most part, only in terms of focusing on its indefiniteness, improbability, or impracticability, concluding that such "idealism" was simply futile. Often it was even conjectured that Eliot must be being satirical, or just not serious in the Zionist aspects of the plot. See Martin, "Contemporary Critics." Susan Meyer, focusing on what she labels the "proto-Zionism" of the novel, argues that Eliot applies the idea of Jewish return opportunistically, primarily in the service of British interests both at home in England and abroad vis-à-vis the "Syrian Question." In my view, however, such a reading does not adequately account either for Eliot's knowledge about Judaism or for the interconnectedness (and urgency) of Eliot's representation of Zionism to the fate of the English in the novel. See Meyer, " 'Safely to their Own Borders.' "

55. See Andrew Thompson, *George Eliot and Italy*, 173–82, for the connections between Daniel and Mazzini. As Thompson characterizes the brand of nationalism espoused by Mazzini, "the State, representing the general will, and the Nation, representing a homogeneous people, should be co-extensive, and physical and ethnological boundaries were seen as the 'natural' confines of states" (180). He also develops Eliot's and Lewes's sympathies for Mazzini and, more generally, for the values of the *Risorgimento*.

56. Crosby, *The Ends of History*, 35.

57. Anderson, "George Eliot and the Jewish Question," 41.

58. Ibid., 51, 52.

59. Hebrew was not a language that any Jews had spoken (perhaps ever and at least since Babylonian times) for everyday use; and Zionism also asked the Jewish people to acquire a territory, to which Hobsbawm adds: "for Herzl it was not even necessary that that territory should have any historic connection with the Jews." See Hobsbawm, *The Age of Empire*, 147.

60. Ibid., 147–48.

61. For this reason, the Diaspora offers a fitting trope for Eliot, combining, as it does, this loss of rootedness to place (which increasingly typifies the modern state for her) with a spiritual and moral basis or means of communication.

62. Gilman, "Black Bodies, White Bodies," 239.

63. Discussions of Eliot's remark range from seeing it simply as an innocuous and unfortunate one to connecting it more explicitly to the treatment of race and its relation to nationality throughout the novel. As will become clear, in my usage I am most concerned with its larger import in the context of the novel: specifically, how it positions Jews as both so-called insiders *and* outsiders and how this positioning speaks to the ambivalent nature of national identity constructed by the text. I should note, however, that this particular racial division does not seem terribly ambivalent to me, something that I try to reinforce as well in terms of my discussion of the treatment of the East in the novel.

64. Christina Crosby, in fact, has argued that Eliot, in her desire to present the English with an alternative model of a responsible national identity palpable to them, goes so far as to make Judaism itself Christian. See Crosby, *The Ends of History*, 12–43.

65. Said, *The Question of Palestine*, 56–114.

66. In terms of the former kinds of ideological "hailings," there is Deronda's trip to the synagogue in Frankfort, where he is asked directly about his parentage by a Jew who will turn out to be an old friend of Daniel's grandfather (415–17); when, later, he describes his feelings in the synagogue to Mirah, she replies, "I thought none but our people would feel that" (424), foreshadowing Daniel's discovery of his Jewish heritage. Similarly, there are numerous examples of the latter, more indirect notings of difference. For instance, Mrs. Davilow muses that "[Daniel] puts me in mind of Italian paintings. One would guess, without being told, that there was foreign blood in his veins" (378).

67. Hall, "Culture, Community, Nation," 353.

68. For more on this trope, see Said, *Culture and Imperialism*, 3–97.

69. Žižek, "Eastern Europe's Republics of Gilead."

PART III   *Itineraries of the Utopian*

1. See Wegner, *Imaginary Communities*, 64.

2. Carter's aim is to write a spatial history that disrupts the teleological thrust of imperial or "diorama" history and its "illusion" of the "all-seeing spectator." In place of such a theatrics, he offers "unfinished maps" and the "prehistory of places, a history of roads, footprints, trails of dust and foaming wakes," which "[recognize] that our life as it discloses itself spatially is dynamic, material but invisible." See Carter, *The Road to Botany Bay*, xxi–xxii.

3. The phrase comes from Paul Gilroy, who uses the experiences of black Atlantic culture to question modern conceptions of nationalism and ethnicity. Like the utopian narratives I discuss, a central aspect of Gilroy's analysis entails reconfiguring the space of modernity. See Gilroy, *The Black Atlantic*, esp. 2–40.

4. See especially Bloch, *The Utopian Function of Art and Literature*, 36–44.

5. This type of utopian impulse coincides with Ernst Bloch's notion of "concrete" utopia, which he describes in contrast to forms of empirical realism: "Where the prospective horizon is omitted, reality only appears as become, as dead. . . . Where the prospective horizon is continuously included in the reckoning, the real appears as what it is in concreto: as the path-network of dialectical processes which occur in an unfinished world, in a world which would not be in the least changeable without the enormous future: real possibility in that world . . . *Concrete utopia stands on the horizon of every reality; real possibility surrounds the open dialectical tendencies and latencies to the very last.*" See Bloch, *The Principle of Hope*, 223.

CHAPTER 4   *William Morris and a People's Art*

1. For accounts of the importance of the sagas to Morris's political development, see E. P. Thompson, *William Morris*, 175–91, and Shaw's essay, "Morris as I Knew Him," in which Shaw assigns Iceland and the sagas a pivotal role, "by changing the facile troubadour of love and beauty into the minstrel of strife and guile, of battle, murder, and death." He goes on, in grand Shavian fashion, to rank *Sigurd the Volsung* the greatest epic since Homer and to claim that "epic was child's play to [Morris]: for pure pastime he translated that schoolboy's curse the Aeneids [*sic*] of Virgil into long lolloping lines that in any other hands than his would have reduced the reader to idiocy, and later on *The Odyssey*: a nobler translation than the tale is worth." See "Morris as I Knew Him," in May Morris, ed., *William Morris*, xxxvii.

2. Etienne Balibar employs the term "neo-racism" to define the racism of decolonization—"of the reversal of population movements between the old colonies and the old metropolises, and the division of humanity within a single political space." Its operation is one of "racism without races": "It is a racism whose dominant theme is not biological heredity but the insurmountability of cultural differences, a racism which, at first sight does not postulate the superiority of certain groups or peoples in relation to others but 'only' the harmfulness of abolishing frontiers, the incompatibility of lifestyles and traditions" (21). While positioning itself as having learned from anti-racism, this meta-racism ultimately leads to the same policy, that of the segregation of collectivities. My interest in this characterization of neo-racism rests in its lineage to the old racism: where the old racism was grounded in a pseudo-biological concept of race, neo-racism takes as its line of demarcation *cultural differentiation*. What the "differentialist revolution" shares with biologistic ideologies is its aim to explain "not the constitution of races, but the vital importance of cultural closures and traditions for the accumulation of individual aptitudes, and, most importantly, the 'natural' bases of xenophobia and social aggression" (26). It is precisely these kinds of closures that we saw operating in George Eliot's texts in chapters 2 and 3. My point with respect to Morris is that in significant and substantial ways he resists and struggles against this kind of cultural nationalism. See Balibar and Wallerstein, *Race, Nation, Class*, 17–28.

3. If anything, this shows the ambivalence of appropriating Morris for the present, since when he is "known" it is in the context of the commodification of his furniture and wares. A perfect example of this is the current craze for Restoration Hardware, where what is being produced is exactly what Morris would have hated: shoddy wares that reproduce the Arts and Crafts style but not its system of production.

4. Two notable exceptions are Stephen Arata's "On Not Paying Attention" and Jerome McGann's " 'Thing to Mind.' "

5. Marx, *The German Ideology*, 53.

6. Thompson, *William Morris*, 106. It should be noted that Morris's own pecuniary situation allowed him never to have to worry about financially supporting himself through his various endeavors. Because of an inheritance from his father, the money for which came from his father's shares in Devon Great Consols (copper and tin mines in the southwest), Morris was independently wealthy, certainly a factor in how he was able to pursue his artistic and work interests pleasurably. Yet, at the same time, Morris was well aware of the advantages he enjoyed and the effects of such privilege. "Look you," he enjoins, "as I sit at my work at home, which is Hammersmith, close to the river, I often hear go past the window some of that ruffianism of which a good deal has been said in the papers of late, and has been said before at recurring periods. As I hear the yells and shrieks and all the degradation cast on the glorious tongue of Shakespeare and Milton . . . fierce wrath takes possession of me, till I remember, as I hope I mostly do, that is was my good luck only of being born respectable and rich that has put me on this side of the window among delightful books and lovely works of art, and not on the other side, in the empty street, the drink-steeped liquor-shops, the foul and degraded lodgings." Quoted in Timo, "News from Somewhere," 3.

7. Strachan, "Around William Morris," 151.

8. Thompson, *William Morris*, 700.

9. A great deal of debate has taken place over the direction of the flows of influence between and among Carlyle, Ruskin, Morris, and Marx. For an endorsement of the Englishness of Morris's ideas, see Clayre, *Work and Play*, 63–78. He also argues, though, that Morris and Carlyle and company were not cut off from continental European ideas, but rather that there was a fluid give and take between the two traditions that came as much from Marx "sharing" Carlyle's ideas, for example, as vice versa. This perspective is advocated by E. P. Thompson as well, who points to Clayre's work as one of the best readings of Morris. I will take up this issue more fully in the second section of this chapter.

10. Morris's critique of the subsumption of all labor under wage labor will form the brunt of his opposition to Edward Bellamy's utopian novel, *Looking Backward*. Morris argues against Bellamy's utopia in terms of his treatment of labor as drudgery and therefore simply a necessity to be reduced—in terms of hours and effort—as much as is socially possible. It is this critical blockage that leads to an overvaluation of regimentation and standardization and the primacy of the machine within Bellamy's utopia. By reducing labor to wage labor in this fashion, Bellamy, according to Morris, remains stuck within the specious precepts of bourgeois ideology, unable to imagine a different and creative relationship to labor. The importance of this distinction in how labor is defined and positioned within the social totality, as well as a more specific discussion of Morris's alternative utopian vision in *News from Nowhere*, will be further developed later in the chapter.

11. Carlyle, *Past and Present*, esp. 226–31.

12. Marx, *Capital*, vol. 1, 481–82.

13. Ruskin, "On the Nature of Gothic," *The Stones of Venice*, 152–230. In part, the nineteenth-century relationship to medievalism was prompted by new scholarship about the Middle Ages, which reexamined medievalism from a more historical approach rather than seeing it as a mythical fairy world. See Thompson, *William Morris*, 22–39; and Chandler, *A Dream of Order*, for a general reading of the medieval revival in England.

14. Raymond Williams places Carlyle and Ruskin in a tradition of "remarkable and admirable inquiry into the values of [their] society," a tradition marked by "open rebellion against Whiggery" and of "opposition to 'civilization.' " In this context he sees Morris attempting to break what he terms the "general deadlock" which Carlyle and Ruskin both reach by "[attaching] its general values to an actual and growing social force: that of the organized working class." See Williams, *Culture and Society*, 137–61.

15. Consequently, a change in current social relations necessarily involves a change in the basis of society, as Morris clarifies when distinguishing revolution from reform: "The word Revolution, which we Socialists are so often forced to use, has a terrible sound in most people's ears, even when we have explained to them that it does not necessarily mean a change accompanied by riot and all kinds of violence, and cannot mean a change made mechanically and in the teeth of opinion by a group of men who have somehow managed to seize on the executive power for the moment. Even when we explain that we use the word revolution in its etymological sense, and mean by it a change in the basis of society, people are scared at the idea of such vast change, and beg that you will speak of reform and not revolution. As, however, we Socialists do not at all mean by our word revolution what these worthy people mean by their word reform, I can't help thinking that it would be a mistake to use it, whatever projects we might conceal beneath its harmless envelope." See "How We Live and How We Might Live" in Morton, ed., *Political Writings of William Morris*, 134.

16. Morris joined the SDF in 1883 and remained a member until 1885. The Socialist League, under Morris's leadership, was formed in 1885 as a splinter group of the SDF. Pivotal to this factional infighting and eventual split was the conflict of personality and politics between H. M. Hyndman, a.k.a. the "Father of English Socialism," and Morris. One anecdote that gets to the heart of their differences involves their respective attachments (or lack thereof) to their top hats: whereas Morris accidentally sat on his when resigning his directorship (of the Firm), Hyndman couldn't be found without his on. In terms of their more substantive political differences, a crucial one was simply the matter of how Hyndman and Morris viewed the workers themselves: while Hyndman rarely hid his contempt for them, Morris put his greatest hopes in them.

17. To prioritize Morris's works subjects them to a kind of division of labor wholly inimical to the spirit and work of Morris as a whole. While I think it is important to grant previously marginalized elements of Morris's oeuvre more attention—such as these shorter political writings—it seems unnecessary to have to do so at the expense of his verse or other works, with the motive of critically ranking their merits. But this said, I would also point to the Icelandic sagas with which I began this chapter as an area ripe for further investigation.

18. Morris, "Useless Work versus Useless Toil," in Morton, ed., *Political Writings of William Morris*, 107. All further page references will be made parenthetically in the text and abbreviated *U*.

19. The opening sentence of "The Society of the Future" (1888) is representative, both in its philosophy of revolution and in its optimism: "In making our claims for the changes in Society, we Socialists are satisfied with demanding what we think necessary for that Society to form itself, which we are sure it is getting ready to do; this we think better than putting forward elaborate utopian schemes for the future" (453). See May Morris, ed., *William Morris*, 453–68.

20. The manliness Morris attributes to the beauty he describes ("which man creates when he is most a man") signals one of the weaker aspects of his thought. His presumption of the artist as male and of beauty as a manly creation is undoubtedly problematic. As I hope to show, however, the structure of work Morris envisions in his notion of creative labor does not depend on a sexual division of labor, and thus can be appropriated for other, less problematically gendered uses. This issue is discussed at greater length in the final section of the chapter on Morris's utopian romance, *News from Nowhere*. On the concept of manliness in Morris, see Bizup, *Manufacturing Culture*, 177–202.

21. In "Communism," for example, Morris draws on this notion of "reasonable needs" in his explanation of what he means by the communist goal of equality of condition among all people: "Which again does not mean that people would (all round) use their neighbors' coats, or houses or tooth brushes, but that every one, whatever work he did, would have the opportunity of satisfying all his reasonable needs according to the admitted standard of the society in which he lived: i.e., without robbing any other citizen" (237). Moreover, he underscores the fundamental centrality of this belief when he ends by saying, "And I must say it is in the belief that this is possible of realization that I continue to be a socialist" (237). See "Communism," in Morton, ed., *Political Writings of William Morris*, 226–40. All further page references will be made parenthetically in the text and abbreviated *C*. In this respect, Morris's characterization of reasonable needs has a deep affinity with Marx's understanding of use-value, which recognizes the historical contingencies of use as well as its inherent ambiguities: "The commodity is, first of all, an external object, a thing which through its qualities satisfies human needs of whatever kind. The nature of these needs, whether they arise, for example, from the stomach, or the imagination, makes no difference . . . Every useful thing, for example, iron, paper, etc., may be looked at from the two points of view of quality and quantity.

Every useful thing is a whole composed of many properties; it can therefore be useful in various ways. The discovery of these ways and hence of the manifold uses of things is the work of history." Marx, *Capital*, vol. 1, 125.

22. Marcuse, of course, makes his observations about the "current unfreedom" of advanced industrial society amid the affluence of 1950s America. His concern is to show the ways in which modern technological apparatuses are used not to realize "freedom from necessity" but rather to more effectively and instrumentally dominate individuals and to perpetuate new forms of control. See Marcuse, *One-Dimensional Man*. Fredric Jameson also discusses Marcuse's analysis of postindustrial capitalism as an environment marked by the "paradoxical context" of "abundance and total control." See *Marxism and Form*, 106–16.

23. Early on in the essay, Morris describes the hope of product as "product worth having by one who is neither a fool nor an ascetic" and pleasure as "pleasure enough for all of us to be conscious of it while we are at work; not a mere habit, the loss of which we shall feel as a fidgety man feels the loss of the bit of string he fidgets with" (*U* 87).

24. Morris, "The Society of the Future," 457. In the same essay, in more general terms, Morris expands on what he means by a free and full life. Responding to the question of what makes men happy, he offers as definition "the pleasurable exercise of our energies, and the enjoyment of the rest which that exercise or expenditure of energy makes necessary to us. I think that is happiness for all, and covers all difference of capacity and temperament from the most energetic to the laziest" (456).

25. Certainly this debate continues and has seen various permutations since Morris's time. The notion of education as compulsory preparation for the production of good workers formed one of the cruxes of resistance in the student movement of the 1960s. More recent debates about educational funding in the United States illustrate the paucity of vision in notions of commercial education and its increasing role in the service of capital. In response to the New York State and City budget crisis in the 1990s and proposals to cut the SUNY system's budget drastically, for instance, the city council's minority leader, Tom Ognibene, defending Giuliani's cuts, quipped, "A lot of those kids don't need to go to college. They can do very clever things with their hands and their bodies" (630). Far from being the exception, sentiments such as this appear to be more and more the rule. See Fitch, " 'Spread the Pain'?"

26. Geoghegan, *Utopianism and Marxism*, 63.

27. In a different context, Fredric Jameson, referring to the work of Schiller and Marcuse, assigns to the hypothetical reconstruction of the past ("a more primitive, a more natural, *original* past") less a *historical* function than a *hermeneutic* one. He goes on to develop the manner in which the work of a political hermeneutic preserves the concept of freedom itself: "Indeed, it is the concept of freedom which, measured against those other possible ones of love and justice, happiness or work, proves to be the privileged instrument of a political hermeneutic, and which, in turn, is perhaps itself best understood as an interpretive device rather than a philosophical essence or idea . . . Thus the idea of freedom involves a kind of perceptual superposition; it is a way of reading the present, but it is a reading that looks more like the reconstruction of an extinct language." See Jameson, *Marxism and Form*, 85.

28. Thompson, *William Morris*, 100.

29. Interestingly, he shares with Eliot the analogy of modern society to gambling. At one point, he describes the system of competitive commerce as one which is "distinctly a system of war; that is of waste and destruction: or you may call it gambling if you will, the point of it being that under it whatever a man gains he gains at the expense of some other man's loss." Morris, "Art and Socialism," in Morton, ed., *Political Writings of William Morris*, 123. All further page references will be made parenthetically in the text and abbreviated *A*.

30. Frye, "The Meeting of Past and Future in William Morris," 308–9.

31. Ibid., 309.

32. Hobsbawm makes this statement in the context of situating Morris and the Arts and Crafts movement within an artistic ideology which sought to link art and the worker through "applied" arts and to extend that ideology outward toward social change. See Hobsbawm, *The Age of Empire*, 233.

33. Morris, "Art and the People," in May Morris, ed., *William Morris*, 383.

34. Morris, "At a Picture Show," in May Morris, ed., *William Morris*, 415.

35. It is this sense of recovery and of a unity that has been fractured that leads to much of the criticism of Morris's vision of utopia. But as I show in chapter 5, in my discussion of Oscar Wilde, the notion of living labor that drives Morris's utopianism does not have to lead to this kind of dialectic. Moreover, as discussed above, it is the hermeneutic rather than the historical function of this reconstruction that is to be emphasized.

36. Morris's "At a Picture Show" is inspired by just such an observation. As he goes on to note, the "public does its art, as it does its religion—by deputy." See May Morris, ed., *William Morris*, 417.

37. Morris, "How We Live and How We Might Live," in Morton, ed., *Political Writings of William Morris*, 155.

38. Ibid., 156.

39. Williams, *Culture and Society*, 159.

40. E. P. Thompson provides some remarkable statistics about the achievement of middle-class hegemony by the 1880s. For example, in the census of 1851, those in the professions numbered 272,000: in 1871, 684,000. He goes on as well to provide numbers regarding the huge upswelling in domestic servants (from 900,000 to 1.5 million), capital investments abroad (they jumped from 210 million pounds to 1,300 million), and the number of shareholders in Indian Railway stock (50,000). He also illustrates the import of these statistics with a triumphant paean from the free-trade advocate John Bright, delivered shortly after the Reform Bill of 1867 passed, which is worth reproducing here: "The aristocracy of England which so lately governed the country has abdicated," he declared. "There is no longer a contest between us and the House of Lords; we need no longer bring charges against a selfish oligarchy; we no longer dread the power of the territorial magnates; we no longer feel ourselves domineered over by a class; we feel that denunciation and invective now would be out of place; the power which hitherto has ruled over us is shifted." What he makes no specific mention of, but is also quite interesting about this particular speech, is that it was addressed to the working men of

Edinburgh, and hence the rhetorical "we" and "us" of the piece is used to bring the working classes within the ambit of the middle class in the process of praising its own achievement of hegemony. Thompson, *William Morris*, 136. For other statistical data, see also Hobsbawm, *The Age of Empire*, 34–55.

41. See especially Carlyle's "Signs of the Times" (1829) where the gamut of his most trenchant social criticism is splendidly laid out, ranging from attacks on educational methods, French positivists, the Bible-Society ("machines even for converting the heathen"), and John Stuart Mill with his Freemason's Tavern, to the institutionalization of thought, culture, art, etc. Carlyle, *Selected Writings*, 61–85.

42. Richard Wolin makes a similar argument about the relationship between Benjamin's aesthetics and politics in his discussion of Benjamin's "materialist theory of experience." See Wolin, *Walter Benjamin*, 213–39; and see also Walter Benjamin, "The Work of Art in the Age of Mechanical Reproduction," *Illuminations*, 217–51; and "The Storyteller," *Illuminations*, 83–109, in which Benjamin develops his analysis of the decline of community and the loss of experience.

43. From this perspective, Morris occupies an identifiable position within the socialist tradition. Like Lukács, he theorizes the identity of subject and object in a particular historical agent. Wilde, on the other hand, belongs much more fully, albeit idiosyncratically, with Adorno and the practice of a negative dialectics.

44. Jameson, *The Cultural Turn*, 135.

45. Benjamin, "The Work of Art in the Age of Mechanical Reproduction," *Illuminations*, 242.

46. Ibid.

47. As I hope to show, the placement of Morris in a trajectory with strong affinities to the Frankfurt School productively shifts the terms of debate about Morris away from whether he falls on the utopian or scientific side of the Marxist divide, or whether he makes visible the gap between knowledge and desire in materialist theory itself, toward a more expansive view of the integrated relationship he maintained between theory and practice, and utopianism and materialism.

48. Meier, *William Morris, the Marxist Dreamer*, esp. 201–44.

49. Morris, "How I Became a Socialist," in Morton, ed., *Political Writings of William Morris*, 244.

50. Perry Anderson, *Arguments within English Marxism*, 173.

51. In "Communism" Morris states the difference thus: "Communism is in fact the completion of Socialism: when that ceases to be militant and becomes triumphant, it will be communism" (*C* 233).

52. Thompson, *William Morris*, 683.

53. Lukács, *The Historical Novel*, 171.

54. These resources were being all too visibly and violently utilized both at home and abroad. During this period, in particular, England was wielding its might in the scramble to "open up" Africa. Morris was acutely aware of the false separation of England's brutal treatment of its colonized peoples from its treatment of its own working-class "natives" and agitators. In a recruitment plea, Morris wryly notes that while socialists may serve presently as mere figures of mockery, this should in no way blind them to the violence driving capitalist society: "But remember that the body of people who have for instance ruined India, starved and gagged Ireland, and tortured Egypt, have capacities in them—some ominous signs of which they have lately shown—for openly playing the tyrants' game nearer home." Morris, "Art and Socialism," 132.

55. Shaw, "Morris as I Knew Him," xxxviii–ix.

56. Even those more open-minded toward the "masses" tended to fall easily into the kind of fear of the mob represented in Eliot's *Felix Holt*, as well as numerous other industrial novels. Emblematic of such a response is a story about Ruskin that E. P. Thompson relates. Ruskin was initially supportive of the Commune until they burned the Louvre, at which point his sympathy toward the working class and their demands ended. From then on he saw them only as a "brutalized, destructive force" beyond the bounds of reason. See Thompson, *William Morris*, 201.

57. Negt and Kluge, *Public Sphere and Experience*, 57.

58. See Williams's *Problems in Materialism and Culture*, 196–212, for a full discussion of these keywords.

59. Quoted in Frye, "The Meeting of Past and Future in William Morris," 305–6.

60. I take this notion of labor as a problematic of value from Michael Hardt and Antonio Negri. They theorize labor as a "value-creating practice" and "in this sense, labor functions as a social analytic that interprets the production of value across an entire social spectrum, equally in economic and cultural terms." This concept points to a similar attempt in Morris to examine the processes of valorization within a capitalist economy and to critique the denial of pleasures and desires within its work ethic. Moreover, viewing labor as constitutive of social value breaks down the kinds of divisions we have seen in the industrial novel between so-called economic and subjective economies. Hardt and Negri, *Labor of Dionysus*, 7.

61. This aspect of Morris is uncannily similar to Marx's description of unalienated labor and communism in the Paris Manuscripts. In the chapter "Private Property and Communism," Marx describes the positive transcendence of private property as a dialectical movement leading toward the emancipation of all human senses and qualities, and including, crucially, the humanizing of nature itself: "Thus *society* is the unity of being of man with nature—the true resurrection of nature—the naturalism of man and the humanism of nature both brought to fulfillment." Morris, I would argue, takes Marx one step further. Morris's future landscape is not simply a "man-made landscape," as Marx had in mind, but a social one. Nature is not so much resurrected; instead, a truly humanized nature is presented, one not dominated for exploitation but rather fully inhabited and respected. See Marx, *Economic and Philosophic Manuscripts of 1844*, 137. For a discussion of *News from Nowhere* as an "ecological society" presaging current mainstream "green" ideas, see Paddy O'Sullivan, "Struggle for the Vision Fair," 5–9.

62. This connection and the following discussion come from Phillip Wegner's analysis of Thomas More's *Utopia*. In the larger context of his discussion of utopian narratives, Wegner also compares Edward Bellamy's *Looking Backward* to Morris's *News from Nowhere*. Like many others, he argues that Morris's *News from Nowhere* ultimately represents an idealization of a preindustrial England, an argument that I try to complicate below. While we differ in this respect, I have drawn heavily on his analysis of utopian narratives in general. See Wegner, *Imaginary Communities*, 27–98.

63. In Wegner's words, "England represents the place where the possibility of 'nationness' itself first takes root; as the historian Liah Greenfeld puts it, 'The birth of the English nation was not the birth of a nation; it was the birth of the nations, the birth of nationalism.'" See Wegner, *Imaginary Communities*, 55; and Greenfeld, *Nationalism*, 23.

64. Patrick Brantlinger charts three shifts in the nineteenth century: the first (1830s–40s) marked by "social cleavage," the second (1850s–60s) by "the cult of progress," and the third (post-1870) by the growth of corporate capitalism and of trade unions. As he argues, these latter developments, as well as "the series of depressions starting in 1873, rendered the old liberal reformist attitudes increasingly obsolete and opened the way for the revolutionary socialism of Morris and Hyndman, the pragmatic socialism of the Fabians, and the welfare state liberalism of L. T. Hobhouse." See Brantlinger, *The Spirit of Reform, 1832–1867.*

65. Morris, "The Society of the Future," 456.

66. Morris, *News from Nowhere*, 22. All further page references will be made parenthetically in the text and abbreviated *N*.

67. See Belsey, "Getting Somewhere," 345. In my reading here, I follow Belsey, who emphasizes the playfulness of the text.

68. In the context of discussing how two novels of 1880s science fiction are refunctioned in *News from Nowhere*, Darko Suvin notes the way in which Morris's text skips over a generation. This amounts to an absence of fathers, which Suvin reads as "an enmity . . . against the generation of the fathers, and by metonymy against patriarchal authority." See "Counter-Projects," 93.

69. Belsey, "Getting Somewhere," 344.

70. See Suvin, "Counter-Projects," 88–97.

71. Bellamy, *Looking Backward*, 148.

72. Morris, "Looking Backward," in May Morris, ed., *William Morris*, 506.

73. See especially chapter 15, "On the Lack of Incentive to Labour in a Communist Society," 77–84.

74. A less churlish criticism of Morris's views on modern machinery might challenge his lack of attention to the relationship between machines and craftsmanship. In addition to all sorts of shoddy goods, goods of a quality never before imagined as possible under craft modes of production are also produced in factories. Modern craftsmanship, for example, is entirely dependent on the industrial infrastructure: cheap, but high quality and durable, electrical hand tools have revolutionized the productivity of carpenters and woodworkers over the past twenty years as did the availability of all sorts of ready-milled lumber and building products after the Second World War. This granted, the world of *News from Nowhere* is still clearly not preindustrial in any meaningful sense: the mode and relations of production could hardly be characterized as feudal.

75. Williams, *Problems in Materialism and Culture*, 204.

76. Morris and Bax, *Socialism*, 288.

77. Walter Benjamin, "Theses on the Philosophy of History," *Illuminations*, 256.

78. Perry Anderson, for instance, claims that "technology, science, schools, novels, history, travel, feminism were each of them products of an entire cycle of bourgeois civilization eradicated from his range of sympathy. Hence the kind of censorship under which they fall—a marginalization or suppression—in *News from Nowhere*." See Anderson, *Arguments within English Marxism*, 169.

79. In this, *News from Nowhere* echoes the opening of "The Manifesto of the Socialist League," which begins: "We come before you as a body advocating the principles of Revolutionary International Socialism; that is, we seek a change in the basis of Society—a change which would destroy the distinctions of classes and nationalities." See Thompson, *William Morris*, appendix 1, 732.

80. Ibid., 792.

81. Ibid., 807.

82. Ibid.

83. Anderson, *Arguments within English Marxism*, 161.

84. Ibid., 162.

85. Thompson, *William Morris*, 810.

86. Anderson does detach Morris from Thompson's view of him in his chapter "Strategies." Here he points to the invaluable contribution made by Morris with regard to the issue of reformism and, concomitantly, his remarkable understanding of the "*structural unity* of the capitalist order." But no connection is made between these strategic insights (displayed so spectacularly, as noted by Anderson, in Morris's detailing of the revolutionary process in *News from Nowhere*'s "How the Change Came") and Morris's utopianism. Rather Morris's strategic brilliance is presented more as a welcome antidote to his utopianism. See Anderson, *Arguments within English Marxism*, 178.

87. Thompson, *William Morris*, 807.

CHAPTER 5   *Utopia, Use, and the Everyday*

1. Marcuse, *Eros and Civilization*, xxi.

2. Ibid., xi.

3. Ibid., xvii.

4. Brecht, *Life of Galileo*, 76.

5. Fredric Jameson makes this point in his essay on pleasure as a political issue, claiming that "the thematizing of a particular 'pleasure' as a political issue . . . must always involve a dual focus, in which the local issue is meaningful and desirable in and of itself, but is also *at one and the same time* taken as the *figure* for Utopia in general, and for the systemic revolutionary transformation of society as a whole." As I hope to show, Wilde adds to this view of pleasure by taking both sides of the equation equally seriously. Thus he not only addresses "politics" through his critique of the constitutive categories of modernity—reified notions of labor, "productive" [heterosexual] sexual relations, technological progress, nationalism, and imperialism—but also provides the beginnings of a vocabulary of pleasure *as* pleasure, an area left largely unexplored by left intellectuals. See Jameson, "Pleasure," 13.

6. Wilde, "The Decorative Arts," 151–52.

7. Wilde, "The House Beautiful," 172.

8. Ibid., 180.

9. Certeau, *The Practice of Everyday Life*, 117.

10. Ibid., 119.

11. Ibid., 117.

12. Other approaches toward Wilde have tended to take a couple of different directions. One is to see Wilde's personality (somewhat ruefully) taking over his principles (as in the case of Richard Ellmann); another is to conflate his personality, specifically his homosexuality, with his principles (and his prose), as critics such as Christopher Craft tend to do. See Ellmann, *Oscar Wilde*, 194; and Craft, *Another Kind of Love*, 106–39.

13. In *The Picture of Dorian Gray*, for instance, this will be expressed as "The artist is the creator of beautiful things." Wilde, *The Picture of Dorian Gray*, 21; all further page references will be made parenthetically in the text and abbreviated *DG*.

14. Richard Ellmann notes that the form of *Dorian Gray* prompts a new set of standards by which to read it. As he distinguishes its form, "Wilde made it elegantly casual, as if writing a novel were a diversion rather than a 'painful duty' (as he characterized Henry James's manner)." Ellmann, *Oscar Wilde*, 314.

15. Sedgwick, *Epistemology of the Closet*, 175.

16. Adorno, "Subject and Object," 499.

17. Arendt, Introduction, *Illuminations*, 42; Benjamin, *Schriften I*, 416, quoted in Arendt.

18. Sedgwick, *Epistemology of the Closet*, 176.

19. For a different reading of homosexual desire in *The Picture of Dorian Gray* that focuses on the sexual intensities of what is disembodied in the text, on "a current of desire whose subject is finally nowhere, and thus everywhere at once" (320), see Jeffrey Nunokawa, "Homosexual Desire and the Effacement of Self in *The Picture of Dorian Gray*, 311–21.

20. Within such a multiform modeling of the subject, Wilde understandably can claim pieces of each of his characters: "Basil Hallward is what I think I am; Lord Henry what the world thinks of me; Dorian what I would like to be—in other ages, perhaps" (quoted in *DG*, 265).

21. As Neil Bartlett mentions, Wilde's description of this den contributes to the emerging documentary school of writing. Middle-class journalists, urban anthropologists, and working-class authors at this time began exploring the down and out for sensational stories and newspaper exposés. Bartlett goes on to note that in fact this same den had been described before by at least two other writers—James Greenwood in an exposé of Tiger Bay for the *Daily Telegraph* and Richard Rowe in his book *Found in the Streets* (1880). The point Bartlett wants to make about the structure of this kind of writing is that it already presumes a great divide between the informant and his/her subject at the same time that it is unsettling: "it creates a picture of an uneasy London, a city in which poverty, vice and violence have a constant presence, in which they could at any moment cease to be simply scandals, reports in the newspaper, and could erupt onto the streets." At the same time, Bartlett draws attention to the fact that in all this literature, with all its claims to the truth, no mention of homosexuals or homosexual culture appears, although, unquestionably, they and it existed and lived and worked within the same trolling grounds as the pimps and prostitutes being exposed. See Bartlett, *Who Was That Man?*, 142–46.

22. Marx, *Capital*, vol. 1, 163–64.

23. Ibid., 164–65.

24. Benjamin, *Illuminations*, 60.

25. Ibid., 67.

26. This is where one can really distinguish Wilde from Morris. While Morris grounds his vision of utopia in the historical present, he nonetheless envisions the overcoming of alienation as a reuniting of subject and object, of the producer with his or her product, of the individual and the community, of the subject with itself, in a condition of seamless identity. Morris's future is a return to a previous unity. It is precisely this that Wilde implicitly rejects. Wilde, in addition to never taking the almost hundred-year leap into the future, as Morris does in *News from Nowhere*, grounds his utopia instead in a principle of nonidentity and asks us to think of a world beyond alienation that is not dependent on a recovery of pleasures lost in the processes of capitalist production. Instead the serial and nonidentical nature of Wilde's utopia emphatically embraces new pleasures.

27. Quoted in Arendt, Introduction, *Illuminations*, 39.

28. For this example and numerous others, see Bartlett, *Who Was That Man?*, 201–5.

29. Ibid., 204.

30. Ibid., 227.

31. Wilde to R. Clegg, April 1891, quoted in Bartlett, *Who Was That Man?*, 46.

32. Wilde, *Lord Arthur Savile's Crime and Other Stories*, 42. All further page references will be made parenthetically in the text and abbreviated *L*.

33. Said, *The World, the Text, and the Critic*, 42.

34. Wilde, *De Profundis and Other Writings*, 120. All further page references will be made parenthetically in the text and abbreviated *DP*.

35. Holland, Introduction, *De Profundis*, 91–95.

36. Bartlett, *Who Was That Man?*, 185–86.

37. Wilde also claims at another point that "Like Gautier, I have always been one of those *pour qui le monde visible existe*" (*DP* 207).

38. Wilde, "The Soul of Man under Socialism," in *De Profundis and Other Writings*, 52. All further page references will be made parenthetically in the text and abbreviated *S*.

39. Quoted in Ellmann, *Oscar Wilde*, 121.

40. See *S*, 29–32. Again, Wilde's sentiments share much with Brecht's aesthetic in this regard. In his writings on epic theater, Brecht counters the idea that emotions can only be stirred by empathy and argues that emotions are historical and hence mutable: "The emotions always have a definite class basis; the form they take at any time is historical, restricted and limited in specific ways. The emotions are in no sense universally human and timeless." See *Brecht on Theater*, 145.

41. Marx, *Economic and Philosophic Manuscripts of 1844*, 128.

42. Ibid., 132.

43. Jameson, "Actually Existing Marxism," 32.

44. Eagleton, *Heathcliff and the Great Hunger*, 339.

45. Jonathan Dollimore also holds that Wilde's aesthetic is one of "tough materialism" and sees his notion of individualism having "less to do with human essence, Arnold's inner condition, than a dynamic social potential, one which implies a radical possibility of freedom 'latent and potential in mankind generally.'" See Dollimore, "Different Desires," 27.

46. The notion of a "new hedonism" comes from Kate Soper's work on pleasure and the challenge it offers to current feminist and Marxist models of the "utopian." She argues for a utopianism that "needs to trouble some of the blander images of pleasure and in doing so associate an anti-capitalist and egalitarian politics with more complex affective and moral understandings." See Soper, *Troubled Pleasures*, 14.

47. Fredric Jameson argues that Bloch's work on the utopian is premised on the idea that "real philosophizing begins at home . . . in lived experience itself and in its smallest details, in the body and its sensations." See Jameson, *Marxism and Form*, 122.

Conclusion

1. D. A. Miller's Foucauldian reading of the nineteenth-century novel in *The Novel and the Police* provides the most compelling analysis of this process.

2. Jameson, *The Political Unconscious*, 152.

3. Eliot, *Felix Holt*, 473.

4. Buck-Morss, *Dreamworld and Catastrophe*, passim.

5. Adorno, *Notes to Literature*, vol. 1, 237.

6. Quoted in Bill Brown, "Thing Theory," 10.

7. For an extended analysis of the role of pleasure in Brecht's oeuvre, as well as its relationship to a certain mode of critical realism, see Jameson, *Brecht and Method*.

8. This is the split that Raymond Williams identifies as "a parting of the ways" in his history of the English novel. Whereas Hardy and Lawrence fall on the side of social realism in Williams's account, James exemplifies the tendencies of psychological realism. See Williams, *The English Novel*, 119–39.

9. Lisa Cohen looks to Madge Garland, British *Vogue*'s fashion editor during the 1920s and 1930s to argue for the importance of rethinking art and labor in relation to modernism. As she writes, "while fashion and other so-called 'minor' arts have now veered into view for scholars of modernism, they still tend to be seen in that context, not for themselves but through the lens of 'high' literary or artistic production. In other words, our understanding of modernism does not yet truly account for the labor and language of endeavors such as fashion." See Cohen, "Velvet Is Very Important," 4.

10. Comaroff, "The Empire's Old Clothes," 32.

11. For a reading of Buchi Emecheta's *The Joys of Motherhood* in relation to Elizabeth Gaskell's *Mary Barton*, see Lesjak, "Authenticity and the Geography of Empire"; for an analysis of a new vision of labor in Kidlat Tahimik's *The Perfumed Nightmare*, see Jameson, *The Geopolitical Aesthetic*, 186–213.

12. For two contemporary formulations of this view of labor, see Spivak, "Scattered

Speculations on the Question of Value," *In Other Worlds,*" 154–75; and Kluge and Negt, *Geschichte und Eigensinn.*

13. This is Susan Buck-Morss's thesis in *Dreamworld and Catastrophe,* in which she compares forms of mass utopia in East and West at what she sees as the moment of their passing, the end of the cold war.

BIBLIOGRAPHY

....

Adorno, Theodor W. *Notes to Literature*. Vol. 1. 1958. Translated by Shierry Weber Nicholsen. New York: Columbia University Press, 1991.

———. "Subject and Object." In *The Essential Frankfurt School Reader*, edited by Andrew Arato and Eike Gebhardt, 497–511. New York: Continuum, 1987.

Amin, Samir. *Eurocentrism*. Translated by Russell Moore. New York: Monthly Review Press, 1989.

Anderson, Amanda. "George Eliot and the Jewish Question." *Yale Journal of Criticism* 10.1 (1997): 39–61.

———. *The Powers of Distance: Cosmopolitanism and the Cultivation of Detachment*. Princeton, N.J.: Princeton University Press, 2001.

———. *Tainted Souls and Painted Faces: The Rhetoric of Fallenness in Victorian Culture*. Ithaca, N.Y.: Cornell University Press, 1993.

Anderson, Benedict. *Imagined Communities: Reflections on the Origin and Spread of Nationalism*. London: Verso, 1983.

Anderson, Perry. *Arguments within English Marxism*. London: Verso, 1980.

Arac, Jonathan. *Commissioned Spirits: The Shaping of Social Motion in Dickens, Carlyle, Melville, and Hawthorne*. New York: Columbia University Press, 1989.

Arata, Stephen. "On Not Paying Attention." *Victorian Studies* 46.2 (Winter 2004): 193–205.

Argyle, Gisela. *German Elements in the Fiction of George Eliot, Gissing, and Meredith*. Frankfurt am Main: Peter Lang, 1979.

Armstrong, Nancy. *Desire and Domestic Fiction: A Political History of the Novel*. Oxford: Oxford University Press, 1987.

Arnold, Matthew. *Culture and Anarchy*. Edited by J. Dover Wilson. Cambridge: Cambridge University Press, 1960.

Arthur, C. J. *Dialectics of Labour: Marx and his Relation to Hegel*. Oxford: Basil Blackwell, 1986.

Auerbach, Erich. *Mimesis: The Representation of Reality in Western Literature*. Translated by Willard R. Trask. Princeton: Princeton University Press, 1953.

Baker, William. *George Eliot and Judaism*. Salzburg: Institut für Englische Sprache und Literatur, 1975.

Balibar, Etienne, and Immanuel Wallerstein. *Race, Nation, Class: Ambiguous Identities*. London: Verso, 1991.

Barrett, Dorothea. *Vocation and Desire: George Eliot's Heroines*. London: Routledge, 1989.

Barthes, Roland. *The Pleasure of the Text*. New York: Hill and Wang, 1975.

Bartlett, Neil. *Who Was That Man? A Present for Mr. Oscar Wilde*. London: Serpent's Tail, 1988.

Baudrillard, Jean. *The Ecstasy of Communication*. Translated by Bernard and Caroline Schutze. New York: Semiotext(e), 1988.

———. "The End of Production." *Polygraph* 2–3 (1989): 5–29.

———. "The Mirror of Production." In *Jean Baudrillard: Selected Writings*, edited by Mark Poster, 98–118. Stanford, Calif.: Stanford University Press, 1988.

Beales, Derek. *From Castlereagh to Gladstone 1815–1885*. New York: W.W. Norton, 1969.

Beer, Gillian. *Darwin's Plots: Evolutionary Narratives in Darwin, George Eliot, and Nineteenth-Century Fiction*. London: Routledge and Kegan Paul, 1983.

———. *George Eliot*. Bloomington: Indiana University Press, 1983.

Bellamy, Edward. *Looking Backward, 2000–1887*. New York: Penguin, 1982.

Belsey, Andrew. "Getting Somewhere: Rhetoric and Politics in *News from Nowhere*." *Textual Practice* 5.3 (Winter 1991): 337–51.

Benjamin, Walter. *Illuminations*. Translated by Harry Zohn. Introduction by Hannah Arendt, 1–51. New York: Schocken Books, 1977.

Bhabha, Homi K., ed. *Nation and Narration*. London: Routledge, 1990.

Bizup, Joseph. *Manufacturing Culture: Vindications of Early Victorian Industry*. Charlottesville: University Press of Virginia, 2003.

Bloch, Ernst. *The Principle of Hope*. Translated by Neville Plaice, Stephen Plaice, and Paul Knight. Oxford: Basil Blackwell, 1986.

———. *The Utopian Function of Art and Literature: Selected Essays*. Translated by Jack Zipes and Frank Mecklenburg. Cambridge, Mass.: MIT Press, 1988.

Bodenheimer, Rosemarie. *The Politics of Story in Victorian Social Fiction*. Ithaca, N.Y.: Cornell University Press, 1988.

Bourdieu, Pierre. *Outline of a Theory of Practice*. Translated by Richard Nice. Cambridge: Cambridge University Press, 1977.

Brantlinger, Patrick. " 'News from Nowhere': Morris's Socialist Anti-Novel." *Victorian Studies* 19.1 (1975): 35–49.

———. *The Spirit of Reform: British Literature and Politics: 1832–1867*. Cambridge, Mass.: Harvard University Press, 1977.

Brecht, Bertolt. *Brecht on Theatre: The Development of an Aesthetic*. Edited and translated by John Willett. New York: Hill and Wang, 1964.

———. *Life of Galileo*. Translated by John Willett. New York: Arcade Publishing, 1994.

————. *Poems 1913–1956*. Edited by John Willett and Ralph Manheim. New York: Methuen, 1987.

Briggs, Asa. *Victorian People: A Reassessment of Persons and Themes, 1851–67*. Chicago: University of Chicago Press, 1955.

Brooks, Peter. *The Melodramatic Imagination: Balzac, Henry James, Melodrama, and the Mode of Excess*. New Haven: Yale University Press, 1976.

Brown, Bill. "Thing Theory." *Critical Inquiry* 28 (Autumn 2001): 1–21.

Buck-Morss, Susan. *Dreamworld and Catastrophe: The Passing of Mass Utopia in East and West*. Cambridge, Mass.: MIT Press, 2000.

Butler, Judith. *Subjects of Desire: Hegelian Reflections in Twentieth-Century France*. New York: Columbia University Press, 1987.

Carlyle, Thomas. *Past and Present*. Edited by Richard D. Altick. New York: New York University Press, 1977.

————. *Selected Writings*. Edited by Alan Shelston. Middlesex: Penguin, 1971.

Carter, Paul. *The Road to Botany Bay: An Exploration of Landscape and History*. New York: Alfred A. Knopf, 1988.

Certeau, Michel de. *The Practice of Everyday Life*. Translated by Steven Rendall. Berkeley: University of California Press, 1988.

Chandler, Alice. *A Dream of Order: The Medieval Ideal in Nineteenth-Century English Literature*. Lincoln: University of Nebraska Press, 1970.

Chapple, J. A. V., and Arthur Pollard, eds. *The Letters of Elizabeth Gaskell*. Cambridge, Mass.: Harvard University Press, 1967.

Clark, Anna. *The Struggle for the Breeches: Gender and the Marking of the British Working Class*. Berkeley: University of California Press, 1995.

Clayre, Alasdair. *Work and Play: Ideas and Experience of Work and Leisure*. New York: Harper and Row, 1974.

Cohen, Ed. *Talk on the Wilde Side: Toward a Genealogy of a Discourse on Male Sexualities*. New York: Routledge, 1993.

Cohen, Lisa. "Velvet Is Very Important: Madge Garland and the Work of Fashion." Lecture, Swarthmore College, March 2, 2005.

Comaroff, Jean. "The Empire's Old Clothes: Fashioning the Colonial Subject." In *Cross-Cultural Consumption: Global Markets, Local Realities*, edited by David Howes, 19–38. New York: Routledge, 1996.

Cottom, Daniel. *Social Figures: George Eliot, Social History, and Literary Representation*. Minneapolis: University of Minnesota Press, 1987.

————. *Text and Culture: The Politics of Interpretation*. Minneapolis: University of Minnesota Press, 1989.

Craft, Christopher. *Another Kind of Love: Male Homosexual Desire in English Discourse, 1850–1920*. Berkeley: University of California Press, 1994.

Crimp, Douglas, ed. *AIDS Cultural Analysis/Cultural Activism*. Cambridge, Mass.: MIT Press, 1988.

Crosby, Christina. *The Ends of History: Victorians and "the Woman Question"* London: Routledge, 1991.

Cvetkovich, Ann. *Mixed Feelings: Feminism, Mass Culture, and Victorian Sensationalism.* New Brunswick, N.J.: Rutgers University Press, 1984.

David, Deirdre. *Fictions of Resolution in Three Victorian Novels: "North and South," "Our Mutual Friend," and "Daniel Deronda."* New York: Columbia University Press, 1981.

———. *Rule Britannia: Women, Empire, and Victorian Writing.* Ithaca, N.Y.: Cornell University Press, 1995.

Davidoff, Leonore, and Catherine Hall. *Family Fortunes: Men and Women of the English Middle Class, 1780–1850.* Chicago: University of Chicago Press, 1987.

Delany, Samuel R. *The Motion of Light in Water: Sex and Science Fiction Writing in the East Village, 1957–1965.* New York: New American Library, 1988.

Deleuze, Gilles, and Félix Guattari. *Anti-Oedipus: Capitalism and Schizophrenia.* Translated by R. Hurley et al. Minneapolis: University of Minnesota Press, 1983.

Delphy, Christine. *Close to Home.* Amherst: University of Massachusetts Press, 1984.

Dickens, Charles. *David Copperfield.* New York: Penguin, 1996.

———. *Great Expectations.* New York: Penguin, 1996.

Dollimore, Jonathan. "Different Desires: Subjectivity and Transgression in Wilde and Gide." *Genders* 2 (Summer 1988): 24–41.

Doyle, Arthur Conan. *The Sign of Four.* In *Sherlock Holmes: The Complete Novels and Stories.* Vol. 1. New York: Bantam, 1986.

During, Simon. "Literature—Nationalism's Other? The Case for Revision." In *Nation and Narration,* edited by Homi K. Bhabha, 138–53. London: Routledge, 1990.

Eagleton, Terry. *Heathcliff and the Great Hunger: Studies in Irish Culture.* London: Verso, 1995.

———. *Literary Theory: An Introduction.* 2nd ed. Minneapolis: University of Minnesota Press, 1996.

Edelman, Lee. "The Future Is Kid Stuff: Queer Theory, Disidentification and the Death Drive." *Narrative* 6.1 (1988): 18–30.

Eisenstein, Zillah, ed. *Capitalist Patriarchy and the Case for Socialist Feminism.* New York: Monthly Review Press, 1979.

Eliot, George. *Daniel Deronda.* London: Penguin, 1986.

———. *Essays.* Boston: Colonial Press Company, 1883.

———. *Felix Holt, the Radical.* New York: Penguin, 1972.

———. *The George Eliot Letters.* 9 vols. Edited by Gordon Haight. New Haven, Conn.: Yale University Press, 1954.

———. *Middlemarch.* New York: Penguin, 1965.

———. *Selections from George Eliot's Letters.* Edited by Gordon S. Haight. New Haven, Conn.: Yale University Press, 1985.

Ellmann, Richard. *Oscar Wilde.* New York: Vintage, 1987.

Epstein, James, and Dorothy Thompson, eds. *The Chartist Experience: Studies in Working-Class Radicalism and Culture, 1830–1860.* London: Macmillan, 1982.

Fanon, Frantz. *The Wretched of the Earth.* Translated by Constance Farrington. New York: Grove Press, 1963.

Felski, Rita. *The Gender of Modernity.* Cambridge, Mass.: Harvard University Press, 1995.

Fitch, Robert. "'Spread the Pain'? Tax the Gain!" *The Nation* (May 8, 1995): 628–32.

Flaubert, Gustave. *Dictionary of Received Ideas*. In *Bouvard and Pécuchet*, translated by A. J. Krailsheimer. New York: Penguin, 1983.

Fraiman, Susan. *Unbecoming Women: British Women Writers and the Novel of Development*. New York: Columbia University Press, 1993.

Frears, Stephen, dir. *My Beautiful Laundrette*. Screenplay by Hanif Kureishi.

Frye, Northrop. "The Meeting of Past and Future in William Morris," *Studies in Romanticism* 21.3 (Fall 1982): 303–18.

Fuss, Diana, ed. *Inside/Out: Lesbian Theories, Gay Theories*. New York: Routledge, 1991.

Gagnier, Regenia. *Idylls of the Marketplace: Oscar Wilde and the Victorian Public*. Stanford, Calif.: Stanford University Press, 1986.

———. "Productive Bodies, Pleasured Bodies: On Victorian Aesthetics." In *Women and British Aestheticism*, edited by Talia Schaffer and Kathy Alexis Psomiades. Charlottesville: University of Virginia Press, 1999.

Gallagher, Catherine. *The Industrial Reformation of English Fiction: Social Discourse and Narrative Form 1832–1867*. Chicago: University of Chicago Press, 1985.

Gaskell, Elizabeth. *Mary Barton: A Tale of Manchester Life*. New York: Penguin, 1986.

———. *North and South*. London: Oxford University Press, 1973.

Geoghegan, Vincent. *Utopianism and Marxism*. New York: Methuen, 1987.

Geras, Norman. "Fetishism." In *A Dictionary of Marxist Thought*, edited by Tom Bottomore et al., 165–66. Cambridge, Mass: Harvard University Press, 1983.

Gill, Stephen. "Notes to *Mary Barton*." In *Mary Barton*, by Elizabeth Gaskell. New York: Penguin, 1986.

Gilman, Sander. "Black Bodies, White Bodies: Toward an Iconography of Female Sexuality in Late Nineteenth-Century Art, Medicine, and Literature." *Critical Inquiry* 12.1 (Autumn 1985): 204–42.

Gilroy, Paul. *The Black Atlantic: Modernity and Double Consciousness*. Cambridge, Mass.: Harvard University Press, 1993.

Gould, Stephen Jay. *Ever since Darwin: Reflections in Natural History*. New York: W. W. Norton, 1977.

Greenfeld, Liah. *Nationalism: Five Roads to Modernity*. Cambridge, Mass.: Havard University Press, 1992.

Grossberg, Lawrence, Cary Nelson, and Paula Treichler, eds. *Cultural Studies*. New York: Routledge, 1992.

Hadley, Elaine. *Melodramatic Tactics: Theatricalized Dissent in the English Marketplace, 1800–1885*. Stanford, Calif.: Stanford University Press, 1995.

Hall, Catherine. "Rethinking Imperial Histories: The Reform Act of 1867." *New Left Review* 208 (November–December 1994): 3–29.

Hall, Stuart. "Culture, Community, Nation." *Cultural Studies* 7.3 (October 1993): 349–63.

Haraway, Donna. "A Manifesto for Cyborgs: Science, Technology, and Socialist Feminism in the 1980s." In *Coming to Terms: Feminism, Theory, Politics*, edited by Elizabeth Weed. New York: Routledge, 1989.

Hardt, Michael. "The Withering of Civil Society." *Social Text* 45 (Winter 1995): 27–44.

Hardt, Michael, and Antonio Negri. *Labor of Dionysus: A Critique of the State-Form*. Minneapolis: University of Minnesota Press, 1994.

Hardy, Barbara. Introduction to *Daniel Deronda*, by George Eliot. London: Penguin, 1986.

Harvey, David. *The Condition of Postmodernity: An Enquiry into the Origins of Cultural Change*. Oxford: Basil Blackwell, 1989.

Haug, Wolfgang Fritz. *Critique of Commodity Aesthetics: Appearance, Sexuality, and Advertising in Capitalist Society*. Translated by Robert Bock. Minneapolis: University of Minnesota Press, 1986.

Hobsbawm, E. J. *The Age of Capital: 1848–1875*. New York: Vintage Books, 1975.

———. *The Age of Empire: 1875–1914*. New York: Vintage Books, 1989.

———. *The Age of Revolution: 1789–1848*. New York: New American Library, 1962.

Homans, Margaret. *Royal Representations: Queen Victoria and British Culture, 1837–1876*. Chicago: University of Chicago Press, 1998.

Homans, Margaret, and Adrienne Munich. *Remaking Queen Victoria*. Cambridge: Cambridge University Press, 1997.

Horkheimer, Max, and Theodor W. Adorno. *Dialectic of Enlightenment*. Translated by John Cumming. New York: Continuum, 1988.

Howe, Irving. "George Eliot and the Jews." *Partisan Review* 46 (1979): 359–75.

Hughes, Robert. *The Fatal Shore: The Epic of Australia's Founding*. New York: Vintage Books, 1988.

Irigaray, Luce. *This Sex Which Is Not One*. Translated by Catherine Porter. Ithaca, N.Y.: Cornell University Press, 1977.

———. *Speculum of the Other Woman*. Translated by Gillian C. Gill. Ithaca, N.Y.: Cornell University Press, 1985.

Jaggar, Alison. *Feminist Politics and Human Nature*. Totowa, N.J.: Rowman and Allanheld, 1983.

James, Henry. *Partial Portraits*. New York: Macmillan, 1905.

Jameson, Fredric. "Actually Existing Marxism." In *Marxism beyond Marxism*, edited by Saree Makdisi, Cesare Casarino, and Rebecca E. Karl, 14–54. New York: Routledge, 1996.

———. *Brecht and Method*. London: Verso, 1998.

———. "Cognitive Mapping." In *Marxism and the Interpretation of Culture*, edited by Cary Nelson and Lawrence Grossberg, 347–57. Urbana: University of Illinois Press, 1988.

———. *The Cultural Turn: Selected Writings on the Postmodern, 1983–1998*. London: Verso, 1998.

———. *The Geopolitical Aesthetic: Cinema and Space in the World System*. Bloomington: Indiana University Press, 1992.

———. *The Ideologies of Theory*. Vol. 2. Minneapolis: University of Minnesota Press, 1988.

———. *Marxism and Form*. Princeton, N.J.: Princeton University Press, 1971.

———. "Pleasure: A Political Issue." *Formations of Pleasure*. London: Routledge and Kegan Paul, 1983.

————. *The Political Unconscious*. Ithaca, N.Y.: Cornell University Press, 1981.

Jay, Martin. *The Dialectical Imagination: A History of the Frankfurt School and the Institute of Social Research, 1923–1950*. Boston: Little, Brown, 1973.

Jones, Gareth Stedman. *Languages of Class: Studies in English Working-Class History 1832–1982*. Cambridge: Cambridge University Press, 1983.

Joyce, Patrick. "The Constitution and the Narrative Structure of Victorian Politics." In *Re-Reading the Constitution: New Narratives in the Political History of England's Long Nineteenth Century*, edited by James Vernon, 179–203. Cambridge: Cambridge University Press, 1996.

Kaplan, Cora. "Wild Nights: Pleasure/Sexuality/Feminism," In *Formations of Pleasure*, 15–35. London: Routledge and Kegan Paul, 1983.

Keating, P. J. *The Working Classes in Victorian Fiction*. London: Routledge and Kegan Paul, 1971.

Kiberd, Declan. *Anglo-Irish Attitudes*. Derry: Field Day Theater Company, 1984.

Kincaid, James. *Annoying the Victorians*. New York: Routledge, 1995.

Kristeva, Julia. *Revolution in Poetic Language*. Translated by Margaret Waller. New York: Columbia University Press, 1984.

Kuhn, Annette, and Ann Marie Wolpe, eds. *Feminism and Materialism: Women and Modes of Production*. London: Routledge and Kegan Paul, 1978.

Laclau, Ernesto, and Chantal Mouffe. *Hegemony and Socialist Strategy: Towards a Radical Democratic Politics*. London: Verso, 1985.

Lafargue, Paul. *The Right to be Lazy*. Chicago: Charles J. Kerr, 1989.

Langbauer, Laurie. *Women and Romance: The Consolations of Gender in the English Novel*. Ithaca, N.Y.: Cornell University Press, 1990.

Leavis, F. R. *The Great Tradition: George Eliot, Henry James, Joseph Conrad*. New York: George W. Stewart, 1949.

Le Doeuff, Michèle. *The Philosophical Imaginary*. Translated by Colin Gordon. Stanford, Calif.: Stanford University Press, 1989.

Lesjak, Carolyn. "Authenticity and the Geography of Empire." *Studies in the Literary Imagination* 35.2 (Fall 2002): 123–46.

Lewis, Reina. *Gendering Orientalism: Race, Femininity, and Representation*. New York: Routledge, 1996.

Linehan, Katherine Bailey. "Mixed Politics: The Critique of Imperialism in *Daniel Deronda*." *Texas Studies in Literature and Language* 34.3 (Fall 1992): 323–46.

Lovell, Terry. *Consuming Fiction*. London: Verso, 1987.

Lukács, Georg. *The Theory of the Novel*. (1971). Translated by Anna Bostock. Cambridge, Mass.: MIT Press, 1985.

————. *The Historical Novel*. Translated by Hannah and Stanley Mitchell. Lincoln: University of Nebraska Press, 1962.

Marcuse, Herbert. *Eros and Civilization: A Philosophical Inquiry into Freud*. Boston: Beacon Press, 1974.

————. *One-Dimensional Man: Studies in the Ideology of Advanced Industrial Society*. London: Routledge and Kegan Paul, 1964.

Martin, Carol A. "Contemporary Critics and Judaism in *Daniel Deronda.*" *Victorian Periodicals Review* 21.3 (Fall 1988): 90–107.

Marx, Karl. *Capital.* Vol. 1. Translated by Ben Fowkes. New York: Penguin, 1990.

———. *Collected Works 1857–1861.* Vol. 28. New York: International Publishers, 1986.

———. *Early Writings.* Translated by Rodney Livingstone and Gregor Benton. New York: Penguin, 1992.

———. *Economic and Philosophic Manuscripts of 1844.* Translated by Martin Mulligan. New York: International Publishers, 1964.

Marx, Karl, and Friedrich Engels. *The German Ideology.* Translated by C. J. Arthur. New York: International Publishers, 1978.

McClintock, Ann. *Imperial Leather: Race, Gender and Sexuality in the Colonial Contest.* New York: Routledge, 1995.

McCormack, Kathleen. "George Eliot and Victorian Science Fiction: *Daniel Deronda* as Alternate History." *Extrapolation* 27.3 (1986): 185–96.

McGann, Jerome. "'Thing to Mind': The Materialist Aesthetic of William Morris." *Black Riders: The Visible Language of Modernism.* Princeton, N.J.: Princeton University Press, 1993.

Meckier, Jerome. "Dating the Action in *Great Expectations.*" *Dickens Studies Annual* 21 (1992): 157–94.

Meier, Paul. *William Morris, the Marxist Dreamer.* Translated by Frank Gubb. Atlantic Highlands, N.J.: Humanities Press, 1978.

Meyer, Susan. *Imperialism at Home: Race and Victorian Women's Writing.* Ithaca, N.Y.: Cornell University Press, 1996.

———. "'Safely to their Own Borders': Proto-Zionism, Feminism, and Nationalism." *ELH* 60 (1993): 733–58.

Mies, Maria. *Patriarchy and Accumulation on a World Scale: Women in the International Division of Labour.* London: Zed Books, 1986.

Miller, Andrew H. *Novels behind Glass: Commodity Culture and Victorian Narrative.* Cambridge: Cambridge University Press, 1995.

Miller, D. A. *The Novel and the Police.* Berkeley: University of California Press, 1988.

Moi, Toril. "Feminism, Postmodernism, and Style: Recent Feminist Criticism in the United States." *Cultural Critique* (Spring 1988): 3–22.

Moretti, Franco. *Signs Taken for Wonders: Essays in the Sociology of Literary Forms.* Translated by Susan Fischer, David Forgacs, and David Miller. London: Verso, 1988.

———. *The Way of the World: The Bildungsroman in European Culture.* London: Verso, 1987.

Morgentaler, Goldie. "Meditating on the Low: A Darwinian Reading of *Great Expectations.*" *Studies in English Literature 1500–1900* 38.4 (1998): 707–21.

Morris, May, ed. *William Morris: Artist, Writer, Socialist.* New York: Russell and Russell, 1966.

Morris, William. *News from Nowhere.* London: Routledge and Kegan Paul, 1970.

Morris, William, and E. Belfort Bax. *Socialism: Its Growth and Outcome.* London: Swan Sonnenschien, 1893.

Morton, A. L., ed. *Political Writings of William Morris*. New York: International Publishers, 1973.

Negt, Oskar, and Alexander Kluge. *Geschichte und Eigensinn*. Frankfurt am Main: Zweitausandeins, 1981.

———. *Public Sphere and Experience: Toward an Analysis of the Bourgeois and Proletarian Public Sphere*. Translated by Peter Labanyi, Jamie Owen Daniel, and Assenka Oksiloff. Foreword by Miriam Hansen, ix–xli. Minneapolis: University of Minnesota Press, 1993.

Nunokawa, Jeff. *The Afterlife of Property: Domestic Security and the Victorian Novel*. Princeton, N.J.: Princeton University Press, 1994.

———. "Homosexual Desire and the Effacement of the Self in *The Picture of Dorian Gray*." *American Imago* 49.3 (1992): 311–21.

O'Sullivan, Paddy. "Struggle for the Vision Fair: Morris and Ecology." *Journal of the William Morris Society* 8.4 (Spring 1990): 5–9.

Pearson, Keith Ansell, Benita Parry, and Judith Squires, eds. *Cultural Readings of Imperialism: Edward Said and the Gravity of History*. New York: St. Martin's Press, 1997.

Plotz, John. *The Crowd: British Literature and Public Politics*. Berkeley: University of California Press, 2000.

Pollock, Griselda. *Vision and Difference: Femininity, Feminism and the Histories of Art*. New York: Routledge, 1988.

Poovey, Mary. *Making a Social Body: British Cultural Formation, 1830–1864*. Chicago: University of Chicago Press, 1995.

———. *The Proper Lady and the Woman Writer: Ideology as Style in the Works of Mary Wollstonecraft, Mary Shelley, and Jane Austen*. Chicago: Chicago University Press, 1984.

———. *Uneven Developments: The Ideological Work of Gender in Mid-Victorian England*. Chicago: University of Chicago Press, 1988.

Prendergast, Christopher, ed. *Cultural Materialism: On Raymond Williams*. Minneapolis: University of Minnesota Press, 1995.

Robbins, Bruce. *The Servant's Hand: English Fiction from Below*. Durham, N.C.: Duke University Press, 1993.

Ruskin, John. *The Stones of Venice*. New York: J. Wiley, 1884.

Ruth, Jennifer. *Novel Professions: Interested Disinterest and the Making of the Professional in the Victorian Novel*. Columbus: Ohio State University Press, 2006.

Said, Edward W. *Beginnings: Intention and Method*. Baltimore: Johns Hopkins University Press, 1975.

———. *Culture and Imperialism*. New York: Alfred A. Knopf, 1993.

———. *The Question of Palestine*. New York: Vintage Books, 1979.

———. *The World, the Text and the Critic*. Cambridge, Mass.: Harvard University Press, 1982.

Sargent, Lydia, ed. *Women and Revolution: A Discussion of the Unhappy Marriage of Marxism and Feminism*. Boston: South End Press, 1981.

Scarry, Elaine. *Resisting Representation*. Oxford: Oxford University Press, 1994.

Schor, Hilary M. *Scheherezade in the Marketplace: Elizabeth Gaskell and the Victorian Novel*. New York: Oxford University Press, 1992.

Scott, Joan. *Gender and the Politics of History*. New York: Columbia University Press, 1988.

Sedgwick, Eve Kosofsky. *Between Men: English Literature and Male Homosocial Desire*. New York: Columbia University Press, 1985.

——. *Epistemology of the Closet*. Berkeley: University of California Press, 1990.

——. *Tendencies*. Durham, N.C.: Duke University Press, 1993.

Seltzer, Mark. "Statistical Persons." *diacritics* 17.3 (Fall 1987): 82–98.

Simpson, David. "Raymond Williams: Feeling for Structures, Voicing 'History.'" In *Cultural Materialism: On Raymond Williams*, edited by Christopher Prendergast, 29–50. Minneapolis: University of Minnesota Press, 1995.

Sinfield, Alan. *Cultural Politics—Queer Reading*. Philadelphia: University of Pennsylvania Press, 1994.

Sohn-Rethel, Alfred. *Intellectual and Manual Labour: A Critique of Epistemology*. Atlantic Highlands, N.J.: Humanities Press, 1978.

Soper, Kate. *Troubled Pleasures: Writings on Politics, Gender and Hedonism*. London: Verso, 1990.

Spivak, Gayatri. *In Other Worlds*. London: Routledge, 1988.

Strachan, Walter J. "Around William Morris." *Contemporary Review* (September 1990): 147–52.

Suvin, Darko. "Counter-Projects: William Morris and the Science Fiction of the 1880s." In *Socialism and the Literary Artistry of William Morris*, edited by Florence S. Boos and Carole G. Silver, 88–97. Columbia: University of Missouri Press, 1990.

Thompson, Andrew. *George Eliot and Italy: Literary, Cultural and Political Influences from Dante to the Risorgimento*. New York: St. Martin's Press, 1998.

Thompson, Dorothy. *The Chartists: Popular Politics in the Industrial Revolution*. New York: Pantheon Books, 1984.

Thompson, E. P. *The Making of the English Working Class*. New York: Penguin, 1980.

——. *William Morris: Romantic to Revolutionary*. New York: Pantheon Books, 1955.

Timo, Helen A. "News from Somewhere: The Relevance of William Morris's Thought in 1990." *Journal of the William Morris Society* 8.4 (Spring 1990): 3–5.

Uglow, Jennifer. *George Eliot*. New York: Pantheon Books, 1987.

Vernon, James. *Politics and the People: A Study in English Political Culture, c. 1815–1867*. Cambridge: Cambridge University Press, 1993.

Vicinus, Martha. "'Helpless and Unfriended': Nineteenth-Century Domestic Melodrama." *New Literary History* 13.1 (Autumn 1981): 127–43.

Viswanathan, Gauri. "Raymond Williams and British Colonialism." In *Cultural Materialism: On Raymond Williams*, edited by Christopher Prendergast, 188–210. Minneapolis: University of Minnesota Press, 1995.

Walkowitz, Judith R. *City of Dreadful Delight*. Chicago: University of Chicago Press, 1992.

——. *Prostitution and Victorian Society: Women, Class and the State*. Cambridge: Cambridge University Press, 1980.

Warner, Michael, ed. *Fear of a Queer Planet: Queer Politics and Social Theory.* Minneapolis: University of Minnesota Press, 1993.

Weedon, Chris. *Feminist Practice and Poststructuralist Theory.* Oxford: Basil Blackwell, 1987.

Wegner, Phillip E. *Imaginary Communities: Utopia, the Nation, and the Spatial Histories of Modernity.* Berkeley: University of California Press, 2002.

White, Hayden. "Auerbach's Literary History: Figural Causation and Modernist Historicism." In *Literary History and the Challenge of Philology: The Legacy of Erich Auerbach*, edited by Seth Lerer. Stanford, Calif.: Stanford University Press, 1996.

Wiener, Martin J. *English Culture and the Decline of the Industrial Spirit, 1850–1980.* Cambridge: Cambridge University Press, 1981.

Wilde, Oscar. "The Decorative Arts," "The House Beautiful," and "The English Renaissance." In *Oscar Wilde in Canada: An Apostle for the Arts*, by Kevin O'Brien. Toronto: Personal Library, 1982.

———. *De Profundis and Other Writings.* Introduction by Vyvyan Holland, 91–95. New York: Penguin, 1986.

———. *Lord Arthur Savile's Crime and Other Stories.* Penguin, 1979.

———. *The Picture of Dorian Gray.* New York: Penguin, 1985.

Williams, Raymond. *The Country and the City.* Oxford: Oxford University Press, 1973.

———. *Culture and Society: 1780–1950.* New York: Penguin, 1963.

———. *The English Novel from Dickens to Lawrence.* London: Hogarth Press, 1984.

———. *Problems in Materialism and Culture.* London: Verso, 1980.

Wolin, Richard. *Walter Benjamin: An Aesthetic of Redemption.* New York: Columbia University Press, 1982.

Yeazell, Ruth. "Why Political Novels Have Heroines: *Sybil*, *Mary Barton*, and *Felix Holt*." *Novel: A Forum on Fiction* 18.2 (Winter 1985): 126–44.

Žižek, Slavoj. "Eastern Europe's Republics of Gilead." *New Left Review* 204 (September–October 1990): 50–62.

———. *Tarrying with the Negative: Kant, Hegel, and the Critique of Ideology.* Durham, N.C.: Duke University Press, 1993.

INDEX

....

Doyle, Arthur Conan, 220 n.9
Drayton, Michael, 82

Eagleton, Terry, 201, 215 n.4, 230 n.24
Edelman, Lee, 218 n.27
Education, 241 n.25
Eliot, George, 13, 141–142, 162, 207–209; *Adam Bede*, 234 n.44; *Middlemarch*, 131, 136; on morals, 234 n.41; reform in, 227–228 n.9; sexuality in, 234 n.44; on storytelling, 234 n.45. See also *Daniel Deronda*; *Felix Holt*
Ellmann, Richard, 185, 247 n.12, 247 n.14
Emecheta, Buchi, 249 n.11
Empire, 16–18, 25, 75–81, 88, 93–94, 99, 112, 114, 128, 137, 186–187, 212–213, 220 n.9, 243–244 n.54. See also *Daniel Deronda*; *Great Expectations*
"English Renaissance, The" (Wilde), 184–185
Enjoyment, 4–5
Eustace Diamonds, The (Trollope), 205
Experience, 63, 66, 118–123, 137–38, 243 n.42; lived, 9, 22–23; relationship to labor, 9–10

Fabianism, 161–163, 245 n.64
Fanon, Frantz, 99
Faucher, Leon, 221 n.16
Felix Holt (Eliot), 14, 15–16, 18, 23–27, 130–131, 136, 222 n.18, 227 nn.6–9, 229 nn.17–19, 230 nn.22–23; artisanal production in, 74–75; Chartism in, 73–74; gender relations in, 75–81; history in, 227 n.3; landscape in, 63–67, 227 n.4; the mob vs. the mass in, 228 n.14, 244 n.56; narrative mode in, 65–68; nationalism in, 73–76, 80–83; Orient in, 75–81; pleasure in, 80, 83; prophetic mode in, 65–6, 73–74, 81–83; reformism and, 72–73, 228 n.10; sexuality in, 79; working-class culture in, 70–72

Feminism, 13–14, 146; feminist criticism and, 219 n.6
First Reform Bill (1832), 48, 61, 69, 72–73, 224 n.33
Fordism, 159–160
Forster, E. M., 211
Foucault, Michel, 1
Frankenstein (Shelley), 49, 224 n.36
Free trade, 85–86
Freud, Sigmund, 4
Frye, Northrop, 153, 164, 208

Gallagher, Catherine, 2–3, 10, 31, 87, 215 n.3, 219 n.7, 225 n.40, 225 n.42
Garland, Madge, 249 n.9
Gaskell, Elizabeth, 14, 207–209, 221 n.12; anxiety about readership, 220 n.4; letters of, 220 n.4; *North and South*, 23, 33, 211; political economy and, 221 n.7; sexuality and politics and, 221 n.7. See also *Mary Barton*
Gellner, Ernest, 232 n.28
Gender, 13, 37–39, 139; and class, 25, 36, 54, 219 n.5; empire and, 114; experience of pleasure and, 13–14; hierarchies, 18, 79–80, 134; nationalism and, 26; political function of, 3–4. *See also* Sexuality; *individual literary works*
Genealogy, 1–3, 6–7, 14, 19, 206
Genre, 31; as substitute for pleasure, 57
Geoghegan, Vincent, 151–152
Geras, Norman, 104
Gesamtkunstwerk, 153
Gill, Stephen, 221 n.16
Gilman, Sander, 129
Gilroy, Paul, 237 n.3
Giuliani, Rudolph, 241 n.25
Global economy, 16, 85–88, 137; regime of accumulation and, 91–92, 206
Godard, Jean-Luc, 89
Goncourt, Edmond de (Goncourt family), 22–23, 25
Great Expectations (Dickens), 16, 130, 218–219 n.31, 231 n.15; as *Bildungs-*

164–165, 249–250 n.12; separation from culture, 86–97; and subject formation, 9; as "vanishing mediator," 9. *See also* Culture

Labor novel, 1–19, 138, 206; genealogy of, 1–3, 6–7; realism and, 11–12. *See also* Industrial novel

Lacan, Jacques, 4

Lafargue, Paul, 198, 218 n.28

Landscape, 63–67, 227 n.4

Langbauer, Laurie, 232 n.25;

Lawrence, D. H., 211, 249 n.8

Leavis, F. R., 112, 232 n.30

Leisure, 5

Lesjak, Carolyn, 249 n.11

Lewes, George, 235 n.52, 235 n.55

Linehan, Katherine Bailey, 233 n.34

Lodge, David, 211

Looking Backward (Bellamy), 168–169, 238–239 n.10

"Lord Arthur Savile's Crime," 193–194

Love, 191–192, 196

Lovell, Terry, 32

Lukács, Georg, 29–30, 160–161, 219 n.3, 232 n.30, 243 n.43

Luxemburg, Rosa, 223 n.30

Marcuse, Herbert, 149, 181–183, 241 n.22

Marshall, Timothy, 211

Martin, Carol, 235 n.52, 235 n.54

Marx, Karl, 45–46, 63, 143–145, 158, 162, 185, 189–190, 199, 224 n.35, 238 n.9; commodity fetishism in, 104, 240–241 n.21; on factory labor, 221 n.15

Marxism, 14, 146, 158, 198, 208–209; avoidance of pleasure, 14

Mary Barton (Gaskell), 2–3, 14, 15, 18, 23–27, 163, 219 n.5, 222 n.19, 223 n.29, 224 n.38, 225 n.40, 225 n.42, 225–226 n.47, 226 n.49, 226 n.53, 226 n.55; domesticity in, 3, 35–54, 58; female authorial voice in, 32; gender relations in, 36; industrial labor in, 32–36; marriage in, 39–41, 222 n.22; melodrama

in, 15, 26, 43–44, 52–58; nationalism in, 30, 47–49, 58–61; pleasure in, 40–41, 55–56; productive sphere in, 43–50; prostitution in, 37–38; psychological interiority in, 225 n.39; realism of, 43, 61; sentimentalism in, 31–34, 43; sexual desire in, 39–42, 44, 55–58; unions in, 224 n.34; working class in, 30–34, 43, 44–51, 56

McGann, Jerome, 238 n.4

Meckier, Jerome, 231 n.17

Medievalism, 151–155, 158, 239 n.13

Meier, Paul, 158

Melodrama, 15, 43–44, 52–58, 225 n.42, 226 n.52; pleasure and, 55

Meyer, Susan, 235 n.54

Middlemarch (Eliot), 131, 136

Miller, D. A., 249 n.1

Modernism, 209–213

Money, 102–106

Morality, 32

More, Thomas, 137, 158, 165

Moretti, Franco, 16, 81, 85, 87–88, 94–95, 218 n.30, 224 n.36, 228 n.12

Morgentaler, Goldie, 231 n.15

Morris, William, 6, 13, 17, 139–140, 182–184, 198, 207–214, 239 n.14, 240 n.19, 241 n.24, 242 n.36, 249 n.11; applied arts and, 242 n.32; "Art and Socialism," 152–156, 243–244 n.54; Bellamy and, 168–169, 238 n.6; Bloody Sunday, importance of, 160–162, 168; commodification of Morris's style, 143, 238 n.3; "Communism," 148, 159–162, 243 n.51; compared to Benjamin, 157–158; concept of class, 149; critical attention to, 142–143, 158; education in, 150–151; empire in, 243–244 n.54; "How We Live and How We Might Live," 155; Icelandic sagas of, 141–143, 237 n.1, 240 n.17; influences on, 238 n.6; labor as problematic of value in, 165, 244 n.60; Marxism and, 158, 176–179, 243 n.47, 246 n.86;

Morris, William (*continued*)
    masculinity and, 240 n.20; medieval-
    ism in, 151–155, 158; modern society as
    gambling, 242 n.29; national identity
    in, 163–176, 237–238 n.2; needs in,
    147–149, 157, 240–241 n.21; nostalgia
    and, 154–155, 244–245 nn.63; notion
    of progress in, 155–156; on past and
    present, relationship between, 151–155;
    patriarchal authority and, 245 n.68;
    pleasurable labor in, 143–151, 183,
    238 n.6, 241 n.23, 244 n.61; productive
    vs. unproductive labor in, 146–148;
    reception of works, 240 n.17; *Sigurd
    the Volsung*, 141; as socialist, 140–142,
    156–164, 239–240 nn.15–16, 243 n.43,
    243 n.51, 243–244 n.54, 245 n.64; "The
    Society of the Future," 150; tech-
    nology and machinery in, 155–156, 198,
    245 n.74; "Useful Work versus Useless
    Toil," 146–151; utopianism of, 143,
    152–179, 242 n.35, 248 n.26; wealth of,
    238 n.6; women and, 18, 139, 173–174.
    See also *News from Nowhere*
My Beautiful Laundrette (Frears), 212–
    213

Narrative mode, 65–68
Nation: empire and, 25–26; Englishness
    and, 73, 131–135, 165; gender inequali-
    ties and, 26; ideology of, 73, 75, 76,
    81–83, 91, 112, 128–136, 165–166, 175–
    176, 187–188, 232 n.28, 246 n.63; as
    organic community, 129–136. *See also*
    Zionism
Needs, 147–149; 157, 185, 240–241 n.21
Negri, Antonio, 13, 218 n.24, 244 n.60
Negt, Oskar, 13, 60, 163–164, 226 n.55,
    249–250 n.12
New, 214
New Poor Law (1834), 54
News from Nowhere (Morris), 139, 1667,
    177, 179, 183, 216 n.12, 245 n.74,
    248 n.26; gender and sexuality in, 165,

172–174; national identity in, 164–
    167, 175–176; patriachal authority in,
    245 n.68; pleasurable labor in, 168–
    172; revolution in, 168; socialism in,
    175–176; technology in, 246 n.78
North and South (Gaskell), 23, 33, 211
Norton, Caroline, 54
Nunokawa, Jeff, 233 n.36, 247 n.19

Objects, 13–14, 68; object world and, 19,
    189–190
Ognibene, Tom, 241 n.25
Orient, 75–81
Orientalism, 129–130, 186–187
Orwell, George, 217 n.22
O'Sullivan, Paddy, 244 n.61
Owenites, 60

Past and Present (Carlyle), 144
Picture of Dorian Gray, The (Wilde), 139,
    186–192, 247 nn.13–14, 247 n.20
Pleasure, 40–41, 183; aesthetic, 3; as
    antidote to labor, 14; cognition and,
    11–12; consumption and, 13–14; cross-
    class, 49–50; as experience, 5; hedo-
    nism and, 182, 196, 203, 249 n.46; Left
    intellectuals and, 246 n.5; linkage to
    labor, 12–13, 143–151, 164–179, 206;
    melodrama and, 55; opposed to desire,
    4–5, 56–58, 216 n.10; privatization of,
    12; separation from labor, 1–19 passim;
    sexuality and, 182; theory of, 194–197;
    utopia and, 19, 183, 203, 206, 246 n.5;
    value and, 5; women and, 13. *See also*
    Labor
"Pleasures" (Brecht), 210
Poly-Olbion (Drayton), 82
Poovey, Mary, 32–33, 215–216 n.5,
    221 n.7, 224 n.36; on marriage,
    229 n.20; on psychology, 225 n.39
Postcolonialism, 212–213
Private property, 13–14, 46, 105, 199, 202,
    224 n.35
Production. *See* Labor

Productive sphere, 32–33, 43–44. *See also* Domestic sphere; Labor

Productivism, 183

Progress, 72–74, 86, 93–94, 149, 155–156

Prophetic mode, 65–66, 73–74, 81–83

Prostitution, 37–38, 221 nn.16–17

Queerness, 188

Queer theory, 14, 218 n.25

Race, 129–132, 237 n.2; polygeneticism and, 129

Radicalism (political movement), 24, 70

Realism, 17, 30–31, 34, 43, 69, 207–211; aesthetic aspects of, 11–12; British, 3; cognitive aspects of, 11–12, 217 n.22; labor novel and, 1–3, 6, 11–12; relationship to utopian narratives, 137–138; socialist, 209–10; subject matter of, 21–23, 61

Reform. *See* First Reform Bill; Second Reform Bill

Reification, 192–193

Representation, 63–65, 68–69; of economy, 87; relationship of political to literary, 72

Restoration Hardware, 238 n.3

Return of the Native (Hardy), 10

Revolution, fear of, 3, 30–31

Revolutions of 1848, 29–30, 160–161, 228 n.11

Robbins, Bruce, 215 n.5, 217 n.22, 221 n.13, 231 n.21

Rodchenko, Alexander, 209

Romance, 220 n.5, 232 n.25. *See also* Sentimentalism

Rowe, Richard, 247–248 n.21

Ruskin, John, 141–142, 144, 158, 238 n.9, 239 n.14; on Paris Commune, 244 n.56; "Sesame and Lilies," 145; *The Stones of Venice*, 145

Said, Edward, 90, 123, 129–130

Scarry, Elaine, 216–217 n.20

Schor, Hilary, 57, 226 n.51

Scott, Joan, 222–223 n.22

Second International, 149, 178

Second Reform Bill (1867), 15, 61, 69, 72–73, 228 n.10, 229 n.15

Secrets, 40–42, 50–52

Sedgwick, Eve Kosofsky, 186–188, 234 n.44

Seltzer, Mark, 233 n.38

Sentimentalism, 23–24, 31, 34, 43

"Sesame and Lilies" (Ruskin), 145

Sexuality, 4, 13, 18, 36–38, 40–41, 49, 76–81, 182–183, 188–189; history of, 3–4

Shaw, George Bernard, 146, 162–163

Shirley (Charlotte Brontë), 2, 210 n.11

Sigurd the Volsung (Morris), 141

Simpson, David, 216 n.19

Socialism, 140, 156–164, 175, 208–209

Socialist realism, 209–210

"Society of the Future, The" (Morris), 150

Soper, Kate, 13, 249 n.46

"Soul of Man under Socialism, The" (Wilde), 183, 194–195, 197–203

Space, 138, 164–167, 185–186; spatial histories, 88, 91, 236–237 n.2

Sparling, Halliday, 144

Speed, 63–64

Spivak, Gayatri, 249–250 n.12

Stalinism, 178

Stones of Venice, The (Ruskin), 145

Structural violence, 52

Subject, bourgeois, 8–9, 109. See also *Bildungsroman*

Surrealism, 209

Suvin, Darko, 168–169, 245 n.68

Sybil (Disraeli), 2, 220 n.11

Technology, 65, 155–156, 198

Thompson, Andrew, 235 n.55

Thompson, Dorothy, 224 n.32

Thompson, E. P., 142–143, 158, 160, 176–179, 222 n.22, 237 n.1, 238 n.9, 239 n.13, 242–243 n.40, 244 n.56

Totality, 219 n.3

Chapter 2 is a revised version of
"A Modern Odyssey: Realism, the
Masses, and Nationalism in George
Eliot's *Felix Holt*, which appeared in
Novel: A Forum on Fiction 30.1 (Fall
1996): 78–96, copyright NOVEL Corp.
© 1996, reprinted with permission.
A version of the *Daniel Deronda* section
of chapter 3 was published in *Victorian
Identities: Social and Cultural Formations
in Nineteenth-Century Literature*,
ed. Ruth Robbins and Julian Wolfreys
(Houndmills, Basingstoke, Hampshire:
Macmillan, 1996), 25–42, reproduced
with permission of Palgrave Macmillan.
Chapter 5 is a slightly revised version of
"Utopia, Use and the Everyday:
Oscar Wilde and a New Economy of
Pleasure," *ELH* 67.1 (March 2000):
179–204. I thank *Novel*,
Palgrave Macmillan, and *ELH*
for permission to reprint.

Carolyn Lesjak is an associate professor of
English at Swarthmore College.

Library of Congress Cataloging-in-Publication Data
Lesjak, Carolyn
Working fictions : a genealogy of the
Victorian novel / Carolyn Lesjak.
p. cm.—(Post-contemporary interventions)
Includes bibliographical references and index.
ISBN-13: 978-0-8223-3835-2 (cloth : alk. paper)
ISBN-10: 0-8223-3835-1 (cloth : alk. paper)
ISBN-13: 978-0-8223-3888-8 (pbk. : alk. paper)
ISBN-10: 0-8223-3888-2 (pbk. : alk. paper)
1. English fiction—19th century—History
and criticism. 2. Authors, English—19th
century—Political and social views.
3. Working class in literature. 4. Work in
literature. 5. Pleasure in literature. 6. Social
conflict in literature. 7. Economics in
literature. 8. Capitalism in literature.
9. Industrialization in literature.
I. Title. II. Series.
PR871.L47 2006
823'.009355—dc22   2006010447